AUG 1 5 2006

P9-AZV-721

my love
affair
with
modern art

my love affair with modern art

BEHIND THE SCENES WITH
A LEGENDARY CURATOR

KATHARINE KUH

EDITED & COMPLETED BY AVIS BERMAN

ARCADE PUBLISHING
NEW YORK

FIRST EDITION

Library of Congress Cataloging-in-Publication Data

Kuh, Katharine.
   My love affair with modern art : behind the scenes with a legendary curator /
   by Katharine Kuh ; edited and completed by Avis Berman. — 1st ed.
        p. cm.
   ISBN 1-55970-769-0
   1. Art, American—20th century. 2. Art Institute of Chicago. I. Berman, Avis.
   II. Title.

   N6512.K84 2006
   709'.045'07477311—dc22   2005010309

Published in the United States by Arcade Publishing, Inc., New York
Distributed by Time Warner Book Group

Visit our Web site at www.arcadepub.com

10 9 8 7 6 5 4 3 2 1

Designed by API

EB

PRINTED IN THE UNITED STATES OF AMERICA

For all who knew Katharine and in memory of my father

Contents

Preface   *ix*

Introduction: Sorting Out and Summing Up   1

1   Searching and Seeing   41

2   Mies van der Rohe in Chicago   69

3   The Two Vincent van Goghs   85

4   Fernand Léger: Pioneering the Present   95

5   Stuart Davis and the Jazz Connection   113

6   Constantin Brancusi: Elision and Re-vision 121

7   Three Encounters with Bernard Berenson   131

8   Mark Rothko: A Portrait in Dark and Light 143

9   Alfred Jensen: Competing with the Sun   167

10 Clyfford Still: Art's Angry Man   191

11 Isamu Noguchi: In Search of Home   201

12 Mark Tobey in Basel   215

13 A Day with Franz Kline   227

14 Jacques Lipchitz at the White House   239

15 Hans Hofmann in Provincetown   247

16 Josef Albers: The Color of Discipline   259

17 Edward Hopper: Foils for the Light   271

Notes   283

Photograph and Illustration Credits   293

Acknowledgments   301

Publication History   305

Index   307

Preface

Katharine Kuh was always too vehemently involved with life to let death, let alone the opinions of other people, stand in the way of her voice. When she began writing these reminiscences at the age of eighty-seven, she didn't care what the task might exact from her in physical strength or mental energy. I myself was skeptical of the enterprise. Of course, I encouraged her to persevere with the notion of a book, because from years of hearing her stories, I knew and loved the rich texture of Katharine's life. As her friend and literary executor, I was eager to read and help her to publish anything she wrote, but I wasn't persuaded that she had the stamina or concentration for such sustained work. Happily, she confounded me and a number of others who knew her: the prospect of being an author again and the dedication it entailed got her up in the morning and kept her active every day. Katharine's blazing determination trumped my stereotyped expectations of what was possible or prudent for someone of her age and health. When she died, on January 10, 1994, at the age of eighty-nine, she had written three-quarters of this manuscript.

Nevertheless, in the piles of handwritten notes, typescripts, clippings, envelopes, and folders that had been accumulating, Katharine also left essays in various stages of gestation. In addition to writings that had been abandoned and perhaps not destined for publication, other chapters were in a rudimentary state and lacked the analysis and brio she had brought to the polished chapters that unquestionably represented a final summation. Because I had interviewed Katharine extensively about her professional life beginning in 1982 and written about her on several occasions, she asked me to complete her memoirs if she did not live to do so. Yet my primary criterion for including material was that it had to stand as Katharine's writing, expressed in the first-person point of view. If the pages in question had to be augmented so substantially by me as to render them a secondhand research article about the subject, as opposed to a personal account based on Katharine's direct observation, participation, and explication, I did not retain them. If I could not fill gaps and construct transitions as I think Katharine would have, I forfeited the raw information. In my editing, I tried to proceed as a thoughtful conservator would in restoring a fine painting. I refined and polished where needed, but I did not alter the meaning or expression of the essential composition.

However, for the sake of forming a book as a whole, I did have to write extended portions of this volume. In almost all instances, I depended on Katharine's letters, publications, and scrapbooks, along with my own knowledge and recollections. In addition, I had an indispensable resource — a three-hundred-page transcript of an interview I conducted with Katharine throughout 1982 and 1983 for the Archives of American Art's oral history program. For that project, I was supposed to make three or four recordings of Katharine's recollections, but she possessed such scope and mesmerizing recall that I ended up taping her fifteen times instead. Well before the interviewing was finished, we had become friends. Whenever I was unsure of an opinion or an attitude or if Katharine changed her mind about a certain person, event, or subject, I would search through her catalogues, magazine articles, and the oral history until I found the answers or pregnant clues I needed. As a rule, I made a point of expressing the missing thoughts or data in a manner as close to her syntax as I could manage.

While I did have ample primary documentation before me, Katharine took care to suppress several cardinal facts about her early life and career. Had she lived, it is debatable if she would have acquiesced to supplying personal information to an imploring publisher. Katharine had grown up and matured in an age that valued privacy and decorum, discretion above sensation and revelation. When she described Edward Hopper's reserve, she responded to that tight-lipped rectitude with admiration and understanding. Katharine was frank about personal matters to friends, but committing such truths to print was abhorrent to her. Reticent about her private life, she genuinely believed that her own personality was not as central as those she wrote about. As she saw it, the legacy of her writing would be judged in proportion to how directly it reflected an engagement with artists — the source of the experiences that most intensely enkindled her life. She was shocked and baffled that John Canaday, who was chief art critic at the *New York Times* while she was at *Saturday Review,* advocated avoiding all personal contact with artists, lest his impartial judgments be threatened. She objected that impartial judgments could not exist in art because strong emotions and total involvement are prerequisites of understanding. For Katharine, warm familiarity with artists was invaluable in comprehending the vitals of art and transmitting that intelligence to the public. Nothing, she stated, could substitute for the experience of seeing an artist's paintings, one by one, in his or her studio. She buttressed her case by arguing that when studying earlier masters, we long to have secrets unraveled that only personal accounts might have disclosed.

The value of her memoirs, Katharine maintained, lay in her history as the rare confidante of Clyfford Still, as the world traveler who led Hopper to the one place in Mexico that fused with his imagination, as the insider visiting Isamu Noguchi's house in Japan, or as the eavesdropper on the priceless remark, as when she heard Walter Gropius say to Mies van der Rohe, "All that work and what have we got to show for it — the picture window?" In other words, she felt that her writing made a contribution only insofar as it willingly remained subservient to the far more creative forces which were its raison d'être. Katharine also regarded criticism as an offshoot of her real work, which, as she defined it, was "knowing about works of art, whether they were produced in the past or present. Judging them, understanding their condition, knowing how to read an X-ray photograph revealing the layers of an old painting or recognize if a drawing has been reinforced — these are the things that have interested me." What she loved most, whether as writer or curator, was the act of looking and, ultimately, of seeing.

But Katharine's tendencies to the contrary, certain principal facts and details of her life need to be volunteered in order to understand some uncharacteristically elliptical passages in the text. She was born Katharine Woolf on July 15, 1904, in St. Louis, Missouri, the youngest of three daughters of Morris and Olga Weiner Woolf. A native of London and part of a family of English Jews, Morris Woolf was a distant relation of Leonard Woolf. He was brought to the United States as a young boy and became a prosperous silk importer. He, Olga, and their children enjoyed a comfortable life. In 1909 the Woolfs moved to Chicago, and five years later one of the pivotal events of Katharine's life occurred: she contracted polio. The Woolfs were traveling in Europe that summer, and just after World War I broke out, while they were in Geneva, Katharine was diagnosed, paralyzed, and unable to walk. One of her earliest memories of her illness was sitting propped up at the window of the Woolfs' hotel in Paris, hearing the firing of guns in the distance and watching the wounded soldiers, covered in blood from the Battle of the Marne, being transported back to the city in taxicabs.

For the next ten years she had to wear a plaster body cast. At first she was bedridden and then progressed into a wheelchair, but she remained a shut-in. In those days, nearly a century before laws were passed to make schools more accessible to disabled children, she was tutored at home. During these years when Katharine could not walk, Morris Woolf, who collected prints, decided to show her how to catalogue them. (The collection, which contained works by Dürer, Van

Dyck, Goltzius, Haden, Hollar, Jongkind, van Leyden, Legros, Meryon, Millet, Teniers, and Whistler, was donated by Olga Woolf to the Art Institute of Chicago in 1941.) One of Katharine's uncles collected paintings, and he surrounded her with art books. Although Katharine had had no interest in art before, learning about the prints and reading about art was a happy distraction in a childhood that had turned out to be lonely and isolated.

When Katharine reentered school at the age of fifteen, she had to wear a heavy cast under her clothes to support her spine, which was no longer straight. She had recovered enough to walk again, but she limped and her left leg never developed properly. She had to continue exercises and other forms of physical therapy, but no matter how onerous her treatment, she was thrilled to be among people her own age and threw herself into being "normal." Art was put aside: it reminded her of the disease that left her lame and bereft of companionship. She was eager to learn how to live, to be accepted by her schoolmates. Most American teenagers, even well-to-do upper-middle-class ones, were not studying art books and old master prints. No doubt at the urging of her mother, who was a resolute advocate of women's rights, Katharine read *A Doll's House* and was powerfully impressed by it. She vowed that polio was never going to stop her from doing anything again. Nor was she going to reveal that she was physically handicapped unless she had no other choice. She was ready to fight to get what she wanted. She grasped life as a gift.

Katharine was dead set against imparting her medical history in her autobiographical writings, and she was largely successful in evading all discussions of her bout with polio. However, as someone who suffered agonies dragging herself up flights of stairs, it is no wonder that she remembered — and described — the torture of visiting the top-floor studios of Léger and Hopper. Such repeated complaints about climbing a winding staircase seem mysterious and anomalous coming from the pen of someone who was otherwise so tolerant of the quirks of artists' habitats, but Katharine's commentary was merely a function of the aftereffects of polio, which she never publicly admitted. However, in the chapter on Bernard Berenson, she did acknowledge her condition — in all of two lines. I and other readers urged her to explain

Katharine Woolf, about 1919, when she was able to return to public school.
Her clothes hide the body cast she was wearing.

why she and her mother were unaccountably lunching in Boston so often. The reason was that the two were there for frequent appointments with a polio specialist, seeking remedies for ameliorating her condition. On one occasion she was sitting in the doctor's waiting room when another patient, a handsome, urbane man in leg braces, was wheeled in by his manservant. The aide temporarily left the room, and the man, who was reading a newspaper, accidentally dropped it. He turned to Katharine and asked if she would pick it up. Katharine, embarrassed, had to admit, "I can't stoop because I'm in a plaster cast." The stranger rescued the situation with great charm, answering, "Well, with my legs and your plaster cast, we make a good team." Later, looking at a photograph in the newspaper, she recognized the affable man who had chatted with her. He was Franklin Delano Roosevelt.

One of the root reasons for Katharine's love of travel during adulthood no doubt stemmed from her decade encased in a cast, unable to move around. The more intrepid the journey, the more she wanted to make it — if nothing else, it was another proof that she had conquered her disability. Mentally or physically, she would not be incarcerated. She went to Alaska six times, one time sleeping on a salmon fisherman's boat and shooting seal for money to get there; her last visit to India took place in 1978. As *Saturday Review*'s art critic during the 1960s, she was sent on long trips to cover cultural matters in Israel, Turkey, the Soviet Union, Sicily, and Mexico. She reveled in exploring and studying the art of remote regions. When she worked as an art consultant for the First National Bank of Chicago from 1968 to 1978, she visited nearly every branch they had, touring Europe, Asia, and South America to buy and install art. When she wrote about Vincent Willem van Gogh, the artist's nephew, she devoted several paragraphs to his appetite for travel, poking gentle fun at his obsession, but sharing it in a milder form.

After she graduated from high school, Katharine entered Vassar College, which had been chosen for her by her mother, in 1921. Olga Woolf had been to college herself, and was adamant that her daughter have a profession, especially because she was handicapped. Whereas Morris Woolf would say, "Oh, I wish I could wear that brace for you," Olga would take another approach, admonishing her daughter, "Stand up straight, Katharine. You can do it." Katharine looked back on the school with mixed feelings, still boiling over at several classmates' anti-Semitism. Yet it was there that her connection with art intensified into a passion that enveloped her for the rest of her life. Katharine had entered Vassar as an economics major — art at that time still had the smell of the sickroom attached to it. She was not through battling enormous physical problems. In college Katharine remained burdened with a plaster cast wrapped around her entire torso; she required almost daily sessions with a physical therapist.

During her junior year, Katharine spotted what she was sure would be a snap course — a class on Italian Renaissance art taught by a new young instructor named Alfred H. Barr, Jr. Barr, the visionary art historian who would become the founding director of the Museum of Modern Art in 1929, electrified Katharine with lectures and

Katharine in Alaska, 1941, on her own, leading a liberated life.

opened her eyes to a whole new world. In his fervent teaching, he never isolated art, but integrated it with history, design, industry, psychology, and society. Barr was only two years older than Katharine and most of the other students. While "he talked our language," she remembered, "he was light-years ahead of us." Katharine was so inspired by him that she immediately changed her major to art history, taking all the art courses she could. Barr's ideas and approach would influence her for the rest of her career. When Katharine became a curator at the Art Institute, she collaborated with Barr and her counterpart at the Modern, Dorothy Miller, on exhibitions. Friends and spirited competitors, Barr and the Modern are leitmotifs in Katharine's memoirs — as museum director and institution, they appear throughout her memoirs in frequency second only to the Art Institute and its director, Daniel Catton Rich. But Barr is always first in Katharine's estimation and enthusiasm as the person who most acutely changed attitudes toward twentieth-century art, toward museums and their practices, and, above all else, toward the meaning of the word *art* itself.

If Katharine's allusions to polio were so discreet as to be invisible, there is absolutely no acknowledgment of her love life in these memoirs. For all her eagerness to converse about her passion for art, she was implacably silent about her love affairs, stubbornly separating the professional from the personal. As in the case of her medical history, her romantic attachments must be fleshed out to add context and psychological understanding to her motivations.

After Katharine finished Vassar, she moved back to her parents' house to earn a master's degree in art history at the University of Chicago. She also declared that her decade of wearing the body cast was over. Living like other girls and going to dances was all she wanted. (She had not had boyfriends because of her condition — aware that someone putting his arm around her would be repelled by the heavy plaster support, Katharine was too embarrassed to encourage such situations.) Rebelling against the body brace was the beginning of a freer life for Katharine. While she was in Chicago, she met George Kuh, a businessman some years her senior, and the two were instantly attracted to each other. A widower, George Kuh was tall and athletic — he had been a football player in his younger days — and was chief operating officer of a large clothing firm. He represented the strong, masculine, unencumbered presence her illness had denied her. Katharine wanted to pursue her studies and moved to New York in 1929 to begin work on a Ph.D. at New York University. Within a year, however, she dropped out of school to marry George Kuh.

Katharine loved her husband. But George Kuh had a son from his first marriage, and try as Katharine might, the little boy did not accept her easily. Her new situation proved full of difficulties, and she was too young and inexperienced to handle any of them. George Kuh's son was still traumatized by his mother's death and needed psychiatric help. Katharine was overwhelmed, unable to deal with the emotional complexities posed by her role as stepmother. Furthermore, because of the curvature of her spine and related deformities, Katharine was advised by her doctor not to have children. The tension of getting along with her stepson in difficult circumstances, coupled with her disappointment at being told she could not have her own child, ate away at the marriage. Those anxieties were exacerbated by her move into George Kuh's house in the suburb of Highland Park, on the North Shore. As the mistress of a large house — someone who was supposed to entertain and supervise household help — Katharine, who was never domestic under the best of circumstances, found herself in prison all over again. She felt too young to be stifled as a matron with a child and a large establishment. Trying to escape, Katharine worked in the art section of a bookstore and lectured and taught small classes. All of which made her husband unhappy: he felt that her work took her away from her real job as a wife and mother. Her in-laws disapproved altogether. When she bought a lithograph by Toulouse-Lautrec, they made fun of it. Stung by the cruelty and bitterness of that episode, Katharine never forgot having to put the print in her dresser drawer and hiding it from everyone else's eyes. While she still cared for her husband, she could not go on any longer; she left Highland Park and moved into a small hotel in Chicago. The Kuhs officially separated in June 1935. In November Katharine opened her gallery. In 1936 her divorce became final.

Katharine pretty much decided from then on that she would not marry again. She enjoyed occasional affairs in her younger days with

Katharine and George Kuh, about 1931.

some of the artists she met. As an unattached and single woman sitting alone at her desk, she was regularly propositioned at the gallery, and remembered with some amusement the writer Nelson Algren, who demanded that she go to bed with him within hours of their first meeting. When she refused, he became indignant, left Katharine at the door, and never spoke to her again. Her lovers were often married, a situation that seemed to suit Katharine as well as her partner. In 1938, Katharine began a passionate affair of several years with the painter Carlos Mérida, whom she showed in her gallery. Mérida was married and resided in Mexico. He had met Katharine in Chicago while exhibiting at the gallery, and the two fell in love. In order to see him more, she decided to take a house in San Miguel de Allende and teach at the same school as Mérida during the summers. They had a life together during the summer months, and continued when Mérida would come to Chicago. Their relationship was serious. Mérida, who called her "Kata," warmly inscribed a number of paintings, drawings, and watercolors to her. In her reminiscences, Mérida appears either as an artist represented by the Katharine Kuh Gallery — and the hero of one of her favorite anecdotes about Chicago know-nothingness when

Carlos Mérida, one of Katharine's great loves. She agreed to teach summer school in Mexico to be near him.

he flummoxed the overbearing members of the archconservative organization Sanity in Art — or as her guide to Mexico, impersonally showing her around. She never revealed the true nature of their relationship in anything she wrote.

By the late 1930s, Katharine had also gotten to know a number of prominent African-American artists and other key figures in the Chicago Renaissance, most notably Richard Wright and Katherine Dunham. (Dunham fondly remembered Kuh as someone who helped her negotiate the perils of mingling with the culturati of white Chicago.) She was interested in — and chased — Horace Cayton, a catalytic writer, scholar, and social activist, but her pursuit came to nothing. Katharine later told me that she had been foolhardy and that Cayton was right to rebuff her. An interracial sexual relationship would have been "too dangerous" for him. She praised Cayton's restraint in the face of her bad judgment. That said, Cayton was known to have had multiple affairs with all sorts of women. In Katharine's case, he simply may not have found her to his liking. Regrettably, other than a glancing reference to the black artist Charles Sebree, whom she showed in her gallery, Katharine did not include more observations about the members of the Chicago Renaissance in any of the surviving manuscripts.

Katharine joined the Art Institute in 1943, and was hired by Daniel Catton Rich, the director from 1938 to 1958. By then, her relationship with Mérida was largely over. Judging from all her writings about Mies van der Rohe, it is clear that she was very attracted to him, but nothing romantic happened between them. In the late 1940s, possibly while on a trip to Los Angeles together to visit Walter and Louise Arensberg about their art collection, Katharine and Dan Rich began a romantic relationship. Just three months older than Katharine, Rich was married with several children and there was no plan or hope of divorce. He remained the enduring love of her life, and Katharine often fantasized about Dan leaving his wife. She always said that Dan was the one man she would have married. But Rich didn't want to be separated from his family, and the scandal would have cost one or both of them their jobs. Strangely and surprisingly, their affair, which most everyone in the museum staff and board of trustees seemed to know

Daniel Catton Rich in 1939, a year after he became director of the Art Institute of Chicago. About ten years later, he and Katharine formed a bond that only death would break.

about as the years went on, was accepted without penalty to either, perhaps because the two worked so well as a professional team and enriched the Art Institute with many superb exhibitions and works of art.

Theirs was a union of mind, art, heart, and sensibility, and it ended with Rich's death in 1976. (Rich's wife, the former Bertha Ten Eyck James, had died in 1968. When, in 1970, Rich moved to New York City, he and Katharine maintained separate apartments, but remained devoted to each other.) Though Dan and Katharine were a perfect match in their engagement with art, their temperaments could not have been more different. Whereas Rich, as a museum director, behaved with prudence and tact, Katharine was often fierce in delivering her opinions and unabashed in voicing her disagreements. Their arguments would ring throughout the corridors of the Art Institute. As Thomas M. Messer, the former director of the Solomon R. Guggenheim Museum and a close friend of Rich's, said, "He bore her outbursts stoically."

Dan Rich was an important personage in Katharine's career, and she wanted to leave it at that in her writing. She was evasive about his central role in her emotional life. Above all else, she wanted to make certain to credit him for his brilliant tenure as the director of the museum, always positioning him as the colleague and boss with whom she collaborated closely. Their travels together were often made on behalf of the museum, and after Rich's resignation in 1958 her decision to leave a year later with the advent of a new director she distrusted seemed altogether logical. Dan and Bertha Rich were long dead when she began writing her memoir, but Katharine strongly believed that her personal relationship with Dan needed to remain undiscussed and not interfere with their achievements in the museum world.

These dynamics of rebellion and freedom extended to Katharine's personal circumstances and aesthetic preferences, but not necessarily to larger gender-related issues. She was an independent woman, happier living a life of the mind rather than one filled with elaborate domesticity or financial security. (Morris Woolf had been an avid investor in the stock market, and lost his money in the Depression. Katharine could not rely on the financial ease of her childhood to cushion her.) In the 1930s she supported herself and her gallery, and as a critic and art consultant drew a salary until the late 1970s, but nonetheless never thought of herself from a feminist perspective. In her own gallery, she simply pursued what she wanted to do without the label of "woman dealer." But after Katharine joined the Art Institute as a female employee, she realized that she was being paid about half as much as men doing similar jobs. In the mid-1940s, she became a curator, the editor of the museum's bulletin, and a lecturer with the education department. She still made less than men with fewer responsibilities. Later on, when she understood how valuable to the museum she had become, she fought for a just salary. The inequities, however, did not begin and end with the issue of money. The Art Institute was in charge of the 1956 Venice Biennale, and Katharine did all the work for it, organizing the entire show. Traditionally, the person who assembles the exhibition for the American pavilion is the U.S. commissioner to the Biennale and the one who helps determine which artists will receive its coveted prizes. Katharine took it for granted that she would be commissioner. No woman commissioner had ever represented the United States to date, and the government authorities were not ready to break with tradition. They decreed that Dan Rich would be the U.S. commissioner, and so he was.

In both New York and Chicago, Katharine knew and respected many women artists. She bought and showed their work, befriended many of them, and wrote extensively about them. Among this group were Anni Albers, Georgia O'Keeffe, Louise Nevelson, Claire Zeisler, Charmion von Wiegand, Mary Callery, Gertrude Abercrombie, Julia Thecla, Leonore Tawney, Toshiko Takaezu, Hedda Sterne, Dorothy Ruddick, Norma-Jean Bothmer, Elise Asher, Ellen Lanyon, Martyl, Dorothea Tanning, Denise Hare, Perle Fine, Claire Falkenstein, Margo Hoff, and Nancy Spero. In 1947, in the first large survey show of con-

Katharine hoisting a glass with her fellow workers at the Venice Biennale, celebrating the installation of her exhibition at the American Pavilion, 1956.

temporary American artists that Katharine and her colleague Frederick Sweet organized for the Art Institute, 42 out of the 252 artists shown were women, a marked increase over any previous exhibitions of modern art at the museum. However, Kuh and Sweet were people of their time, well before the era of consciousness raising. They perpetrated sexual stereotyping in the catalogue they wrote for the show; their patronizing classifications of most of the women artists would never have been countenanced if they had been applied to the men. Maud Morgan and Margaret Tomkins, for example, were described as housewives raising young children, and any woman married to another artist was always identified in terms of her husband, whereas none of the wives or offspring of the men were cited, only their professional attributes or affiliations were listed. Even Katharine's great friend Hedda Sterne was primarily characterized as the "wife of cartoonist Saul Steinberg." As the years went by, Katharine steadfastly encouraged and mentored many young women critics, curators, scholars, and art historians, including myself. She recognized — and railed against — individual injustices, but she did not interpret them as emblematic of larger political structures until she looked back on her life in the 1990s. The primary battle as Katharine saw it was to get pioneering and often unpopular art accepted and vindicated, whether it was made by a woman or not. And usually, in her view, it was not.

For the last three or four years of her life, polio, Katharine's old nemesis, returned with a ferocity that would have vanquished a less stubborn spirit. Katharine was housebound when she wrote these memoirs. She suffered from post-polio syndrome, experiencing overwhelming muscle weakness and aching. Her vertebrae began to contract, plunging her into spasms of pain and making it even harder for her to walk. Her skeleton was compressing, and had she not mercifully died in her sleep, her lungs would have been crushed between her rib cage and vertebrae within a year or two. Naturally, sitting for long periods of time in a library to verify hunches, check details, or update information would have been extremely uncomfortable for her. I, along with friends at the Art Institute, would occasionally help her look up items she needed, but most of what she wrote was from memory. And that memory was astonishing. In the process of preparing the various chapters of this book for publication, I spent many hours among Katharine's papers in the Archives of American Art, the Art Institute of Chicago, and the Beinecke Library of Rare Books and Manuscripts at Yale University checking facts, adding and comparing dates, and clarifying thoughts. All of it confirmed to me that her recall could be trusted.

The editing of the memoirs took more time than I expected, for emotional reasons. I first began to work on assembling the manuscript a few months after Katharine's death, which in hindsight was too soon. I mourned her, and felt her absence. I was so reverent about her literary project that I didn't feel entitled to change or omit a word, and loyally tried to keep every line in the order that she wrote it. Her essays had taken on the aspect of sacred texts that I dared not despoil. I gingerly corrected factual inaccuracies, but didn't evaluate the prose with enough rigor. I was an admirer and a mourner, but not a critic. Such attitudes, I knew, were doomed to impair the manuscript. I had to put it aside.

Years later, when my judgment became clearer and feeling I could function as a stringent reader, I returned to the manuscript. I could reshuffle, add, and cut with confidence and discernment as I hope Katharine would have wished. As I did so, Katharine came back in all her force and feistiness. The more strongly I shaped the manuscript and brought it to a viable conclusion, the more I discovered that for me Katharine had never died. Now that her testament is finally before the public, I hope readers will recognize that we are indeed missing something extraordinary by her absence — her knowledge, her flinty integrity, her humility, and, in her phrase, her open eye.

Avis Berman

my love
affair
with
modern art

Introduction
Sorting Out and Summing Up

My life has been a long vista dominated by the fecundity of art, and I was privileged to be the friend of several artists who are now a part of history. They are all dead now, and I feel impelled to record various personal experiences and encounters. These memories, I hope, will help humanize these outstanding men and contribute to a fuller understanding of their achievements. In remembering and writing, I am also trying to question the present as much as to repossess the past, though reliving the momentum of the latter has been an exhilarating occupation. Analyzing the world I've known — one dominated by art museums, curatorial adventures, art education, and, supremely, artists — has reinvigorated me.

When I focus on puzzling aspects of twentieth-century art, it is chiefly as a participant and eyewitness. My goal is to offer firsthand observations that in most instances have not been published before, and which with my death would otherwise pass into oblivion. As I look back, I find myself disputing many established beliefs and practices of a modern world emerging from a celebrated nineteenth century into an even more dynamic twentieth. I consider problems presented by fakes, faulty attributions, and copies, and ponder the uneasy union of democracy and art, of manipulative donors and thwarted museums. These and other inquiries can erode long-accepted credos.

When I stop to think how and why I came to know such a variety of artists so well and often informally, I realize that it was due partly to my dogged longevity — I was born on July 15, 1904 — and partly to a shifting professional life, almost all of which was associated with art. As a dealer, museum curator, obsessive traveler, and art consultant, I have worked constantly with artists. I have taught the history of art, lectured widely — too widely perhaps — labored on government projects in assorted countries, and tangled futilely with obdurate bureaucracies, our own included. Predictably, I've written several books. For eleven years I was art advisor to a large international corporation and I served for nineteen years as art critic on a national magazine. You might say I've been an art bum. For considerably more than half a century, I've carried on a love affair with this curiously introverted world.

Veering only once and for less than a month, I was persuaded in Chicago during World War II to become more "socially conscious" and join a training group, which was eventually to land me in a public venereal disease clinic as an investigator. Peremptorily fired, I was accused of too much curiosity — I couldn't get enough of listening to the prostitutes tell stories about their lives — and too little performance. So back to art.

My first close acquaintance with painters and sculptors was the natural outcome of opening the Katharine Kuh Gallery in Chicago in November 1935. There I showed the work of dozens of artists, often while they were still struggling for public recognition. I think immediately of Alexander Archipenko, Lázló Moholy-Nagy, Fernand Léger, Stuart Davis, Isamu Noguchi, Paul Klee, Joan Miró, Ansel Adams, Edward Weston, and Josef Albers, who had one of his earliest exhibitions in America at my gallery.

The Depression was roaring along, and I, newly separated and on the verge of divorce, decided that this was the moment to become an entrepreneur. I wanted to be a pioneer in my own backyard, but, more crucially, I wanted to live a life I believed in after a stultifying existence on the North Shore, where my in-laws made fun of what I cared about and I was a complete failure at being domestic. I wanted to make a total break from five years of surburban married life, and I had been fascinated by the avant-garde in art for a long time. These were heady years, with the emergence of one great movement after the next, and I was determined to try to understand them.

I leased a very beautiful space at 540 North Michigan Avenue in the Diana Court Building, so called because of the Carl Milles fountain of Diana in the inner court that the gallery faced. The rent was fifty dollars a month, a sum rarely covered by sales. I had no financial backing during the entire life of the gallery, a fact that ensured my independence but also long hours of work because I couldn't afford

The Katharine Kuh Gallery, December 1937, during the run of an exhibition of sculpture by Alexander Archipenko. Katharine is sitting behind her desk. Photograph by Edmund Teske.

help. Armed with an M.A. in the history of art plus credits toward a doctoral degree, I was bold enough to conduct private classes in the rear of the gallery, hoping to cover expenses. Eventually the lectures did stimulate a number of budding Chicago art lovers to become serious collectors, but I can't pretend that the majority of my students were scholarly paragons. My morning classes were usually filled with well-to-do housewives, and after one session, after I had talked for an hour on Velázquez, one woman told me that the artist sounded "just fascinating." She urged me to get in touch with her the next time he came to Chicago so that she could "arrange a soirée" in his honor.

During the 1930s the term *modern art* was anathema in the Midwest — a label of opprobrium. To sell contemporary work was an uphill push all the way, and only a blithe neophyte would have been brash enough to consider trying it. It almost seemed as if the daring imagination that Chicago had expended on commerce exhausted its ability to cope with visual innovations other than in the field of architecture, which, to be sure, depended on the city's industrial life. Some years later, when I was a curator at the Art Institute, I encountered the opposite dilemma. By then a handful of wealthy trustees (who were also avid collectors) blindly championed modern art to the exclusion of the past, even opposing the acquisition of a Tintoretto. They found it "old-fashioned" and out of step with contemporary life. Modern art had become chic.

I supported my gallery both by teaching and by running an employment bureau for commercial artists. When Japanese-Americans came out of the internment camps and Jewish refugees arrived from Europe, the bureau provided free services for them. And only at that time did I begin to understand the enormity of Nazism. Until then I'd been somewhat skeptical of the rumored atrocities. One minor incident undid me, involving a young woman who came into the gallery with her small son, who was about four years old. She was an interior designer, recently escaped from Munich, and was in dire need of work. As we were talking, two policemen arrived, hoping to sell tickets for a benefit. After one glance the little boy stood at attention, saluted, and piped out "Heil Hitler." His Jewish mother tearfully explained that to save his life, she had been forced to depend on this stratagem. Now, any uniform rang a bell for him.

During the Depression all employment bureaus were in trouble, but especially those catering to artists. I still relive my despair on hearing the art director of a midwestern drugstore chain offer to pay a typographical designer ten cents an hour. Without the WPA and other New Deal projects, the entire art world would, no doubt, have crumbled into oblivion, but the terrible predicament we were all in created a certain camaraderie. Charles Sebree, a young artist whom I represented, regularly stole hundreds of postage stamps from the gallery and then resold them. When I confronted him with the problem, he said it would be "dishonest" for him to pretend that his behavior might change. "After all," he reminded me, "we are good friends." And believe it or not, he continued to steal, though of course, honestly, and I continued to show his work.

To economize, I brought lunch from home each day and dutifully addressed and stamped all monthly announcements myself. Scratching along without monetary or secretarial help, I ran the place as a solo operation and, despite both hostile and apathetic resistance from the public, found the whole experience an exciting adventure. There were, of course, constant headaches, such as an organization unique to Chicago hatched in 1936 called "Sanity in Art." Spurred on by Eleanor Jewett, the art critic of the *Chicago Tribune,* Sanity in Art turned my place into its number-one target. Sanity in Art was like an aesthetic "Moral Majority." It was a rabid movement of art vigilantes with its object to have the most reactionary art, and only American art at that, shown, bought, or collected in Chicago and the rest of the Midwest. In turn, the group was intent on eliminating the practice of modernism — any deviation from its rigid provincial code attracted explosive verbal onslaughts. In my case, the attacks were physically threatening as well, as when someone smashed the glass window of the gallery to register disapproval of an exhibition of Joan Miró. Jewett was a great-niece of Colonel Cyrus McCormick, president of the International Harvester Corporation and the *Tribune*'s archconservative publisher; she was given the job through her family connections.

Her training in art history was nil — she had majored in agriculture in college, but she dropped the curriculum and left the university rather than study animal breeding. However, her position was invulnerable. So there I sat, an easy butt of her poisonous if pusillanimous barbs. The *Tribune* had an enormous circulation and most people in the city took it as the word of God.

I'll always remember a run-in with Sanity in Art and Carlos Mérida, the Guatemaltecan painter who lived in Mexico, when he was in Chicago for one of his frequent exhibitions at my gallery. Carlos, a charming man of meticulous manners who lived into his nineties, had become deaf in his youth, but he always communicated with considerable dexterity. Contemplative and somewhat remote, possibly due to his disability, he was also extremely worldly. At one time he had lived in Paris, where he shared a studio with Modigliani and came to know several other important European artists, which may explain why he never joined Mexico's ardent "return to its Indian roots" movement. His paintings were indebted to both Europe and Latin America. They often were subtle abstractions dependent on simplified Mayan symbols. As he grew older, his work became more geometric and rigid; it was the earlier paintings that I've always found more interesting. He could condense the ground shadow of a flying airplane into a spatial image that unexpectedly recalls native lore.

Despite his deafness, Mérida responded enthusiatically to jazz, to its beat and complexity. Above all, he admired Duke Ellington. On one occasion in Chicago, he was persuaded to consult a well-known specialist who told him that fenestration surgery could substantially improve his hearing and his ability to enjoy music. After much thought, he decided against it. Deafness protected his privacy and permitted him to live in an idealized dream world. He saw the affliction as a decided plus.

One incident almost persuaded me he was right. During an exhibition at my gallery, Carlos was sitting near his paintings reading the newspaper when two or three much behatted, overweight ladies invaded the premises. They approached the desk where I was working and asked if he was the artist whose work was on the walls. They then announced they represented Sanity in Art. With my gallery established as a prime destination on the group's intimidation list, I was sometimes forced to call the police because the members would interfere with business. But the meeting with Mérida was peaceful. The women approached him, exploding with anger, and noisily denounced his paintings, which were not explicitly representational, as "meaningless garbage." Carlos, a man of great refinement, elegantly dressed in imported English clothes, couldn't hear a word and interpreted their passionate gestures as signs of admiration. Thanking them profusely, he kissed their hands. They left totally befuddled, and I took care not to enlighten him on their comments. He was one of the few artists I knew who doubted his own work, wondering aloud whether it had any value. "*Quién sabe?* — as my ancestor, the Indian, would say," was his answer when his paintings were discussed.

It must have been the beginning of September 1939, when I was traveling by train from the Mexican town of San Miguel de Allende to Chicago. I'd been teaching a history of art course in what was then a largely forgotten Baroque town (now it is a tourist mecca). The small art school where I taught, inflatedly called Escuela de Bellas Artes de Universidad de Mexico, catered mainly to Americans on vacation. Of all my peripheral jobs related to art, this was the most frivolous, but nonetheless it was mind-stretching. Though attendance at the school depended more on the students' holiday plans than on any serious commitment to art, the several summers I worked there were an education for me.

Along with learning Spanish, I came to realize how baffling the mores of any foreign habitat are. I kept wanting to fathom the simplest "whys." Why was an awkward nineteenth-century Gothic cathedral dominating the main square in an otherwise exuberantly Baroque town? Why were sophisticated Viennese pastries a specialty in an isolated settlement some two hundred miles from Mexico City? Exquisitely made, these delicate cakes were hawked in the zócalo for a centavo or two, less than one American penny. True, they were covered with flies, but even so, how had this worldly recipe arrived and thrived in San Miguel? And then there was my neighbor, who raised bulls and occasionally performed in the ring, too. He also appeared to have a

monopoly on water in the town, though he was only rarely in residence. Could it have been because his property was on a hill and water flowed from there? He was handsome and a bit condescending
where art was concerned. From him I learned that the bullring is a
world of infinite shadings and endless protocol. I studied the entire
operation, but for some reason was never able to master its fine points
with the same precision that I bring to baseball. Both at their best can
be living works of art, and frequently both have provided themes for
works of art.

The school, located in a rehabilitated monastery, was oriented
around a spacious patio. Chiefly Mexican, the faculty was impressive,
featuring such serious artists as Mérida, Rufino Tamayo, and Pablo
O'Higgins, but, as I recall, we spent more time in the cantina than
in the classroom. The Mexican artists came chiefly to enjoy a relaxed
summer away from Mexico City. I closed my gallery during the
hottest months because even in the best of weather, the Katharine
Kuh Gallery was scarcely a magnet for the Chicago public.

After the first summer I bought a small house, located directly
above the town, for sixty-five dollars. The taxes were seventy-eight
cents a year. I installed a bathroom (I believe that there were only sixteen others in San Miguel then), a kitchen, a small swimming pool,
and a roof garden, where we had memorable dances with mariachis
playing until morning. Vast supplies of tequila were consumed. After
several summers, I regretfully sold the house and retreated from Mexico. It was too tempting, too demoralizing, too removed from reality —
too much drinking and too many affairs and intrigues. A Mexican Indian maid, Carmen, lived in the house with her five little boys, though
precisely where they all slept I never discovered, or perhaps I preferred
not to. Sometimes she took the children up to the roof for a serious
session of delousing. They sat quietly enduring the process, while I
worried that they were too passive. Did they need more orange juice
(something unknown before I came), more fresh vegetables, fewer
starches? Why were they so well behaved?

Carmen's husband came to call occasionally. By way of polite
conversation he once asked me after I had just arrived from Chicago,
"Señora, how is the revolution going in your country this year?"

Those were the days when Mexico was on fire and most artists were engaged in embracing their indigenous Indian heritage at the same time they urgently denounced colonial Spanish influences. I, like many Americans, was attracted to the country largely because of this popular art revolution, not to mention the beauty of the landscape and the economical life there. One could live pleasantly on next to nothing. At that time, Rivera, Orozco, and Siqueiros were heroes to us, not just for their communal emphasis on murals and fresco, but equally for their judgmental messages endorsing native life and culture. It may all seem dated now, but then, in the 1930s, the Mexican movement in politics and art was a rallying cry for liberation from the status quo.

From Mérida I learned more about Mexico than from any other source. He was the first to open my eyes to the meaning of Baroque art and architecture. He recognized San Miguel as a forgotten treasure trove of sumptuous examples. The Baroque, flourishing in eighteenth-century Mexico, came late to that country and was refreshingly opulent in and around San Miguel. Here, then, was an ideal setup for authentic art education: no slides, no drone of information, no darkened, sleep-inducing room. Carlos's engagement with San Miguel's architecture was authentic. He rapidly dispelled my prejudices against the Baroque that had been instilled during my student days when we were led to believe that the word was synonymous with "decadence." At its best, it can become an organized, if riotous, assemblage. Vaulting, curving, receding, advancing, the Baroque duplicates life itself.

Carlos was also my cicerone in Mexico's daily events. He and I were sitting in the town square one morning when a horse-drawn wagon lumbered by. In it lay the corpse of a young Indian boy who had been caught probably stealing a chicken. Carlos went on to explain, "In your country, death is accidental. In mine, it is incidental." That was well over sixty years ago, and death is no longer accidental in my country.

By the time I was on the train traveling back to Chicago, after several summers as a householder and teacher in San Miguel, I was beginning to feel like an old-timer in Mexican lore, but how wrong I was. Our neighbor to the south is not that easy to decode. I was sitting in the so-called club car drenched in heat and soot, for that was before air travel or air conditioning. Across from me sat a middle-aged Mexican man who after a short time invited me to have a beer with him. It turned out that he was one of the top executives at the Carta Blanca Beer company and was on his way to the office in Monterey. His English was fluent and he was an engaging conversationalist, very much a man of the world who had traveled widely and was curious as well as cultured. I told him a bit about my gallery and he in turn explained the beer business to me, but his interests also included music, literature, and archaeology.

After exchanging business cards as he left the train in Monterey, I gave this convivial interlude no further thought. So I was quite unprepared the following February when one morning I arrived to open the gallery and found him waiting at the door. He said he was in Chicago on a personal matter and hoped that I would have dinner with him that evening. All went agreeably, and after dinner he asked if he could come up to my apartment and discuss a matter that had preoccupied him for some time. He then informed me that he had a wife and young son, both of whom meant a great deal to him, and that for some years he shared one night every week with his mistress, who had agreed that should she meet him in public with his wife, she would make no sign of recognition. After this cool recital and having shown not an iota of sentiment, he invited me to become his second mistress and to abide by all the same rules, except in this case he would finance my gallery and move it, along with me, to Mexico City. It would retain my name, and it would continue to feature avant-garde European art. In addition, he would provide for a secretary, an assistant, good catalogues, and other amenities. We would have a pleasant relationship, I would not be so overworked and underfinanced as in Chicago, and the entire project could light up his life and, he hoped, mine as well. I was speechless. That this civilized and articulate man could so totally have misread me and, in turn, I, after several hours of conversation on the train, hadn't the foggiest notion what he was thinking, unnerved me.

I explained to him that I led two lives — one personal, the other professional, and he wanted to take over both ready-made, tied up in a neat package. I didn't need a secretary or an assistant. I didn't want a gallery in Mexico City; I wanted it in Chicago. Moreover, I didn't think his forecast of our personal life together was too alluring, and so the answer was no. He, showing not a sign of disappointment, immediately put on his overcoat, kissed my hand perfunctorily and left. I never heard of or from him again.

After that proposition, I realized how little I had learned about Mexico and how many strata of society could entangle an innocent gringa. As I look back, what never ceases to amaze me are the unpredictable adventures that enliven the life of an art zealot, because I am convinced that it was the gallery more than the "gal" that brought him to Chicago. As far as I was concerned, my indignation also had more to do with the gallery (of which I was inordinately proud and protective) than with my personal self-esteem. For me it would have been a double prostitution; for him, two rejuvenating midlife hobbies.

There are other snapshots from the life of my gallery that come to mind. Ansel Adams, young, thin, taut, and unsure, traveled to Chicago in November of 1936 for an exhibition of his photographs that I was giving him. He needed money, and what with the show being far from a sellout, I scrounged around to arrange a portrait commission for him. The sitter, Rosette Lowenstein, was an imperious and wealthy older woman who was something of an art patron. She'd never heard of Ansel Adams, who was then more or less an unknown entity, but she was ready to give him a chance. He toiled over the assignment, finally coming up with numerous proofs, most of which were undeviatingly honest. The lady wore pince-nez spectacles, which he insisted she wear — considering them to be an integral part of her personality. She had an aggressive, angular, but remarkably strong face. He photographed her with the same cold precision that he might have brought to one of his California peaks. Hard light, bouncing back from eyeglasses and well-coiffed hair, played over her craggy features, which seemed projected almost as if in a movie close-up. The trial proofs were rejected, and the finished photographs never made. I suppose we cannot even estimate how many important works have been lost under similar circumstances.

Nor have I forgotten the circus watercolors and drawings by Alexander Calder, which sold, as I recall, for twenty-eight to thirty-six dollars each. One was paid for on time (in three-month installments) by a young professor who later became Senator S. I. Hayakawa of California. And then there was a January day when Edward Weston arrived from California during a subzero blizzard. He was sockless, in sandals, and without a topcoat. I also had two famous writers stop by to see one of my Klee exhibitions. First came Henry Miller, whom I had never set eyes on before. He made a hasty survey, darting from one picture to another with a kind of unfocused, lilting speed. He then stopped at my desk to ask me if I could spare one hundred dollars. He needed it to continue his trip to the West Coast, he announced without embarrassment. In those terrible days of the Depression, that sum represented two months' rent for the gallery. When I refused, he snapped, "That's it!" and sped out of the gallery. I never saw him again. Some days later, an older man and a heavyset woman dutifully studied the Klees, all the while hissing *Schrecklich, schrecklich!*" to each other. The disapproving visitors were Thomas Mann and his wife, who were briefly in the city. *The Magic Mountain* was one of my favorite books, and I still find it sad that the man who wrote it failed to comprehend Klee's hidden world.

A year or two after I opened the gallery, a wondrous windfall came my way. In fact, the Depression and the general know-nothingness about contemporary art were not all bad news. Incredible opportunities occasionally presented themselves, most memorably the auction of paintings from the estate of the pioneering collector Arthur Jerome Eddy, who had been a heavy purchaser of works of art from the Armory Show. For some inexplicable reason, the sale was held at a third-rate establishment on Wabash Avenue in January 1937, with no fanfare whatsoever. Fortunately for me, it was a massacre, with fine works going for nothing, because the auctioneer had no idea what he was selling. The first thing he said was, "What am I bid for this Tinpansky?" It was a handsome Expressionist painting by Kandinsky, a 1909 landscape of a church in Murnau. The auctioneer suggested twenty dollars. I nodded, and he said, "Sold." He asked me my name and because I didn't want to say who I was and be recognized as a professional art dealer, I replied, "K.K." When a 1909 Fauve painting of Murnau by Kandinsky came up, the auctioneer said, "Anyone willing to give five dollars for this?" I raised my hand, and he said, "To K.K." From then on, whenever no one else wanted a work, he would jokingly say, "How about K.K.?" and I would nod. He thought I was a lunatic. Thanks to his breezy ignorance, I acquired ten pictures — the two Kandinskys, four Jawlenskys, two Man Rays (a rayogram and a painting, each for ten dollars), a Gabriele Münter, and an early color

Ansel Adams, on November 9, 1936, the day that he and Katharine had their pictures taken by an automatic photo machine.

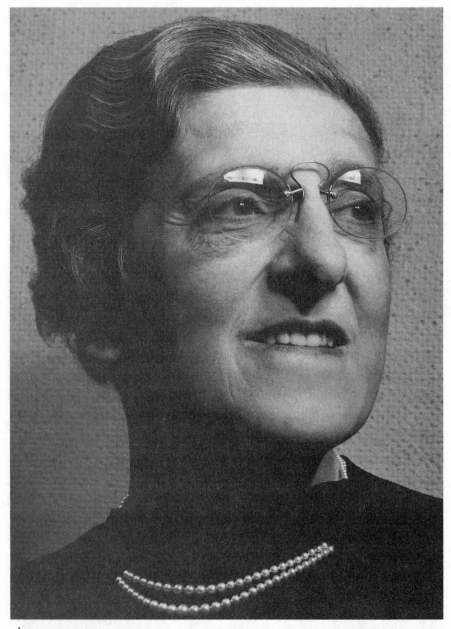

Ansel Adams, *Portrait of Rosette Lowenstein*, 1936. Ansel Adams
made luminous and searching likenesses of Rosette Lowenstein during
his stay in Chicago. She rejected every portrait Adams offered
because she felt they didn't flatter her. Adams, said Katharine,
"didn't ask her for a cent" for his work.

lithograph by Bonnard — all for the sum of $110. This unexpected bonus kept the Katharine Kuh Gallery on an even keel for the rest of the year. I asked $350 for the Expressionist Kandinsky and sold it to an architect who loved it so much that he decided to keep it for himself instead of passing it on to one of his clients. The Fauve oil painting of Murnau, also by the artist that the auctioneer jocularly referred to as a "Tinpansky," has remained on my wall ever since. Prices, then as now, are interesting social barometers having nothing to do with the quality or staying power of art, but as cultural guideposts they provide valuable telescopic information. And when, to be sure, has art not performed as a reliable adjunct to history?

After America entered World War II and communication with European artists the gallery represented became impossible, Daniel Catton Rich, the director of the Art Institute of Chicago, hired me to go to work for the museum. Eventually I became the first curator of modern painting and sculpture; ironically, the museum had never bought a single work of art from me when I was a dealer. Here again, midwestern resistance to modernism posed problems, chiefly with the trustees, most of them businessmen, and with the press, dominated in many cases by these same men or their relatives. As before, my personal contacts with artists continued. I arranged exhibitions of their work, bought their paintings and sculpture, wrote about them in various catalogues, and continually visited their studios in this country and abroad, but I was no longer the blithe free agent of the gallery days. Knuckling down to institutional regulations was tedious, as were the frequent and seemingly endless staff and committee meetings. Yet traveling for the museum was a rewarding plus.

I remember a long and at times arduous trip in 1947 when I drove alone throughout the entire country in search of works eligible for an exhibition of American abstract and surrealist art to be held at the museum. In those days roads and motels were not crowded, but a good number of them were decidedly primitive. In Idaho and Washington State, I stayed in woodland cabins pieced together with occasional nails — no bathroom, no amenities whatsoever. But even in such isolated spots, I sometimes came on interesting artists who were supporting themselves in unexpected ways — farming, brick-making,

Vasily Kandinsky, *Houses at Murnau*, 1909. In January 1937, when this early Fauve painting by Kandinsky was sold at auction, Katharine bought it for five dollars. She held on to the picture for the rest of her life.

running restaurants, finishing furniture, filmmaking, and house painting. A few of the best merely existed as hermits.

The trip was an extraordinary eye-opener, a concentrated slice of American artists struggling for recognition in what we euphemistically call the heartland. The exhibition finally opened in January 1948, and included some 250 artists, many of them already securely established but almost as many unknown. Stopping at their homes after grueling days of driving and finding kind hospitality left an indelible imprint and not infrequently cemented the start of a long friendship. My overall impression was of warmth, loneliness, and pride in survival.

Whereas the best of all curatorial duties involved working with artists, architects, and designers, the most painful experiences I had at the museum hinged all too often on relationships with possible donors. Collectors can be charming, knowledgeable, ambitious, or vulgar; they

The Art Institute of Chicago, front entrance on Michigan Avenue,
around 1950.

also can be entertaining or deadly boring. If they have amassed splendid works of art through inheritance or their own ingenuity, they become marks for equally avaricious curators and directors. There were instances when I invested time, emotions, and fantasies in such pursuits — the most memorable relating to Walter Arensberg and his superb modern collection of Brancusis, Duchamps, Picassos, Mirós, Braques, and Klees, which eventually went to the Philadelphia Museum of Art. Arensberg was a remarkable man, a mercurial character who outwitted one institution after another. Both museum and university trustees camped on his doorstep in Hollywood, California. During two or three forays I made to the Arensberg home to catalogue the collection for an exhibition opening at the Art Institute in October 1949, there was scarcely a day that a delegation from one place or another wasn't ushered in. There everyone sat, making a bid for the collection, in that fabulous living room, with its strangely torn drapes, fine Oriental rugs, and numerous Duchamp paintings packed in among other historic modern works. Walter was engaging, but he dangled his victims unmercifully. I finally realized that he enjoyed this cat-and-mouse game, which gave color to a California life he found tedious after the celebrated salon he hosted in New York. Louise Arensberg was an equally strong character, but less volatile. She impressed me as withdrawn and tense. It was Walter who braved the public, yet, as a couple, they were always a closely integrated team, more interdependent because they were childless. Just months after Louise died, Walter followed her.

Among the university presidents, museum directors, and curators hoping for bounty were Dan Rich and me. Dan got along well with Arensberg, because they both enjoyed discussing the alchemy of ghosts and both were seriously interested in poetry. Arensberg had earlier been a practicing poet, and Dan likewise had tried his hand at it. I was mesmerized by this capricious character who my midwestern gullibility led me to believe was favoring the Art Institute in his con-

Louise and Walter Arensberg with Marcel Duchamp, August 17, 1936, at the couple's house in Hollywood. Photograph by Beatrice Wood.

The sun room in the Arensbergs' house, with a view into the living room. To the left of the door are Picasso's *Man with Violin, Violin and Pipe* by Georges Braque, and *The Newborn* by Constantin Brancusi; to the right of the door are *Maiastra* by Brancusi and *Chocolate Grinder No. 2* by Duchamp. Seen through the door is *The Soothsayer's Recompense* by Giorgio de Chirico.

siderations for the future. After all, wasn't he trusting us with the first full-scale exhibition and catalogue of his collection? Little did I understand his strategy. From letters in various archives, I have recently learned that he agreed to the exhibition in large part in order to obtain a professionally prepared catalogue at no expense to himself. Even before I embarked on writing it, I now believe he had decided where the collection would eventually go, and it was not to the Art Institute of Chicago. He doubtless felt that with this publication in hand, he would be better equipped to dazzle numerous other institutions and thus raise his bargaining power with Philadelphia. As a donor he was prepared to demand certain concessions that would facilitate keeping the collection intact under his and his wife's names, thus assuring a degree of immortality. He even wanted the future museum installation to replicate as closely as possible the highly personal arrangement in his home, but it was a pipe dream to expect that such intimacy would be simulated in a public exhibition area. The collection was of such superior quality as to speak for itself — the simpler the setting the better.

I still flinch with pain when I think of how coolly I was used, but it was more the loss of Arensberg's friendship than of the collection that wounded me. I had enjoyed knowing him — he turned each day that we worked together into an adventure. Although he had no specific reason to break our association, unless perhaps to facilitate an easy alibi for dumping us, the moment the catalogue was completed and the exhibition returned to California at the end of 1949, he refused any further contact with me and turned his back on the Art Institute. Repeatedly, I tried to find out why. Even the health food routine at his home, consisting of little more than nuts and dates at lunch or the inevitable pre-dinner bourbon and revoltingly sweet ginger ale (when I was secretly yearning for a scotch on the rocks), had not blunted my affection for this charismatic man. I believed I was his friend, and not merely a useful tool. In December of 1950, after the Arensbergs formally agreed to donate their collection to Philadelphia, I wrote to see if I could visit them again chiefly as a friend, but I was ignored.

Not long afterward, Duchamp, who knew all about these machinations, sent me a postcard asking if the Art Institute would like a sculpture of Leda by Brancusi. This one — there are two — was from the estate of the prescient modernist collector Katherine Dreier, whom he advised for many years. I've often speculated whether his generous gesture wasn't a way of solacing my pain. At no other time in my years as a curator did I receive an offer of such magnitude on a postcard. The document itself was a true Duchamp ready-made.

As I look back, I realize that Walter, with his circuitous and unpredictable charm, knew exactly how to ensnare me. He kept me on edge by forever changing his mind. Earlier he had given the collection to the University of California, but retrieved it when that institution failed to toe the line. For him altercations were the spice of life, as I found from the moment of my first visit to the Arensbergs in June

1948. Even working on the catalogue was never easy — the couple was opposed to removing works from the walls, so this wasn't a scholarly or accurate enterprise in the least. But it was a listing, which had never been made, of everything in the house that could be considered a work of art, plus whatever information I could get out of Walter. Minus shoes, I'd totter on the furniture trying to approximate correct measurements. There was art behind beds, under beds, in the pantry, in the bathrooms, and early Duchamp paintings crowded together on every wall of Walter's bathroom. I remember how perilously I balanced on the rim of the tub to study them. And there were the threats to our show. Several times Arensberg changed his mind about the Art Institute. I'd appear at their front door at nine in the morning, and Walter would tell me to go away. "No exhibition!" But then he'd relent. Could it have been a trace of guilt that caused his ambivalence?

In 1920 the Arensbergs moved to Hollywood from New York, where Walter had kept up a famous salon built around Duchamp, Picabia, and all kinds of creative people. They often drank straight through the night and, like spark plugs, kept reigniting one another, but Louise "rescued" Walter, or so she told me. In a way, what she really did was destroy him. After being torn away from that life, he never wrote poetry again. In Hollywood he was isolated; he had only two pastimes there — buying art and proving that Francis Bacon wrote Shakespeare. Louise Arensberg always seemed to be wringing her hands as if in the midst of a secret tragedy. I believe she was ill with cancer, and rubbing her hands may have helped alleviate the pain. Her intelligence was veined with flint, covered up by a kind of well-bred femininity.

During April of 1949, on my last trip to the Arensbergs in California, Duchamp came to visit. Walter, who hung on his every word, hadn't seen him for some thirteen years. We were waiting all day and finally he arrived, this legendary figure, cool, impervious, and invariably polite. He calmly walked around the first floor, looking impartially at his own works and those of other artists, most of which he himself had bought for the Arensbergs when he was acting as their private agent. Commenting on only one of his own works, *The King and Queen Surrounded by Swift Nudes,* he said, "It holds up."

Man Ray, a close friend of Duchamp, was living in Hollywood with his wife, Juliet. For some reason (I believe Walter disliked Man's work), the artist was not welcome chez Arensberg. Walter didn't even want Duchamp to see Man Ray while he was hosting him, but Duchamp escaped each day by taking a stroll away from the house and had Man secretly pick him up in his car. Marcel always quietly did whatever he wanted. The Arensbergs ate very sparingly and, let me add, peculiarly. Lunch consisted of some dates and raisins and perhaps a hard-boiled egg, and dinner wasn't much better. I imagine that Duchamp was often as hungry as I. When I was cataloguing works of art in his room (I had permission from the Arensbergs to open all drawers, closets, and cabinets), I found a small erotic plaster sculpture by his brother, Raymond Duchamp-Villon, hidden in his bedside table because of its fragility. Next to it were some Hershey bars, bought, I presume, surreptitiously on the artist's outings with Man Ray.

Walter, who hated Frank Lloyd Wright's architecture, never merely liked or disliked — he either detested or was enthralled. He drove Duchamp and me on a memorable expedition to see nearby examples of Wright's work, always deliberately showing us the least successful. Constantly taking his hands off the steering wheel while talking to Marcel in the backseat, he finally embroiled us in an accident. He slammed into the car ahead and then proceeded to excoriate its driver, who was in no way at fault, but who was nonetheless intimidated. Duchamp remained hors de combat. I was badly shaken.

Another day the three of us made a brief expedition to Walter's next-door neighbor, the dealer Earl Stendahl. Along with splendid examples of modern art, his gallery was the main source of Walter's pre-Columbian sculpture. Just how Stendahl maneuvered this vast and, I judge, forbidden cargo across the border was never explained. The visit was not entirely reassuring. Remedial treatment on early stone carvings was going on at quite a pace. As we left, Duchamp muttered, *"Dangereux."*

Walter Arensberg's repudiation of our friendship was lacerating, but if he was my Waterloo, Chester Dale was Dan Rich's. No two men could have been more unlike than Arensberg and Dale. Where Walter was manipulative and highly cultivated, Dale was raucous, demanding — a law unto himself — but both shared a virtual passion for art and were equipped with responsive eyes. And both received good advice — Arensberg from Duchamp and Chester Dale from his first wife, Maud, an artist and connoisseur. Arensberg was the more adventurous. Along with Duncan Phillips, they were America's most significant modern art collectors during my era.

When Chester Dale was still not widely known as a collector, he and Dan became friends — or so Dan thought. Whenever Dan was in New York, no matter how busy, he always found time for Dale. One auspicious day in 1943 he returned to Chicago with the announcement that Mr. Dale had agreed to a long-term loan of fifty-two contemporary works from his fast-growing collection. The Art Institute gave the deal considerable publicity and installed the paintings with great care. A year later Chester Dale was elected to the museum's board of trustees, which at that time was far from an inclusive group. In fact, it was more like a private club in which this new member was something of an anomaly. The paintings remained on loan for nine years and we took for granted that they were a permanent fixture. Several of the rarest canvases on view were by Braque and of such high quality as to be almost impossible to duplicate. With each passing year, prices steadily increased, making it doubly difficult for the museum to approximate replacing them. But we on the staff were lulled by naïveté and wishful thinking. When suddenly, with no preliminary warning, Dale announced that the collection was to move immediately to the National Gallery in Washington, we at the Art Institute were in a state of shock and Dan was decimated. Losing the Braques was a serious blow to the museum because it was too late to replace them and, to this day, Braque's representation at the Art Institute has never quite caught up. The precipitous removal of the entire group was not unlike having an arm amputated.

From later evidence it would seem that the entire Dale transaction was pretty cold-blooded. He made the loan to us while waiting for the National Gallery to change certain bylaws that prevented the acceptance of works by living artists. For him Chicago was merely a convenient stepping-stone to enhance his name and social stature while also acting as a constant provocation for the National Gallery to hasten the liberalization of its policies. The Washington museum's national status held out more important recognition for him, and despite having served for some time on the Art Institute's board, he was not faintly interested in the future of the museum. He resigned the same year he moved the collection.

All of which set me to questioning why collectors collect. There are all the obvious reasons: love of art, social and civic recognition, even occasionally monetary profit. Many collectors, to be sure, are motivated purely by generosity; the welfare of the community is often a top priority. With Walter Arensberg this was partly true when he first contemplated the idea, but eventually his drive focused on preserving his name in history — not unlike the drive of so many creative artists. He clearly looked on his collection as a planned work of art and demanded that it remain intact as one unified conception and not as a group of individually created objects for which he was in no way responsible. The collection became more important than its intrinsic parts while the reason for collecting bowed to the process of collecting. In addition, despite extensive paid advice from Duchamp, Arensberg considered the assemblage his own personal achievement. His identification with the collection was obsessive; this man was ready to sacrifice friendship, kindness, fair play, and even his word on its altar.

For Chester Dale and certain other famous collectors, their underlying drives were essentially the same. They too were involved in assuring their names a safe spot in history, but Dale, a tough trader who elbowed his way through the ruthless Curb Market and made huge profits from financing railroad and municipal bonds, wanted immediate recognition during his lifetime. Social approval, power, and entry into an otherwise closed world drove him. His insatiable desire for recognition and constant admiration never ceased to goad him. But it was not all one-sided, and we in the museum world were equally guilty. Yet for us it was, in a way, obligatory. Our American form of government forces museum personnel to court possible donors with endless blandishments and thus to lend ourselves to the whole sorry performance. We depend on donors to provide the lifeblood of our institutions, and no matter how difficult they can be, they are preferable to unenlightened public officials. In many European countries, art is subsidized by the government. Not so in the United States. Even the paltry sum allotted to the National Endowment for the Arts has occasioned degrading political interference.

Theoretically, art should blossom under what we commonly think of as political freedom, but the contrary is often true. I don't mean to suggest that repression fosters creativity, but I sometimes doubt that government participation is productive. When we try against severe odds to enlighten our public servants, we're caught in a labyrinth of sleazy politics. We are forced to endure much that is benighted in order to attain an occasional triumph. As for the general public, the idea that art is for everyone, regardless of personal sensitivity or the benefit of an experienced eye, is questionable. Everyone, to be sure, is entitled to intelligent exposure to the visual world, but the uninformed public per se cannot be the final arbiter for art, any more than it can for science. Our own Congress, for which art and morality are too often oversimplified and mindlessly confused, is a glaring reminder. As a rule, if an artist is worth his salt he is in advance of his times and not necessarily accepted by the general public or its political representatives. According to Daniel Halévy, Degas once said, "Art for the people! How dreary!" Some of the most perceptive connoisseurs of art have been autocrats, most conspicuously the Italian Renaissance popes and the princely families from which they came. They may have been good or bad rulers, but they weren't worrying about nudity or perversity when they backed Michelangelo and Leonardo. Nor were those potentates of Persia and India when they commissioned manuscript illuminations as erotic as they were refined.

Art is never a typically democratic process, whether from the viewer's or the artist's point of departure. It's a lonely business and at best embraced by solitary individuals. Still, I believe it is worth the boredom of reviewing works by innumerable shallow exhibitionists in order to winnow out even one authentic voice. Slowly a Giacometti, a Mondrian, a David Smith emerges, followed even more slowly by a small perceptive public. The only hope, whether for the artists or their audiences, is a more active innovative breakthrough in public art education. Then gradually, a patient but, I hope, not passive eye will be better able to distinguish between authentic invention and the meretricious.

I have been reminded again and again that democracy has yet to resolve its relationship to art. During the summer of 1972 while vacationing on Cape Cod, I spent a day in Boston at the Museum of Fine Arts, and wrote an article for *Saturday Review* about a politically motivated installation I saw there:

> Two small enamel cloisonné Chinese vases (vintage twentieth century) were reverently labeled as purchased by President and Mrs. Nixon during their recent trip to China and subsequently given to their daughter and son-in-law, the Edward Coxes. It seems that during late June, Tricia lent the vases to the museum in a ceremony honoring the institution's reinstallation of its splendid Chinese collection. All the more reason to be shocked at finding these shoddy little tourist items on exhibition there and all the more reason to question the relationship of art and politics. Three other questions arise: Are these knickknacks the best works modern China can produce? In the President's large entourage was there no advisor with some knowledge of art? And most important — why should a well-established institution genuflect to such pedestrian objects regardless of their original owners or lenders? Each transcendent Chinese work in the Boston museum was demeaned by the presence of these pitiful offerings.

Because the Associated Press picked up the story and spread it throughout the country, the Boston papers fastened on my criticism as page-one news and the ridiculous little vases were widely reproduced. I, innocent as the dawn, had no idea that my words were being published nationally and were causing both the White House and the Museum of Fine Arts considerable discomfort. It was only after a Boston reporter tracked me down on Cape Cod that I gleefully discovered how one of my pieces at last had hit the mark and was actually being read. By then the Boston museum's curator of Oriental art was making it clear that he had nothing to do with accepting the loan and had not known about it in advance. In a few days the vases disappeared and the cabinet in which they had been placed as precious objects accompanied by a prominent gold card thanking the lenders was removed. That the entire obsequious performance backfired was a plus for quality — and a later ordeal for me. The Nixon White House did not forget my effrontery. Although I did not have the honor of making the infamous "enemies list," I was punished for what I wrote. For the next few years, my tax returns were audited with a ferocity and tenaciousness rivaling that expended on the financial records of Al Capone.

While I was in the Soviet Union in 1963 for several weeks writing a *Saturday Review* piece about art in Communist Russia, the only time I found myself envying citizens there was during my visits to the conservation laboratories of various museums. Well financed by and dependent only on the government, these departments were far larger and more specialized than ours in the United States. In Moscow's Tretyakov Museum, an entire group of highly trained conservators was devoted only to the restoration and preservation of icons. The same was true of works on paper, oil paintings, sculpture, decorative arts, and architecture. These well-equipped laboratories far outstripped ours in the number and often quality of their highly trained specialists. In every other way, the handling of art in the Soviet Union was shockingly regressive. Government subsidies backed paintings and sculpture of the lowest possible denominator, with emphasis always on heavy-handed propaganda. In the foreseeable future, American museums are probably better off depending on private donors than on Congress. But the time, energy, ingenuity, and hopes lavished on wooing collectors are prodigious and demand a kind of aggression not always characteristic of the best curators and scholars.

One episode encapsulated the entire dilemma we faced when it came to propitiating collectors. Dan Rich gave a lecture for a group affiliated with the Art Institute called the Society for Contemporary Art. It was through this organization that the museum acquired many outstanding modern works. Speaking informally, Rich discussed what he would buy were he a private collector. For example, he preferred Picasso to Braque and at midcentury already recognized the Spaniard as the leader of Western art. At the end of his talk, Leigh Block, an Art Institute trustee, and his wife, Mary, collared me to state emotionally that the museum no longer need expect to inherit their collection. They looked on Dan's preference as an insult to them personally. The Blocks were known as prolific collectors who had acquired especially important works by Braque. In this case the identification with their own holdings was irrational: they demanded that even freedom of speech be muzzled. Before and after the Blocks' deaths, the museum inherited a few fine works but by no means the entire collection nor even the heart of it, despite the fact that from time to time we at the Art Institute had advised the Blocks.

There are collectors and there are people who buy art. Quantity does not necessarily make a collection. Overall quality is mandatory and so also is an overall plan that precludes as well as includes. Authentic collectors aren't easily seduced; there is a discipline behind their acquisitions. To make a collection such as the Arensbergs and Duncan Phillips did demanded more than a love of art and available funds. In my opinion, the Blocks were not sufficiently disciplined or knowledgeable to become authentic collectors.

I also owe much to collectors. One of them, Muriel Kallis Newman, would have made a first-rate curator. In Chicago, she was among the first to recognize the meaning of Abstract Expressionism and crowded her living room with top works by Pollock, de Kooning, and their colleagues. The first time I visited her, the impact was almost destabilizing. There she was — a very pretty young woman, eyes shining, words tumbling out and all of them making excellent sense, and there was that living room heralding the best of the newest. I learned much that day. She not only bought the works of these men. She had become their friend as well, and through countless conversations came to understand what made them the rebels they were. Though she is very much alive and still lives in Chicago, she has already willed her collection to the Metropolitan Museum of Art. There were many reasons the Art Institute lost out. Because she was a woman and an unconventional young collector who didn't need piles of money to buy well in a field where she was an early convert, the trustees of the museum ignored her. When the cultural history of our own century is finally written, it may demonstrate that trustees lost as much as they gained for their institutions.

A generous donor to the Art Institute and one who also helped open my eyes was Maurice Culberg. Culberg fell in love with Dubuffet's early work and started buying it when the artist was largely unknown. He had never met Dubuffet, but he reacted sharply to the brutal if deceptive innocence of his images. Culberg offered to give a Dubuffet to the Art Institute if we would choose one from the artist's studio the next time we were in Paris. That's how Dan and I met Jean Dubuffet. He fascinated us. Insinuous, wary, he moved with feline grace and had a way of flattering one more by his manner than his words. Firmly planted in this world, he shrouded himself in an artless guise.

Later Dubuffet came to Chicago for a long visit specifically to get acquainted with Culberg, his undemanding patron. The two men became warm friends, though they shared only one interest in common, the artist's paintings. Some years later when Culberg was dying of cancer, Dubuffet created small works of art for his hospital room. One I remember above all others — a shimmering collage of feathers that was all Dubuffet, but more a salute to life than his usual bow to disintegration.

Culberg gave because he liked to give. He demanded no special attention, no soft soap. I told him at one time how much I admired a certain Miró — *Personages with Star*, painted in 1933. His response, "Do you want it?" It came to the museum the next day.

As a rule, though, Chicago's entrenched conservatism made any attempts to bring the Art Institute into the mid-twentieth century a daily frustration. I must admit to developing a martyr complex, part of which was my own doing. I was a total loss as a diplomat and rarely able to cope calmly with the frequent crises. When, for example, Willem de Kooning's great painting *Excavation* was offered as a gift, it was very nearly turned down by the trustees. They reluctantly accepted, but only with the stipulation that the canvas not be shown for a decade, an agreement we of course rejected. A large Jackson Pollock called *Greyed Rainbow* fared no better. Once acquired (for a pittance), it incurred the wrath of many Chicago art patrons and particularly of the *Tribune*. Dubbing me "Kuh-Kuh" in a headline that read "Kuh-Kuh Must Go," the paper reported on the purchase, which took place in 1955, as a civic calamity. (Four years later I resigned from the Art Institute, moved to New York, and became art editor of the *Saturday Review*. After I had been writing about six months for the magazine, the *Tribune* asked me to contribute a monthly column, a roundup of art in New York. I hunted up the old clipping and sent it to the paper, with a one-sentence note — "Kuh-Kuh cannot come to your aid.") However, I think the charade that most upset me had to do with *Edge of August*, a fine painting by Mark Tobey from 1953. Considering it a frivolous indulgence, but not wanting to alienate the staff entirely, the trustee committee decided to flip a coin and leave the decision to chance. Our museum lost; the picture was soon bought by the Museum of Modern Art.

There were nevertheless compensations, chief among them the stimulation of working with artists and living with art. After I left the museum and was living in New York, I sometimes found myself dreaming about certain favorite works almost as if they were abandoned children. That curators can become overattached to their "wards" is no doubt true and not always healthy, but it is a hazard of the profession. Often underpaid, overworked, and, unlike university professors, lacking the safeguard of tenure, museum curators make up for their insecurity by fiercely identifying with the works in their charge. I actually became physically sick when our paintings were vandalized, which, alas, happened all too often in Chicago.

The problem of vandalism in Chicago was especially rampant immediately after the Second World War, much of it resulting from deranged visitors who were often ticked off by contemporary works. One morning we arrived at the Art Institute to find an important nineteenth-century American portrait with its eyes gouged out, and only a week later several oils by Léger were viciously slashed. Then someone spat on a large painting by José Clemente Orozco. These mutilations made me realize that no matter how much glass distorts a work of art, it was obligatory as a protective measure, at least in Chicago. All of which explains why so many of the museum's fine paintings are still incarcerated behind that unfortunate material, no matter how cruelly the practice distorts the artist's original intention and diminishes the viewer's pleasure.

The Art Institute's collection was not immune to vandalism even when its paintings were far from home. One day Dan and I were having a Campari on the terrace of a small bistro in Rome. Across the street was a kiosk with the latest newspapers on view. My eyes kept focusing on a familiar image that resembled a late Renoir in the Art Institute. And that, alas, was what the picture was, reproduced on page one because it had been stolen the previous day while on loan to the Louvre. Dan left immediately for Paris. After legal headaches, suspense, and all manner of worrisome details, the Renoir was recovered. But the canvas had been cut from its frame. It was restored, but it is a wounded survivor that should never travel again.

The most agonizing experience I ever suffered over works in peril began on April 15, 1958, when we received an emergency call from New York with the horrifying news that the Museum of Modern Art was on fire. *A Sunday on La Grande Jatte,* by Georges Seurat, often considered the Art Institute's supreme masterpiece, was on exhibition there, along with one of our canvases by Juan Gris. The hours we spent waiting for authoritative news suggested the ordeal of relatives hovering outside an operating room. It was unreal. To think of the *Grande Jatte,* probably the outstanding French nineteenth-century painting in America, destroyed or even seriously damaged was intolerable. We girded for action. Dan Rich and Louis Pomerantz, the museum's conservator of paintings, dashed off to New York while I manned the long-distance telephone in my office and immediately called friends in New York who, after a hurried visit to 53rd Street, rang back to say the sight was not reassuring. The street was closed off and all that could be seen were flames, smoke, and multiple fire engines.

Georges Seurat, *A Sunday on La Grande Jatte*, 1884–86. The *Grande Jatte* is the Art Institute's most celebrated work of art. Katharine always asserted that it was also "the greatest nineteenth-century French painting in America."

Because of the ever-present threat of vandalism at the Art Institute, we were forced to encase many paintings in glass, which, of course, made large ones inordinately heavy. Surrounded by its glass and special housing, the *Grande Jatte* weighed about five hundred pounds. Sitting in my office and waiting for word from New York, I didn't know whether to worry about this problem or to be relieved that at least the painting was somewhat protected from smoke. For an unnamable reason I felt guilty, as if we at our museum were personally to blame. Never again would I be a party to lending works of art without considerable soul-searching. Though a late Monet belonging to the Museum of Modern Art was completely burned and a Boccioni painting severely damaged, our paintings miraculously came through in good health — this despite the *Grande Jatte*'s unwieldy frame, which I worried would be too heavy to move in an emergency. (Needless to say, we learned our lesson, and the trappings of several large paintings were subsequently redesigned.)

Eventually, Dan called from New York to say that the Seurat was safe. Safe too was the painting by Juan Gris, lent to another exhibition on view. I had almost forgotten about it in my anxiety about the *Grande Jatte*. Dan further reported that the staff, workmen, and firemen, led by Alfred Barr and René d'Harnoncourt (the museum's first and current directors), had rescued every Seurat in that large retrospective exhibition. By all odds the most difficult, because of its size, weight, and extremely secure installation, was the *Grande Jatte*. It was carried into the Whitney Museum of American Art, then located immediately adjacent to the Modern on West 54th Street. The entire operation was heroic, especially given that the Modern's own permanent collection was also in jeopardy.

Despite the *Grande Jatte*'s being unharmed, a serious argument ensued between Alfred (then the Modern's director of collections) and Dan and me. I urged that the Seurat be returned to Chicago immediately; Alfred wanted it to remain in New York until the Seurat show could be reinstalled and the Museum of Modern Art revitalized. Always a thoughtful strategist, he saw this as a potential vote of confidence; for me, it was tempting fate too much. The *Grande Jatte,* the keystone of the exhibition, had never before left Chicago since its arrival at the Art Institute in 1924, and this time only because the exhibition was a joint enterprise of the two museums. The show had opened first in Chicago to enthusiastic acclaim. Dan felt that we owed the Museum of Modern Art its proper share of this costly exhibition. When he agreed to leave the painting in New York, I must admit to my dismay.

It was a particularly difficult decision for Dan. Under great pressure he had earlier lent Toulouse-Lautrec's *At the Moulin Rouge* to an exhibition at a New York private club because a potential donor (backed by one of our trustees) insisted. Again an unparalleled painting, it was damaged. The injury was not serious, yet it was entirely unnecessary. Works of art are always vulnerable, and exploiting them for political or social prestige is unpardonable.

Later, in a similar situation when I almost capitulated myself, it was these past memories that saved me. John U. Nef, a distinguished professor at the University of Chicago and a man conversant with art, was planning some sort of private Chagall show. He wanted to borrow *Birth,* our early painting depicting the artist's imaginary birth, but its impaired condition had forced us to put it on the nonlending list. For a period of several weeks, scarcely a day went by when I wasn't hounded about that canvas. A charming and erudite man, Professor Nef stooped to every device to force my hand, appealing to our trustees, to Chagall, to my friends and enemies, to threats and blandishments, all so that I'd agree to jeopardize a work of art.

The terrifying fire at the Museum of Modern Art persuaded me that one of the most serious dangers art faces today, more immediately threatening than wars and natural disasters, is the event we would come to call the blockbuster exhibition. Because of this modern and not always fulfilling phenomenon, paintings and sculpture circumnavigate the globe and in the process are exposed to innumerable haz-

Katharine, Marc Chagall, and Dan Rich at the Art Institute of Chicago, 1958. *Birth*, the painting by Chagall that occasioned Professor Nef's relentless pressure, is behind them.

ards: sudden changes in temperature and humidity, the possibility of political and physical upheavals, thefts, storms at sea and in the air, and, worst of all, the daily wear and tear of travel. Constant packing and unpacking, galleries crowded with countless visitors pushing, breathing, and perspiring, can contaminate fragile works of art. Unless this ceaseless travel stops, we'll have little left for future generations.

Such perils were rare before American museums began their unprecedented expansion. When they were the private domains of the elite, they were relatively safe if likewise musty and usually empty of visitors. When dynamic young directors like Dan, Alfred, the Guggenheim's James Johnson Sweeney, and A. Everett "Chick" Austin of the Wadsworth Atheneum began widening art museum parameters with a zeal never equaled before or since, the situation changed drastically. Adding departments and services, rethinking art education, insisting on reliable scholarship, innovating, innovating, innovating, these directors were their own worst enemies. Their efforts were involved with serving a large general public, but as they succeeded beyond all expectations they found insurmountable problems. The more they humanized their institutions, and the more art became accessible to the layperson, the larger, more costly, and complicated their institutions became. Money had to be raised, architects consulted, donors placated, staffs pacified, and soon these creative men were floundering in an administrative maelstrom. And not one of them was a good administrator. It was the art itself that held them. The successful monsters they created were their nemeses.

Museum directors today, if accomplished, are adroit managers who keep the peace among temperamental disparate groups, operate internationally, and are always circumscribed by monetary demands. This generation of directors are not so much innovators as diplomats balancing complicated and often opposing forces. Museums are now more efficient than in my day but less fulfilling places to work. While he was director of the Whitney Museum, John I. H. Baur explained to me after holding the job a relatively short time that he was numb from all the petty problems that were destroying his relationship with art. Earlier he had been a curator of American painting at the Brooklyn Museum, where he acquired some of that institution's finest early canvases. When his predecessor, Lloyd Goodrich, retired from the directorship of the Whitney in 1968, Baur took over, having previously been the associate director. Yet little did he anticipate the daily grind of total administration. The joy was gone, and he confessed he hoped to retire as soon as possible — and that, indeed, is what he did.

What are museums to do? Grow larger and larger? Take in more and more funds to support ever-expanding superstructures? I would advise the reverse. Museums could increase their effectiveness, at least for the foreseeable future, by delving deeper into holdings that could yield valuable surprises. Today it is education rather than entertainment, enlightenment rather than theater, that is mandated. The hype and the mobs have broken down dusty old barriers, but now we must use our gains for more rewarding ends. All the familiar staples — lectures, books, symposia, conducted tours, even perhaps those dreadful talking machines — do have their uses, but the time has come for more in-depth solutions. Historical, scientific, and technical aids can free art education from its past dependence on stereotypes. Education departments as such should be abolished. Each curator must develop his or her own educational program and give it the same priority accorded to acquisitions and highly touted exhibitions. Works that have been taken for granted for years, on reexamination in new contexts, can yield surprising secrets. It is no longer merely exposure we want, it is an intelligent understanding of what makes a work of art. Somehow we must develop new ways of bringing an interested public to a fuller understanding of visual experiences. Often the most difficult works to understand are the most rewarding.

In the late 1950s, after consulting a number of international authorities on conservation, we decided to have the *Grande Jatte* cleaned for the first time. Imagine our amazement to discover, once surface film had been removed, two small figures hidden in the upper-right corner — some eyes found three — that were presumed to be the artist and his mistress. In the first half of the century we relied too often on only visual and structural elements to explain an artist's work. It was form, line, color, space, distance, and motion that were basic. My generation in America was trying to free itself from the sentimentally narrative "art appreciation" common to our period. For us, Van Gogh's ear became a cautionary symbol, his art swallowed up in his tragic story. Moreover, art was too often relegated to the province of ladies' clubs, where it was suffocated in uplifting emotions. We decided that what you see makes more sense than storytelling myths. We were trying to supply an understanding of art from a rational professional stance. Today the emphasis has become equally lopsided, as has occurred with the *Grande Jatte*. In my time it was explained in purely formal terms; now it has turned into a battleground for industrial, social, political, and psychological issues, depending on who is interpreting it. Its structural meaning is rarely mentioned.

For the staff of the Art Institute, the uncovering of the two portraits was electrifying. We began to understand for the first time that Seurat was more than a formalist involved with the scientific breakup of color; he was suddenly a very young man with human emotions. On the occasion of a 1984 symposium at the Art Institute devoted to the *Grande Jatte* on its hundredth birthday, a number of contemporary scholars examined the painting from every angle, but not one mentioned the hidden portraits or what they reveal. The canvas was there, tangible, before their eyes. Could it have become so familiar as to obviate further looking? Or were their theories about nineteenth-century economics more influential than visual evidence?

The *Grande Jatte* was cleaned after it returned from the Museum of Modern Art. Just before it was covered by glass and hung on the wall again, I was sitting on the floor in an empty gallery studying it at leisure, a luxury I had rarely enjoyed before. Dan had already left the Art Institute to become director of the Worcester Art Museum and I too had recently resigned and was due to leave shortly. Though I'd never met the newly appointed director, John Maxon, I was convinced that it would be impossible for us to work together, and my hunch was confirmed soon enough. He was in Chicago that day for a preliminary visit and found me on the floor peering at the *Grande Jatte*. By way of introduction he observed, "I've always considered this painting a bit overrated."

Traveling in search of art or later in search of stories about art for *Saturday Review* gave me further opportunities for working relationships with artists. While assembling a collection for the First National Bank of Chicago, I went on global jaunts to South America, the Near East, Asia, Europe, and the Caribbean as well as all over the United States. These were voyages of discovery that provided familiar and unfamiliar geography with a unifying web of art, a web of ceaselesss gossip and generous hospitality that knew no national boundaries. Architects on Cape Cod sent me to their counterparts in Bombay; curators at London's National Gallery offered introductions to their associates in the museums of Ankara and Jerusalem. A Dutch dealer in old master paintings smoothed my way to collectors stretching from Paris to Warsaw and Geneva to Athens. But above all, artists directed me to other artists, for, like members of a great floating freemasonry, they interact and intercommunicate with one another. More than in other creative professions, I have always felt that visual artists, when their work sparks a mutual empathy, react with tenacious loyalty.

In retrospect, I scan the years and fasten upon two upsetting defeats. One took place in India, where I traveled under the joint aegis of that country and our own with an assignment to organize an exhibition of contemporary Indian art to be shown in America. Visiting dozens upon dozens of studios and galleries, as well as museums, art schools, and the odd collector, I returned with recommendations that were eventually so diluted by the interaction of the two government bureaucracies that the whole project became impotent. In Alaska, the site of my other failure, I experienced a far more bitter disappointment. It was again at the hands of the government — this time our own, acting alone. Commissioned by the Department of Indian Affairs to investigate the state of totemic Indian artifacts in Alaska and then advise on preservation and restoration, I wrote a detailed and passionate report in 1946, following it up with frequent earnest nudgings. But nothing was ever done, which may help to explain why our most distinguished native heritage was allowed to crumble and, in great part, to vanish.

However, it is not ultimately about my career or its high points and downfalls that I want to write. I realize that though my life was devoted to intense visual experiences, it has, in a sense, remained on the periphery of art. The source of art is never the critic, curator, dealer, or historian: it is the artist. Overwhelmingly, the core of this book is lodged in the lives and works of the many creative personalities I was privileged to know. The essays about them are summations by an eyewitness, distillations of my own observations, but my comments are always bolstered by verbatim comments from the artists themselves, and it is my earnest wish that their voices emerge from these pages with authenticity. Unless otherwise indicated, all quotations are drawn from letters to and conversations with me, plus occasional interviews I conducted with the artists for this book and for *The Artist's Voice*, a collection of interviews I published in 1962. Their immediate reactions to daily events, their manner of living, the kinds of houses, studios, and friends they chose, their attitudes toward their art and the public, will all act, I hope, as source material. If these essays go beyond corroborating already familiar facts to supply wider knowledge about the art of this century, and if they debunk overeasy assumptions that have appeared unchallenged in recent publications, then they will have served their purpose.

Often the most casual occurrence may have large meaning. I think immediately of why Edward Hopper painted so many rooftops in the untypically Mexican town of Saltillo, why Mark Tobey left the United States to settle permanently as an expatriate in Switzerland, why Mark Rothko tempestuously gave up teaching, why Mies van der Rohe refused to live in the buildings he designed, what Léger thought of Dubuffet's paintings.

To compare the various artists is to realize how differently they worked and believed. Some were insecure to the point of paranoia; others, even while totally neglected, were convinced of their own worth. Some counted on moods and inspiration; others regarded art as a normal, matter-of-fact occupation. Some were irrationally self-centered, others self-deprecatory. Some were silent and withdrawn, others very much of the world. I found no stereotypes and, in turn, sought veracity. I agree with Voltaire that "to the dead one owes only the truth."

1
Searching and Seeing

What exactly is an art curator? From my experience, curators can be anything they want as long as they conform at least nominally to the bureaucratic folkways of museum life. Committees, trustees, complaints, social interruptions, and the discreet pursuit of possible donors are all part of the game, but aside from these distractions, each curator is a potential self-invention. To be sure, scholarship, experience, and a commitment to using one's eyes both for looking and seeing (quite different processes) are prerequisites, yet there are no rigid boundaries.

The job can involve excitement, frustration, delight, romance, fulfillment, and deep disappointment. To pursue a painting (a superb early Poussin), as I did once for over a year, only to lose it to another museum (the Minneapolis Institute of Arts), can be devastating. Now it seems unimportant to me, for, after all, the canvas is readily accessible to the public whether or not it hangs in Chicago or Minneapolis. In either case, it will be cared for, preserved, studied, and shown in proper surroundings, all services dependent on curatorial initiatives. It is, however, the search, the tracking down, and final snaring of a work of art that I find the headiest curatorial experience. When successful, the joy of the hunt can be overwhelming, and not only because of a competitive victory — there are more palpable rewards. Curators need no personal incomes to acquire great collections or to be surrounded many hours each day by splendid trophies. Their homes can be seedy, but a large part of their lives are spent with masterpieces that would set any private collector to salivating.

The best curators become obsessed: they identify with the works they defend if not as personal possessions, at least as deep-seated attachments. When I left the Art Institute of Chicago in 1959, after some sixteen years, many as curator of modern art, I dreamt constantly of certain favorite works. I was literally haunted by them. Now, after thirty-five years, I still am. Curators are, as Duchamp might have said, "ready-made collectors." I think immediately of my colleague Carl Schniewind, who was originally a private collector before he became curator of prints and drawings at the Art Institute. He was a passionately involved scholar from whom I never ceased learning. One day, at a boring museum luncheon, he overheard a guest discussing a recently purchased print dress and he suddenly came to life. The word *print* galvanized him. He even named his dog Print! Though he was a fine scholar, he was much more; his total commitment to and joy in the works he handled literally kept him alive. Far from well, he worked five days a week at the museum and then remained bedridden every weekend.

Put very simply, a curator's job is to take care of, teach about, and acquire works of art. These are the obligations (better called privileges), but how these duties are pursued is a matter of individual ingenuity. In the United States today, the term *curator* is bandied about so heedlessly that any dilettante who arranges the most meager sampling of art appropriates the title. To make matters worse, the noun now poses as a verb, actively inciting freelance novices to claim a professionalism sadly lacking — not unlike a first-year intern posing as an experienced surgeon. The debasing of the title points to all the trappings of pseudo-scholarship. Because art is an inexact and volatile study, it demands knowledge of the past, if only to validate any serious preoccupation with the present. One must have points of comparison and continuity. I think of Harold Rosenberg, who wrote beautifully about contemporary art but not always persuasively. Although he understood, perhaps clairvoyantly, its sociological implications, his visual expertise rarely antedated Cézanne.

English curators are frequently called keepers, but "keeping" is a far cry from recent practices in American institutions, where the popular pastime of selling works from permanent holdings can become scandalous. The sudden metamorphosis of museum directors and curators into masters of finance partly resulted from the startling escalation of art prices during the 1980s, though the practice has been known for some time. We've all had our hand in it; not keeping but selling — termed "deaccessioning" in polite museum language — has become the order of the day. There was always the alibi, sometimes legitimate, that the dollars gained would be spent on more important works, but who is to say that a Monet is more important than a Matisse or a David Smith than a Miró? Despite qualifying circumstances like date, condition, size, medium, provenance, and of course the specific need of the museum involved, who is all-seeing enough to make these final judgments before history has had its say? And even history can be unreliable. To review at random the economic status of works by such well-known artists as, let's say, Turner and Botticelli, is to realize how unpredictable fashions in art are. There were periods not so long ago when both men were largely ignored. During the late nineteenth century, the English Pre-Raphaelites reinstated Botticelli, and Turner's resurrection owed much to his importance for the Impressionists. Once they were elevated to stardom, he acquired similar status.

Recently I encountered a canvas by Thomas Eakins that the Art Institute sold many years ago in order to acquire a larger, more important painting by the same artist. I don't know what "more important" means, but I do know that the cast-off work still seemed very interesting to me and, at least from hindsight, should have been kept. Perhaps a bit of focused fund-raising to ensure the purchase of the larger canvas would have been wise. Together the two paintings might have enhanced each other; alone they are single experiences. And how is it possible to have too many paintings by America's greatest nineteenth-century artist? Try to buy one today. Museums would be wise to keep much of what they have, since they may never get a second chance. Of course, I'm referring to works of acknowledgable even if debatable importance. Occasionally, straight trades can be advantageous but, as soon as money (often large sums) changes hands, comparative evaluations become more and more hazardous.

What keeps curators most on their toes is the thrill of the hunt, as they compete for works of art in the national and international market. In the early years my new department at the museum was a stepchild where funds were concerned, but eventually we hit on a splendid though tiring acquisition technique. By a vague barter and trade system, we advised and frequently traveled with private collectors who in return gave the museum certain key works. A number of the Art Institute's memorable twentieth-century paintings and sculpture were added in this way. Yet on numerous occasions when unburdened, I operated alone and, if my luck held, jubilantly came home with the booty. However, there was constant competition.

In my experience, the best informed and most stubborn art sleuth was Alfred H. Barr, Jr., the first director of the Museum of Modern Art. He seemed to know unerringly where every available modern work was located, whether in the United States or abroad. He kept voluminous files, and no clue was too elusive for him to follow. Many years ago, during the mid-fifties, the Paris art dealer Katia Granoff announced she had a cache of late Monet paintings all related to the artist's now famous pond and surrounding gardens at Giverny. From the photographs she sent to me, I reserved what seemed the best canvas and assured her I was coming to Europe shortly and would make a decision after seeing the paintings themselves. Flying to Paris from Switzerland in 1956, I arrived at my hotel late one night to find an urgent message from Alfred. He wanted me to call him no matter the hour. I haven't the vaguest idea how he tracked me down. He informed me he had visited Katia Granoff during the past few days and purchased several of the Monets both for the Museum of Modern Art and for certain trustees he hoped would in turn give or leave them to the museum. His overall strategy in assembling the Modern's extraordinary collection was an ongoing project. Only today, decades since his active participation ended, can we begin to comprehend how astutely he coordinated his plans. What he could not acquire for his institution he recommended to various trustees who, in many cases with his help, assembled enviable collections. In turn, from time to time, they either bequeathed or gave these works to the museum, as he had anticipated. It is not surprising that art acquired in this way was adroitly geared to the institution's permanent collection. That, of course, was the original plan. Gaps were gradually filled as earlier promises materialized. Even now, years after his death, the collection and the museum still belong to Barr — the direct result of his long-range vision. The institution faces two acute problems today: first it must articulate its own definition of "modern," and then it must plan for the new century with the same urgency Barr lavished on the twentieth. I hope that its present architecture, which always reminds me of a glorified department store, is no harbinger of the future.

In any case, Alfred had phoned to tell me that he wanted *Iris*, the painting I had reserved. I assured him I was due at the gallery at ten the next morning and would let him know the outcome as soon as possible. What was my surprise when I arrived to find Alfred pacing up and down in front of the gallery. Oblivious to the cold rain sweeping across the Seine, he waited outside while I entered that musty cave to be first led through a closet with an unmade bunk bed that obviously had just yielded up Katia Granoff, who was slopping around in a frayed bathrobe. I must confess that I felt completely superfluous. Eventually we reached a larger room and there at last were the paintings — alive with turbulent pigment and luminosity. I often wondered how Alfred could have imagined I would turn down that wonderful painting, especially after he was so hell-bent on getting it.

I received another message from Alfred during the time I was working with Walter and Louise Arensberg in Hollywood, cataloguing the collection that we at the Art Institute vainly hoped to inherit. One day, Walter returned in high excitement from a visit to Earl Stendahl's gallery. There he had just purchased two sculptures by Brancusi — *The Fish* and *Torso of a Young Man*. How Barr got wind of this sale almost immediately is a mystery but, electrified by the news, he promptly contacted me to find out which version of *The Fish* was involved. At that point, he was negotiating elsewhere for the larger one and he wanted assurance that he was not being bypassed. Over the long-distance phone, he sounded like a deeply concerned parent worried about the well-being of his child. Alert to each nuance in the complexities of collecting, to every breath of gossip that might affect his carefully annotated files, he followed all conceivable leads.

Another visit to Paris and a different art activist, this one more lighthearted: I was walking along the rue de Rivoli when I ran into James Johnson Sweeney, then the director of the Guggenheim Museum. He was exuberant because only that morning he had made a historic scoop, a windfall of four major sculptures by Brancusi that he'd been after for some time and which today still form the backbone of the Guggenheim's sculpture collection. While we celebrated with a brandy or two, he confided that the price for all four came to one hundred thousand dollars, a very sizable sum at that time. He already anticipated trouble with certain trustees, but I was drooling with envy. To have such freedom to invest in superb works of art without the debilitating ordeal of first persuading a lay committee composed chiefly of businessmen seemed little less than nirvana to me. The hours spent in this kind of lobbying were bruising and, to be frank, I was far from adept at the process. Often the more I urged the stonier my reception. I still regret certain splendid works that slipped from our hands — paintings by Mark Tobey and Bradley Walker Tomlin (both now in the Museum of Modern Art), by Baron Gros (in the Metropolitan Museum's collection), by Breughel, and a sculpture by Rodin (the work was deemed pornographic). The Breughel was eliminated because the president of the museum found it "too lugubrious." Though Sweeney's personal income permitted him to assemble a fine collection of his own, he identified with the works he bought for the museum even more intensely. It was not ownership but the scent of the hunt that drove him, as well as his total commitment to the visual world.

A visit to James and Laura Sweeney's East Side Manhattan apartment was a rarefied experience. Mies van der Rohe had designed the interior, which was both stark and handsome. Not even an ashtray sullied the spacious living room, furnished sparsely with only Mies's designs.

On the stark white walls, I remember two paintings: *Metamorphosis* by Picasso and a superb Mondrian. From time to time, these canvases were retired in favor of two or three other masterpieces.

Barr responded to works of art with repressed intensity and a formidable wealth of knowledge, Sweeney with ebullient emotion and an implacable eye. Both dared to break with tradition, both were pioneers in their field, but Barr almost single-handedly overturned museum practices throughout the world. After him, stodgy airless galleries packed with competing works of art no longer existed. He introduced a new kind of showmanship with emphasis on well-designed dynamic installations. Employing innovative techniques, he hoped to engage the viewer in a total experience. For Barr the viewer was the public: his target included art specialists, but it was chiefly the intelligent layman he addressed. He integrated films, photography, architecture, and product design into the museum experience. In addition he was also the first to concentrate on a long series of literate art catalogues that were both scholarly and yet nontechnical enough to interest the more casual museum visitor. He and his colleagues revolutionized museum catalogues.

What I always found startling was the contrast between Barr's quiet persona and the radical concepts he introduced. Soft-spoken, polite, preoccupied, he was almost always under attack by the press as an arrogant "tastemaker." Demoted at one point by his own trustees, he pressed on. His office and title changed, but he never wavered from his mission as our century's foremost art impresario. He was totally committed to the museum he founded and to a public he hoped and indeed helped to educate.

My own pursuit of a Brancusi sculpture was filled with roadblocks. After the Manhattan dealer Curt Valentin died in 1954, his most faithful clients were invited to preview his stock before it was offered to the general public. I went to New York as soon as possible, but Jim Sweeney had already outmaneuvered me and reserved an early sculpture by Brancusi that I yearned for. Back in Chicago, I mourned my loss, but after six months of silent waiting, I inquired as to the status of the sculpture, only to be told it was still reserved by the Guggenheim Museum.

Six months later I received the same answer, but shortly after that, in 1955, Sweeney released the piece and we in Chicago immediately bought it.

Though this idol-like figure titled *Wisdom*, seemingly enveloped in ritualistic silence, was accompanied by little or no provenance, I had never doubted its authenticity. One needed only to compare it to the various versions of Brancusi's *Kiss* to recognize unmistakable stylistic parallels. Of course, it could have been the work of a clever imitator, but its contained, primitive power pointed to no one but Brancusi. Its blocklike form and suppression of all detail were characteristic of the artist's early stone carvings.

After I resigned from the Art Institute and returned to the museum on periodic visits, I would notice that *Wisdom* was not on view. I subsequently learned that it was no longer considered a work by Brancusi. This didn't make it any less interesting for me, but it was now far less valuable for the museum. It seems that the Brancusi scholar Sidney Geist had, after learning that Brancusi had rejected the sculpture, decided that it was not correctly attributed. His opinion carried justifiable weight because of his previous excellent research on the artist. In his monograph on Brancusi's work, published in 1967, he assigned the object "doubtful status." Then, to my amazement, a more current article by Geist and the 1983 reprint of his monograph categorized *Wisdom* as an original sculpture by Brancusi. Dumbfounded, I immediately wrote to him for further information. He explained that the carving had indeed been fully reinstated as authentic. *Wisdom* had rejoined an exclusive canon. This drastic change, he added, was precipitated by valuable new data that had recently surfaced and provided fuller, more detailed information about the sculptor's early work. All of which leads us to believe that the study of art is suspended between knowledge and intuition; both are obligatory. Neither functions reliably without the other. Where art is concerned, there are no absolutes.

A man once came into my office at the Art Institute with two small drawings labeled "Picasso." Both seemed to me of no importance whatsoever. Even in his teens, Picasso was beyond this kind of puttering, or at least so I thought. To make certain, however, I suggested we send photographs of the drawings to the artist. I must

Constantin Brancusi, *Wisdom*, c. 1908. Opinions as to whether or not the
author of this sculpture is indeed Brancusi remain divided.

confess I never expected an answer, but in due time the photos were returned and on each was written *"C'est de moi, Picasso."* We can only guess how many third-rate works are incorrectly dubbed fakes! The problem with authentication is that it has always been too dependent on qualitative judgments. We are unwilling to believe that a great artist might have a bad day. How humble I felt after receiving those photographs back from the artist!

The whole idea of authenticity is a nagging question. How are we to judge Leonardo's *Last Supper* in Milan? Is there a single brush-stroke by the artist still visible after innumerable restorations? This fresco, a veritable icon of Western art, has endured repetitive blows from both man and nature. In addition, we are told by Leonardo's contemporaries that the painting was unusually fragile even from its inception, perhaps due to inadequate drying of its plaster ground. Are we then to think of this masterwork as an original painting by Leonardo or a copy from many different times and hands?

We at the Art Institute were at one time considering the purchase of *Saint Serapion,* a very fine religious composition by Zurbarán, and the museum had arranged for the painting to come to Chicago on ap-proval. Each day we were more enamored of it, but finally we returned the painting to its New York dealer, David Koetser. Using ultraviolet inspection, we had found that the surface of the canvas was generally abraded and that the saint's left hand had been completely repainted. In addition, parts of the saint's ear, jaw, and neck had been retouched. Many years later, I spotted *Saint Serapion* hanging in the Wadsworth Atheneum in Hartford. It struck me as more beautiful than ever and, since then, I've wondered what constitutes authenticity. Had there been no ultraviolet examination, there would have been no doubts. But how can we eliminate the advances of modern science and technol-ogy? These are, of course, added tools. Our final judgment of a work of art must embrace ever-increasing considerations. We cannot accept only what we see; what we know is important too. As the history of art lengthens, the job of a curator becomes more and more demanding.

During the forties, my curatorial duties included leading an art class for the Women's Garment Workers Union in Chicago. Once a week

Francisco de Zurbarán, *Saint Serapion*, 1628. The Art Institute of Chicago deliberated about buying this incandescent canvas by Zurbarán, but declined on account of worries about its abraded condition. Katharine later questioned the wisdom of that decision.

after work, I met for two hours with about twenty-five members, most of them Polish immigrants. For the first few sessions, it was rough going, but as I look back I think those early defeats taught me more about the interplay of art and life than all the erudite seminars I ever attended. The women, who spoke in broken English, had put in a hard day of factory work before the class convened, and most were considerably older than I. In my naïveté, I thought they were there to learn about the history of art, and I was vacillating over whether to start with the Greeks or Giotto. In any case, after the first meeting the group visibly diminished; after the second, there were only nine members left. I appealed to them for enlightenment. What was wrong? One of them volunteered that the women were disappointed; they wanted to know what colors went well together, how to make a small room look big, how, in short, to improve their homes. I explained that I was not an interior decorator, but that I very much wanted to adjust to their needs without sacrificing all emphasis on art. From that day, they started calling me "Teacher," and together we slowly worked out a heartwarming solution. Instead of meeting in a dreary room at the union, I arranged that our classes be held at the Art Institute, in a different gallery each week. None of them had ever before visited the museum. At first they were overawed but, as they began to relax and relate to the single work of art we investigated each session, they melted. Their enthusiasm encouraged others to return and shortly the class was back to its original size.

I tried to select a work each week that needed no preliminary knowledge to capture their interest. For instance, one evening we concentrated on Van Gogh's painting of his bedroom at Arles. I asked them only one question: "What does this canvas tell you about the artist who painted it and also lived in this room?" They argued among themselves, they compared, they responded to the immediacy of the work, and gradually they began to see. Caught up in authentic emotional reactions, they decided that the artist was poor and lonely. But they went beyond the obvious to question why he would have wanted to paint this shabby little room and above all why he had depended almost entirely on the color yellow, though his ultimate message was filled with sadness. We never mentioned chronology, historical progression, technique, or even the names of the artists. Only the work of art itself mattered. They were learning how to see; I was learning that all enrichment from art is not dependent on erudition. Eventually the museum gave the class a group membership. My heart soared when unexpectedly, at some evening opening or other, I'd hear, "Hi, Teacher!" and there, across the gallery, a few of my ladies were waving to me.

Yet there is no doubt that, in the long run, we cannot survive without the baggage of history. We can learn to look, but to see is another matter. One looks first and sees later. Looking is an ocular affair; seeing demands total integration, both conscious and unconscious. While doodling at the telephone, you glance across the room and suddenly see a familiar painting in a surprisingly new ambiance. At times,

Vincent van Gogh, *The Bedroom*, 1889. Van Gogh's moving depiction of his surroundings at Arles made an equally meaningful impression on the working women who were Katharine's students.

the less diligent you are, the more receptive. Seeing is the result of intuition and knowledge, of concentration and dream, of strong emotional reaction and, not least, of flexibility. As different contemporary art movements proliferate, evaluating them demands more than an understanding of the latest current events. We need what endures from the past to understand discoveries of the present, some of them mind-boggling, some déjà vu. To sort them out cogently demands perspective.

For example, take the difference between Cubism, which forever changed our way of seeing, and German Expressionism, which did not. Both emerged early in the present century. As Cubism broke with the past, it forced us to define our world in totally new, multifaceted, always fractured dimensions. It foretold the future, but it also responded to the cultural factors that had spawned it — chiefly the art of Cézanne, African carvings, and the overlay of a fast-paced, mechanized world. The Germans, on the other hand, turned back to a more distant past and to Matthias Grünewald, their sixteenth-century ancestor, whose searching indictments of mankind have never been equaled. Why did German artists reactivate their long love affair with Expressionism precisely when they did, and why does this highly emotional and, at times, overcharged form of art periodically grip the Western world? Is it war angst, moral breakdown, guilt, disillusionment, or all of these that stoke the fire? In Germany, where Expressionism has thrived on and off for some four hundred years, it assumes national proportions. But unlike the Cubists, the Expressionists did not change the course of recent art. What they tell us has been said before and better, for who can compete with the likes of Grünewald or Van Gogh?

As for history, is Hieronymus Bosch less important to our understanding of Surrealism than Freud? Though the Surrealists never borrowed Bosch's religious themes, they were affected by his wildly erotic and often sadistic images. Picasso, the most influential artist of our century, was also the most observant art historian. From El Greco to Velázquez, from Guido Reni to Ingres, he commented on and incorporated the discoveries of famous predecessors. A veritable compendium of the past, his works borrowed from legendary figures, if not always stylistically, at least referentially. The fact that Picasso, along with Braque, was responsible for Cubism, universally acknowledged as modern art's pivotal movement, in no way diminished his loyalty to the past. But he did what he wanted with it, fitting it to his own needs as he explored it. By both contrast and continuity, by irony and satire, he made us see artists like Velázquez and Grünewald as emblems of their own times and as extensions of ours.

The study of art history can be deadly and often is. Slides, technicalities, and splitting hairs over minor details of chronology often alienate more than they instruct. Without the original work of art and the personal stab of response, it can all be reduced to little more than a lifeless routine. Attending museums, visiting exhibitions, and traveling frequently are helpful but costly. The entire process of learning about art demands leisurely assimilation. There are no shortcuts. In 1951 the first all-embracing Caravaggio exhibition opened in Milan. Dan Rich and I had planned to spend two or three days there but, after our first encounter with the show, we decided to stay considerably longer. This panorama of his life's work stunned us. (At that time, and even today, paintings by Caravaggio are rarely seen in the United States.) In addition, the exhibition included those contemporaries and followers he had directly influenced. It was our first authentic introduction to the Caravaggisti.

The show was open from morning until late at night with brief intermissions, and, because it was very large, two strategically located bistros provided rest areas for argument and sustenance. We spent day after day in those galleries, hypnotized by Caravaggio's elliptical brilliance. Both Dan and I were familiar with his work and his brief, if lurid, biography from routine study, but we were not prepared for the impact of the real thing.

Though his paintings are usually based on standard religious themes, they are always idiosyncratic, as indeed he was himself. What other artist in history could have conceivably been forced to flee his home because of a murder he committed over a game of tennis? Possibly apocryphal, the story has been repeated too often not to take seriously. When finally, at the age of thirty-nine, Caravaggio ended his exile in Naples and headed for Rome, he never got beyond the beach where he landed. There, disoriented and ill, he died of fever. Caravaggio's paintings, as operatic as his life, are curiously modern. His understanding of the "common man" pre-dates that of Rembrandt. His focus on dramatic light and shade is cinematic, recalling the haunting films of Bergman. The drama of his performers puts much contemporary Expressionism to shame. Above all else, it is Caravaggio's ability to project a sense of space, out and away from the flat surface of his canvas — a space at once alive, palpable, and embracing — that attracts modern viewers. Operating on many visual levels, Caravaggio's space revolutionized the Renaissance conception of perspective.

For me those days in Milan were only the beginning. I went looking for Caravaggio relentlessly, even traveling to Sicily to see the late works painted while he was in exile. Unforgettable were two very large compositions in Messina, both physical wrecks but still persuasive. I dedicated an entire visit to Rome solely to pursue Caravaggio through myriad dark churches and chapels where, for a small fee, I was allowed to turn on the lights. These voyages were for me a form of living art history far removed from any semblance of slide lectures or footnotes. Art history is often augmented by an artist's preparatory sketches, but what has always amazed me is that no drawings or sketches by Caravaggio have ever been found. Are we then to presume that his monumental interlocking compositions were designed and executed without preliminary studies? If so, he was a magician as well as a genius.

If art grows from history, it also grows from art, although at times they can be one and the same. The art of the twentieth century owes much to the nineteenth century and Cézanne, but even more to two cataclysmic events and two iconoclastic thinkers. World Wars I and II, terminating in the birth of the atomic bomb, shattered any concept of "life as usual," while at the same time the radical discoveries of Einstein and Freud undermined long-held convictions.

Far worlds and unknown horizons were opening up as the demands of international warfare precipitated an all-consuming technology: the machine became the leitmotif of modern art and the airplane superseded the recently invented automobile as an even more liberat-

ing extension. Yet it was such mind-boggling abstractions as space re-
lations and the buried unconscious that most uprooted us. These new
preoccupations played havoc with art as well as with our lives. If the
nineteenth century explored the science and mysteries of natural light,
it was the twentieth that concentrated on the equally mysterious dimension of space as an all-embracing conception. How to depict this
fugitive element and yet never confuse it with distance or perspective
became a constant challenge to contemporary artists. As for the widespread influence of Freud, one need only refer to Surrealism and its
manifold offshoots. Freud's convictions infiltrated painting and sculpture with devastating impact. Medieval symbols of sadism and magic,
no longer reflecting religious themes, unlocked our secret egos.

The first fifty or sixty years of this century were innovative, especially the earlier decades. The impact of primitive art, in all its diversity, freed artists to return to their roots and eliminate nonessentials.
Whether the art was by children, African natives, or the insane, the result was liberation from conventional studio good manners. Keeping
up with the inventions, discoveries, and predictions of this period was
a ceaseless race. Especially in the 1940s and 1950s, it was popular to
damn "modern art" and its protagonists, who were denounced as
Reds, though their art was anathema to Communist thinking. (When
I was visiting the Soviet Union in 1963, I was daily lectured about
modern art, especially that by Picasso and the Russian Kasimir Male-
vich, as being "immature." When I asked to see their work, hidden
away in storage, I was abruptly refused.) Earlier, our own government
had joined with polite society, most of academia, and the average
American citizen likewise to heap scorn on the "new vision." But un-
deterred, the upheaval went on. By the 1960s, acceptance in the
United States had already turned the art revolution into history and a
degree of economic delirium. A banker once told me that he knew of
no stock that could compete with the rapid monetary appreciation of
a Kandinsky painting. Of course Kandinsky was still a nonperson in his
own country in 1963. Attitudes toward art are often tumultuous. It is
an area in which the layperson, even when minimally, if at all, informed, feels it is right to pronounce instant judgments. Because of its
very nature, a work of art can be observed in a split second. To read a

book, see a theatrical performance, or listen to a musical composition demands time.

The two halves of our century confront each other as antagonists. The later years have forged few, if any, momentous landmarks. Chiefly reactive, they have either rejected or retooled vital prior commitments. But the first half, an epoch of indomitable invention, has changed our vision forever and set the pace for an entire era. Picasso emerges as its dominant influence, while Marcel Duchamp has become the catalyst for the later years. However, I often wonder if the spirit of anti-art is a misunderstood message from Duchamp. I believe he was not an anti-artist as much as an anti-painter.

Art can be either a harbinger of the future or a recapitulation of the past. Early on, Cubism and Surrealism mirrored as well as foretold the breakup and re-creation of our inner and outer worlds. Such artists as Picasso, Braque, Mondrian, Ernst, Kandinsky, Duchamp, and perhaps Pollock invented visual concomitants of the myriad technical and scientific advances of the period, which is not to downplay equally distinguished painters and sculptors of the time who were possibly less clairvoyant.

After World War I, we still believed in the future, and Dada was a direct European result of the disillusionment during and following years of indescribable brutality. Yet its nihilistic fury embodied regeneration. We actually tried to create the future by bashing the past. Dada, always considered anarchic, was in reality an expression of moral indignation. After World War II, and even more so after Vietnam, we ceased to believe in endless possibility, and our art reflects this vacuum. Minimal art is precisely that — minimal, and often an expression of little more than cool denial. I'm not always in agreement with Mies van der Rohe that "less is more." In the zeal to remove all semblance of seduction, minimalism and conceptual art reduce our appetites on a diet of emotional and visual bread and water.

Photography and twentieth-century art are intertwined. A steadily growing interest in the camera paved the way for abstract painting. Why be tied to realism if a small machine can do it better? Or can it? And what precisely do we mean by realism? Are we referring, say, to a painting that closely reproduces nature or to one that frankly looks like a painting? How to compare an abstract mobile that moves with a static sculpture that vividly suggests motion, or a fool-the-eye painted version of cloth with a nonobjective collage that has real cloth incorporated into it? In short, is art its own subject or is the natural world its subject? And why can't both exist simultaneously as, of course, they often do?

What has repeatedly surprised me about the art of our century is its close interaction with other arts. In recent years, conceptual art has turned to words as basic supports, while earlier, performance art attempted to extend the boundaries of the theater. Today, installation and site-specific art juxtapose psychological and sociological setups backed by a modicum of interior design. During the twenty-first century, can these disparate tendencies coalesce into a dynamic new movement concentrated on reassessing and widening the boundaries of visual art?

Painting, as such, is intermittently promoted today. Considered fossilized by Duchamp and his followers, pigment and often color per se are taboo. Any concession to intuitive emotions is stifled in favor of rigidly reductive methods. The brush is often superseded by three-dimensional installations that are sometimes more related to sociology than to visual enrichment. But not to fear — the wheel turns inevitably and what is now forbidden blossoms tomorrow, yet never precisely in the same way. Each period leaves its mark on the history of art. Postmodernism, a movement we have not completely shaken off, was an apt label, for this art not only came after, but its initial impetus was a reaction against the century's early dynamic discoveries. What is missing today is any provocative prediction of the future or substantial understanding of the present, unless the contemporary love affair with the minimal is a revolt against superabundance.

Emblematic of contemporary thinking is conceptual art. You might say it's the opposite of Expressionism, which in all its manifestations encourages full rein to emotional involvement. Without the early multidimensional investigations of Cubism, conceptual art might never have developed. Cutting itself loose from eye involvement, conceptual art depends on the legacy of Duchamp, on stray words used ironically, and on mental concepts divorced from eye appeal. What counts is cerebral intention. The artist need only outline his or her plan of action, and not necessarily even supervise its execution. The written word supersedes the hand, while any evidence of direct personal engagement is sublimated. The logical next step is computer art and final subservience to the machine. The antithesis of Van Gogh and, of course, the Abstract Expressionists, against whom the conceptualists are rebelling, the movement is incarcerated in a straitjacket of its own making. Any visceral delight of eye contact is discouraged, and I, for one, feel handicapped by such narrow prerogatives. Not long ago, I talked with an independent curator working on an exhibition of conceptual art for a California museum. She hoped to limit her material to conceptual art dating from what she termed its "golden years," roughly between 1965 and 1975. The projected show was growing too large for its allotted space, but the idiosyncracies of her theme served her well. "Fortunately," she said, "one of the artists involved stipulated that his work could not be exhibited, but only described verbally in the catalogue."

It is important to remember that Duchamp, the father of the movement, renounced art as his life work early on. After his death, we discovered that he had secretly returned to it, but for many years, except for certain minor gadgets, he devoted himself to chess and to the careful preservation of his own art legacy. It was curious to find this pioneering Dadaist devoting his old age to the preservation of works originally intended as expendable. The whole meaning of Dada is subverted by this scramble to turn anti-art into respectable art history. Duchamp's disgust with the paraphernalia of painting and with the duplicity of the art market, despite later being involved in art dealing himself, sparked his renunciation. Could his own brilliant wit and complicated double, even triple, meanings have left him burned out while still at the beginning of his career? His standards were high, his pioneering messages complicated, and he found himself at odds with the whole idea of sensuous appeal. Too easy, he claimed. For Duchamp, constant innovation was mandatory — otherwise, why persist? He was always less regimented, more inventive, and a far more astute observer than his followers.

If the second half of our century has not produced an art renaissance, it has at least added vastly to the literature on art. New scientific tools and more serious scholarship are uncovering valuable secrets of the past, but in the process, marginalia has become a formidable escape hatch. This is the age of the footnote. To quote endlessly from acknowledged sources isn't always reassuring, for, unless the source is impeccable, inconsistencies multiply. These days, I find factual errors I noticed years ago reappearing as accepted history and often magnified by repetition. The most dangerous sources are autobiographical, for here wishful thinking sometimes replaces less flattering facts. Personal records can be as self-serving as they are illuminating, as misleading as they are revealing, for immediacy is not a guarantee of authenticity.

The machine and technology transformed the art of our century no less than its overall history. Every aspect of our lives, our bodies, environments, government, and relationships were irrevocably changed. When I think of the impact of the machine, I scarcely know where to start, but one spring afternoon in 1950 will do. I was walking along a tree-lined residential street in Chicago with Buckminster Fuller when he assured me that, at some point during our lifetimes, there would be no further need for stodgy apartments or conventional houses such as we were passing by. We'd been visiting a friend who lived in one of these Stone Age structures. According to Bucky, new technological achievements would soon free us from antediluvian housing, offering instead architecture without walls, windows, rigid divisions, roofs, or foundations. Talking a mile a minute, he envisioned future dwellings supported by verticals like trees and surrounded by some chemical process that would allow residents to look out but not be seen within. Climate control, privacy, and fluid space would all be guaranteed. Bucky was convinced that his projection was realistic. He was infatuated with the machine and believed in its total reliability. It became almost a religion with him. Looking ahead, he saw technology as the supreme hope of the future; for him its failure was unthinkable. After all, at midcentury, before pollution had become a household word, we believed in progress as our birthright.

Bucky had come to Chicago to give a lecture at the Art Institute on his Dymaxion House. If his geodesic dome, made of aluminum and Plexiglas, was not as utopian as his "tree house," it was nonetheless a brave gamble with the future. In 1992 the American Physical Society reported in its newsletter that seven years before, a group of chemical physicists at Rice University discovered that a sixty-atom cluster of carbon they had just produced remained uniquely stable. Assuming that the molecule had a perfectly symmetrical form like a soccer ball, the Rice scientists thought that their new molecule would probably resemble a geodesic dome, so in honor of its creator, they named the special C_{60} cluster "buckminsterfullerene" or "buckyball" for short.

Bucky might have been delighted but never surprised about being eponymous with a new class of pure carbon. All the doubters, and there were many, would have been astonished. In 1948, when the architect was at Black Mountain College, the photography historian Nancy Newhall shot him in a gallery featuring his two- and three-dimensional designs for future inventions. With a faintly seraphic smile, he introduced his half-art, half-science melange. Because of Fuller's monetary and personal problems, the dome was never mass-produced as intended, but two prototypes were built. There was also a variation tailored to Bucky's needs in Carbondale, when he was in residence at the University of Southern Illinois. Ultimate vindication did not come until 1992, when the Dymaxion House, which had been given to the Henry Ford Museum in Dearborn, Michigan, was put on view for the first time since the 1940s and assumed its rightful place in American architectural history.

In a small compound surrounding the Dymaxion residence in Carbondale, Bucky had also designed his own original version of a Japanese garden. To visit him was to emerge from the rather grubby atmosphere of the town of Carbondale to the otherworldliness of his carefully planned environment. When I was traveling to Carbondale frequently as part of a program to acquire works of art for the university campus, Bucky's home became a refuge for me, especially from the endless and usually aimless faculty meetings. I was always struck by a bronze portrait of him by Isamu Noguchi, his best friend. A gift from the artist, the bust was installed in an extraordinary library that wound around a section of that free-flowing house. If the lack of privacy ordinarily provided by doors and separating walls might have driven the average person, including myself, to despair, the uninterrupted sense of space was exhilarating. The library books, stretching almost from floor to roof and made accessible by an electric swivel chair that ascended and descended like an elevator, were an integral part of the house's overall design. Bucky was very proud of this chair and insisted I try it.

Fuller's speech at the Art Institute started at five and was to be followed at seven-thirty by a small dinner at the Cliff Dwellers Club, across the street from the museum. As the curator in charge, I had invited a few architects and designers, but the dinner never took place. Bucky talked without interruption for more than five and a half hours. The audience gradually melted away, but he was oblivious. It was as if, there on the platform, he was explaining to himself precisely what he was after. As he talked, new ideas were born and he followed each one wherever it led. Through it all, his trust in a future dominated by scientific discoveries was inexhaustible.

In his day, Fuller was not alone in his optimism. Artists like Léger and Moholy-Nagy, if not as single-mindedly, also found inspiration in the machine. So too did Duchamp, Klee, and Picabia, though with tongue in cheek — these three men were more ironic observers than believers. Both in Europe and later in the United States, the machine and technology were favorite subjects treated with affection, awe, sarcasm, humor, and fear by an unending parade of artists. Léger, who was gassed in World War I, claimed that for him war was "a reality which was both blinding and new — a complete revelation to me both as a man and as a painter." He claimed to be the first modern French painter to use the objects of his time as artists of other centuries had used theirs.

If Léger and Bucky were enamored of technology, Duchamp and Klee were more skeptical but equally involved, and indebted too were the Cubists, Futurists, Dadaists, and Surrealists. As I look back, mechanization, with all its ramifications, emerges as the dominant force in the art of our first half-century. Duchamp was philosophically opposed to the very stimuli that Léger and Bucky respected. To him, technology was not the great hope of civilization — it was a weapon that threatened the future of its inventors. Yet without Duchamp, pop and op art might never have developed. Eventually the painted light of the Impressionists and the fervent pigment of the Fauvists drove him away from any semblance of accepted procedures. Far better, he thought, was an art of conjecture, of intellectual questioning, of an underactive hand restrained by both chance encounters and a new chemistry of seeing. What you see is not what you get in Duchamp. He was after more evasive relationships.

When he was in Chicago in 1949, Duchamp called for a moratorium on painting. He told a group of reporters, "Modern painting has

Katharine and Duchamp on the grand staircase of the Art Institute, October 1949. No doubt collaborating with the photographer, Katharine poses so that her left leg, which was paralyzed and deformed by polio, is obscured.

had one hundred years of life and that's the end of it. Let's have a gap for fifty years; there's no reason for going on. There will be painters, there will be collectors but in another form — probably a totalitarian form." His sentiments had not changed, as I was to find out in 1961, when I moderated a symposium on contemporary art at the Philadelphia Museum College of Art. The subject was "Where Do We Go From Here?" and I remember only two other participants, Louise Nevelson and Marcel Duchamp. Louise was terrified of Duchamp — she called him "The Mind." He, cool as ever, listened calmly to the other participants and to their enthusiastic words about the Abstract Expressionists, who were popular at the time. Finally he took to the podium with a brief message urging painters "to go underground for the duration." That is exactly what he himself had done, but for him the duration turned into the better part of a lifetime. That evening in Philadelphia, Duchamp was referring to a duration when emotional and self-revealing expression was the "ism" of the moment. Abstract Expressionism, with its reliance on personal reactions, was still paramount. He disdained any dependence on lavish pigment, denouncing it as "self-indulgent." He wanted the hand to bow out and the head to take over.

At the height of his fame, Duchamp had seemingly ceased all art activity. I asked him why — was it possible that he could no longer compete with himself? At first the idea surprised him, but, after a moment or two, he said, "Possibly." It was not just the fame of *Nude Descending a Staircase* that thwarted him. The very nature of his art was constricting, and its emphasis on the cerebral may have narrowed his choices. He had hoped to extend the parameters of painting and sculpture with the ready-made, a shorthand and usually satirical comment on the ramifications of our culture. Often by only the slightest alteration, he presented prosaic mass-produced objects as philosophical metaphors. He toiled for years over his undisputed and, he claimed, never-finished masterpiece, the *Large Glass,* which featured the complicated takeover of man by technology, or was it vice versa? This melding of human being and machine, he once told me, was unexpectedly enhanced by the accidental cracking of the *Large Glass* during handling. It made the interaction seem less explicit: evidently even the mechanical was not impervious to fate.

Duchamp always remained ambivalent toward the machine. He saw it consuming and subsuming the hand that conceived it. As it borrowed human emotions, it transformed them into a logical progression. Duchamp saw, and never without biting humor, the successful conquest of man by the machine and, at the same time, the machine's humanization. For him, these forces combined to produce a new entity in a robotlike world in which mechanical precision made humanity almost superfluous. In his view, technology had organized erotic reproductive impulses so efficiently that the fluid thus produced became the machine's life-giving source. No one other than Duchamp and occasionally Picabia predicted our supersonic age in such implacable terms, unless it was Rube Goldberg. I think Duchamp would have been amused to learn that the modern computer is now afflicted by viruses. What could be more human? Is it now the machine's turn to capitulate to man?

One of the more direct art assaults on the machine took place during the 1960s, when a Swiss artist named Jean Tinguely popularized a kind of kinetic sculpture devoted to self-destruction. More accessible than philosophical versions by the earlier men, Tinguely's pieces were quite explicit, which may explain their immediate popularity and early oblivion. He built tangles of constructions that, by means of certain mechanisms, were supposed to self-destruct in a blaze of truth. His aim was almost too obvious. I remember a notorious performance that backfired in 1960, when the Museum of Modern Art organized a highly publicized event around the self-extermination of a huge assemblage Tinguely had labored long to create. But no matter how desperately he urged it on, his contrivance refused to explode as planned, and finally only expired with a whimper and the help of some New York City firemen. I suppose we might say it eventually had the last word.

I never met Paul Klee, but I learned more from him than from any other modern artist. He died in 1940 and his small works of mixed media are not always easy to decipher, but his message is timely and wise. His work tells us not to take ourselves or our scientific triumphs too seriously. In his eyes, everything man-made is fallible. With loving care, he invented new combinations of media that would both conceal and reveal his observations. Never aggressive, he depended on what, at first glance, may seem childish but in fact was profound. His small compositions are distillations of human behavior. The machine for him was as fragile as man himself; he made gentle fun of both. Representing the stronghold of technology by spindly lines and pieced-together remnants, he went far beyond caricature to expose the dilemmas of our times. Often he suffused the entire composition with melting color surprises, almost as if no problem was without hidden joys.

For some time, large-scale canvases have been pursued by artists who insist that expansive dimensions offer them greater freedom, or at least a more direct confrontation. I think of the Abstract Expressionists and of op and pop artists, whose paintings have virtually changed the design of recent museums. Architects now adjust dimensions to meet new demands. Not only walls, but elevators, doorways, and storage areas must be rethought. But Klee proved that freedom had nothing to do with size. His was a quiet voice, and his works as a rule were small, but what he had to say contained wider implications than the modesty of his methods might suggest. He was interested in telling us about ourselves, who we are, what makes us tick. The action painters, in contrast, told us about themselves. Klee employed visual metaphors, gentle satire, and cluelike titles to suggest what he wanted us to unravel. For him, the human quandary was a never-ending source of contemplation and the machine merely one aspect of it.

2
Mies van der Rohe in Chicago

Mies asked me to pick him up at his office on South Wabash Avenue late one October afternoon in 1947. We were due at a dinner sponsored by the Renaissance Society of the University of Chicago to celebrate the opening of a Theo van Doesburg exhibition. Because of his affection for both Van Doesburg and his widow, Nelli, who had come from Europe for the occasion, Mies had agreed to design the installation, which reaffirmed his credo of "Less is more." Relying solely on a harmonious spatial balance to set off and integrate Van Doesburg's clean, Constructivist compositions, he confessed that the most time-consuming part of the job had been adjusting the labels. Their positions varied infinitesimally in relation to each drawing, photograph, or design on the wall, for as little as a quarter-inch one way or the other could be crucial with Mies.

After a rather prolonged cocktail hour, the president of the Renaissance Society asked Mies if he knew what was delaying Nelli van Doesburg, since the dinner in her honor couldn't start without her.

Mies was thunderstruck. *"Mein Gott,"* he said, "I forgot her!" The poor lady was waiting in his apartment on the North Side, where she was staying and where he had neglected to tell me to pick her up. He was almost sadistically amused by the episode. Nelli, in a fetching black dress cut low in front, eventually arrived via taxi and found herself at the head of a long table with Mies beside her. She addressed no word, not even a nod, to him.

Later, en route to Mies's apartment, their silence was palpable, quivering on her part with unsaid accusations. Mies, who regardless of any situation, never seemed worried by guilt or personal incidents, finally suggested, tongue in cheek, that I "chaperone" their reconciliation over a nightcap and thus help restore Nelli's equanimity. He always mellowed over his own excellent whiskey, and she, when not upset, was an entertaining, exuberant companion and a woman of considerable determination, but no match for him. Indeed, few women were, perhaps because of the unattainable attraction he was for them. He was invariably courteous, in his own monosyllabic way, yet he trod roughshod over any involvements — emotional or otherwise — that might interfere with his priorities. His pace was measured, heavy, and assured. Only a major catastrophe could disrupt it.

Mies's Chicago apartment at 200 East Pearson Street was sparsely furnished and almost totally unadorned, except for a superb collection of Paul Klees, an early Kandinsky, and a Braque. (Later he bought a sizable group of prints by Munch.) The apartment building itself was small and architecturally undistinguished, but Mies had turned this conventionally arranged flat into his own flow-through environment. The rooms spread out in a spacious sequence because all the intersecting doors between the living room, entrance hall, and dining room had been removed. Though Chicago's handsomest apartment buildings were designed by him, some of them located not far from where he lived, he deliberately never moved into one. He told me that he dreaded the thought of subjecting himself to daily complaints in the elevator, to wails about garbage disposal units or kitchen cabinets.

In his living room I recall a voluminous sofa better adapted to his ample proportions than to mine. I could never lean back and still have my feet touch the floor. In addition, a few examples of his own flaw-

Mies van der Rohe, puffing on one of his omnipresent cigars, 1963.
Photograph by Dick Nichols.

less furniture were included. The room always looked comfortable, lived in, a bit shabby perhaps, but conducive to relaxed conversation. Mies, an affable host puffing away on a large cigar, used words with the same economy that he brought to his architecture, though after a few drinks, he was apt to open up and, despite hesitant English, reminisce about the past or consider the present. I never heard him predict the future or his own ultimate place in history. I think he took it for granted that a spot was reserved for him.

A heavy-set, squarish man with a somewhat impenetrable but thoughtful face that lit up slowly when he smiled (which was not too often), Mies always impressed me as the epitome of old-fashioned masculinity. His deep, slightly gravelly voice, his slow, accented speech, his elimination of small talk, and his quiet self-assurance all contributed to this image. He was so substantial, so impervious, so without ordinary hesitation or equivocation that automatically one felt the presence of an indomitable personality. There was not a shadow of a doubt that he had utter faith in his own work, a confidence that protected him from the need to compete with past or contemporary architects or, for that matter, even with himself. Nothing — from the harshest criticism to the staunchest applause — could alter his convictions.

When he was seventy-eight, he told me that it had taken him "years to find out how to make a clear, honest construction. My entire life has been one trip in that direction." To him individual buildings were merely cogs in his single-minded search. And if an occasional amenity or creature comfort was overlooked, he lost no sleep. Tending to ignore what he considered peripheral details, he concentrated only on structural integrity. "I don't think every building I put up needs to be different, since I always apply the same principles," he said. "For me novelty has no interest, none whatsoever." He was not a rebel nor a member of the avant-garde, but a purist, a classicist who established his own canon and then adhered to it strictly.

Were Mies alive at present, I am sure that he would remain blithely untroubled by the eclectic architecture so fashionable today and by the tendency to denounce the International Style, which he so significantly shaped. The fact that several of his old disciples, most notably Philip Johnson, hastened to throw over all traces of his teaching is not entirely unflattering. Cyclical changes in aesthetic styles are inevitable, but one questions whether such strong denials do not also stem from fears of an invincible force. Mies, always patient, would have ridden out the storm and never vacillated for a moment. He, who believed in the staying power of his own philosophy, had nothing but contempt for nonstructural innovations. He once explained to me that he designed neither for the client nor for himself: "I build for the sake of architecture." Thus I can imagine his searing disgust at postmodernism and its decorative throwbacks to a preindustrialized society. If, to be sure, Mies felt there was only one truth, his truth, he was still less concerned with renouncing the immediate past than with creating a better future. Undoubtedly he would have despised the current emphasis on romantic nostalgia.

Mies came to Chicago in 1938 to head the School of Architecture at Armour Institute, which was shortly to be renamed the Illinois Institute of Technology. Resigning twenty years later to devote all his remaining time to his own architecture, he had already, well before arriving in the United States at the age of fifty-two, been closely involved with education. As the last director of the German Bauhaus in Dessau and Berlin, it was he who finally and regretfully closed the school when Nazi harassment became intolerable. Mies was such a strong and self-contained personality that only the most independent student could have resisted his impact.

Although he taught architecture for several decades, he frequently questioned the process, claiming that all he could hope to pass on to his pupils were his own principles. To eager young Americans these may have seemed surprisingly rudimentary, at least until the budding architects grasped the standards of perfection Mies demanded. "As I have often said," he would tell them, "architecture starts when you carefully put two bricks together. There it begins." The key words were *carefully* and *together.* Mies was of course best known for his steel and glass structures, but throughout his life he also remained faithful to brick. Reminiscing with me a quarter-century after his German pavilion proved a sensation at the 1929 Barcelona Exposition, he observed, "If I'd used brick it would have been equally good architecture (I like brick), but I doubt that it would have become as celebrated."

Mies, unlike his students, had received no academic architectural training, but he did serve apprenticeships under various designers and cabinetmakers. It was the German architect Peter Behrens who most impressed him and under whom he worked for several years. He felt that one learned only by the process of doing, that a conventional education was in the long run less useful than an active apprenticeship. Mies talked frequently about Behrens and also about the Dutch architect H. P. Berlage, both of whom he acknowledged as seminal influences in his early development.

Sometime during the late 1940s, Alfred Barr and Gyorgy Kepes were serving on the jury of a national art exhibition at the Art Institute of Chicago. They specifically wanted to see Mies, whom they both warmly admired. I recall our visit and especially Barr's conversation with the architect about the Barcelona Pavilion and the possibility of the Museum of Modern Art bringing it to America. Mies told us he thought it had been taken apart and stored in separate sections — where he didn't know. When we left, Barr assured Mies that he would pursue the matter, hoping that he might recover the dismantled parts, restore the building under the architect's supervision to its original design, and eventually install it in the museum's garden. This seemed a historic moment to me, and I was already visualizing that ineluctable landmark safely ensconced on West 53rd Street, but, alas, the effort came to nothing. (In 1986, a replica of the German Pavilion was reconstructed as the permanent centerpiece of a public park in Barcelona.)

I first got to know Mies through my art gallery, which I closed during World War II, when it was no longer feasible to represent members of the European avant-garde whose work formed the backbone of my exhibitions. But when Mies arrived in Chicago, the Katharine Kuh Gallery was still humming along, though had I not taught art appreciation classes, I probably would have starved. Almost every year I hosted a show of Paul Klee, whose work never ceased to engage Mies, but had little to no following among Chicago collectors. The newspaper art critics, one a golf reporter and the other a socialite, hysterically opposed to any breath of the new, were even more negative. Meanwhile, Sanity in Art was still threatening me and trying to run my business into the ground. In those days art in Chicago was a lonely and dangerous business.

It was therefore a thrilling occasion for me when this newly transplanted and distinguished architect from Europe fell in love with the Klee exhibition on my walls. Before his visit to the gallery, Mies and I had met casually at a New Year's Eve party, where his attention was riveted on Lora Marx, a sculptor recently divorced from the Chicago designer and art collector Sam Marx. Lora was smitten at first sight, and she remained, with occasional interruptions, his closest companion until his death thirty years later. At the time of the exhibition, works by Klee often sold for less than three hundred dollars. I acquired a very fine mixed-media painting from 1927 for $127, so Mies was also able to indulge himself. I often remember him walking around one of my Klee exhibitions, examining each picture with total concentration, all the time muttering in that deep voice of his, *"Wunderschön, wunderbar."* After that, he came to the gallery frequently, sometimes accompanied by Walter Peterhans or Ludwig Hilberseimer, two

German colleagues he had invited to teach at Illinois Institute of Technology.

In 1943 I was hired by the Art Institute, and later that year I inherited a small department involved exclusively with interpretative exhibitions. Here we tried out various experiments, hoping to explain art in visual rather than verbal terms. The room assigned to the project was badly proportioned and poorly lit, the result of awkward earlier remodeling, but funds for turning it into a viable space were practically nonexistent. What I didn't want was a slick modern background; what I hoped for was a flexible design that would lead the visitor discreetly from one explanatory idea to another and yet not dominate the heterogeneous material on view. It was urgent that the room take on added dimensions while still lending itself to an intimate, almost private experience. With my hands empty and my spirit eager, I went to Mies for advice, wondering if one of his advanced students might not supervise the renovation. To my complete amazement he volunteered to take over the entire job.

At this time — six years after he had settled in Chicago — Mies was fifty-eight and highly respected throughout the world, but he addressed himself to the design of that modest gallery with the same unfaltering standards that he brought to his most important architectural commissions. No detail was too negligible for his scrutiny. Each small problem he explored exhaustively, regardless of how long it took. Whatever time he could steal from his own work (he was then designing the campus of the Illinois Institute of Technology), he spent at the museum, patiently mulling over alternative possibilities that only arduous hours of trial and error resolved. To watch him immersed in a final decision, always puffing away on a large cigar — the Art Institute arranged a special dispensation permitting him to smoke — revealed more about his working methods and his unremitting search for the ideal solution than all the analytical studies about him.

On three walls of the gallery he installed a group of horizontal wood panels that were to serve as backgrounds for changing exhibits. He gave the same dedicated attention to the quality, color, and grain of the wood as to the precise position and relationship of the panels. He was, after all, the first resolutely modern architect who recognized the humanizing influence of luxurious materials. As early as the Barcelona Pavilion and the Tugendhat House, he had demonstrated that structures of uncompromising quality were not necessarily flawed by rich marble or wood. Quite the contrary — they were enhanced. For days he moved the panels back and forth, up and down, sometimes spending an hour or two on an alteration of less than an inch. And it was always and only his eyes that he depended on. No theoretical proportions, no preconceived directions froze his design into early rigidity. He just sat there looking, looking, silently smoking, relating each element in the room to a projected harmonious unity.

Enmeshed in the process of selection and rejection, he was involved with the tangible, yet no artist was ever more abstractly oriented. His architecture has been compared to Mondrian's paintings, but that he was directly influenced I doubt. Each man, bent on a common goal, was trying to substitute order for the chaos around him. Stripping away all nonessentials, they exposed the basic geometry of form and space and in so doing virtually created a new kind of liberated space. Moreover, each relied only on horizontals and verticals to achieve a beautifully measured equlibrium.

The first time I visited Crown Hall, one of the buildings Mies designed for the Illinois Institute of Technology, I was struck by the uncanny marriage of interior and exterior space. Inside the predominantly glass structure, one does not merely look out; one feels that the outside actually floats in. Nowhere in the entire building do conventional barriers block the expanding space. This sense of freedom is exhilarating, and for me it remains one of the two most beautiful buildings in Chicago: the other is Frank Lloyd Wright's Robie House. True, Crown Hall has been criticized for that very openness, which doesn't always provide the privacy classroom activities sometimes require. Never much concerned with what he considered to be the "personal whims" of his clients, Mies occasionally overlooked immediate demands in favor of structural probity. He was involved with an almost ethical obligation to the principles of organic architecture. Above all he believed in the oneness of a building and unequivocally avoided all applied ornament or decoration. "The interior and exterior are one — you can't divorce them," he insisted. "The outside takes care of the inside."

Much as I admired him, I was not entirely indulgent when it came my turn to be uncomfortable. I was living in a new apartment building designed by a young architect who had studied with Mies and was then a devoted disciple. It was a beautiful space that adhered closely to the teachings of the master, but it was marred by one defect. In those days when air conditioning was not prevalent, the Miesian preference for windows that slanted inward and only opened partially was a severe trial when Chicago's weather turned torrid. Ventilation was almost nil, and at times I came close to suffocating. Yet it is important to remember that this fenestration, when conceived as a glass wall, contributed to a harmonious and continuous horizontal rhythm that the architect particularly wanted.

One hot evening Mies was visiting me and because he was mopping his brow, it seemed a ready-made moment for complaint. But I couldn't win. His recommendation: buy a small electric fan, put a board in the window, install the fan on it, and thus blow fresh air into

Crown Hall, Illinois Institute of Technology, Chicago. Completed in 1956, Crown Hall housed the School of Architecture at the ITT, so the building meant a great deal to Mies. The interior is completely open — a dramatic example of Mies's ability to create a rigorously clear structure.
Photograph by Hedrich-Blessing.

Mies van der Rohe in Crown Hall. Photograph by Hedrich-Blessing.

the room. How would that look? I queried. Certain that his solution would not jeopardize the structural honesty of the building, he triumphantly reminded me that this makeshift arrangement need obtain only during warm weather.

One event surrounding Mies was supremely memorable. Not

long after he arrived in Chicago, I found myself seated between him and László Moholy-Nagy at a Hull House dinner in honor of Frank Lloyd Wright. Before Mies settled in Chicago, Moholy had already established himself as director of a progressive art school called the Chicago Bauhaus. It was based on its European precedessor, where Moholy had taught, too. Because both men were originally connected with the German Bauhaus, I naturally expected a warm encounter. Though Moholy greeted the architect effusively, Mies stonily ignored him, later telling me that he couldn't condone the younger man's appropriation of the name and curriculum of the Bauhaus without having first consulted with him. It seems that according to a Bauhaus statute, the title and academic program of the school were to revert to the last director in the event that the institution closed. Not only Mies, but various Bauhaus instructors, including Josef Albers, who by then was also living in the United States, were incensed that Moholy had appointed himself their spokesman in America and in a sense the official source for transmitting their educational theories. Because Moholy was backed by Walter Gropius, the founder and first director of the Bauhaus, he doubtless felt that he needed no further endorsement. Mies, reticent but authoritative, also found Moholy's effervescent aggressiveness offensive. When I saw the two men together, the scene always reminded me of a sturdy elephant brushing off a high-spirited puppy.

Frank Lloyd Wright arrived very late for the dinner. We were all seated and waiting for him when, followed by a small entourage, he dazzled us as he swept in with his ubiquitous cape flowing behind him. Once he was seated at the speakers' table, he spied Mies and peremptorily ordered that he be moved to a place of honor beside him. Like an amused schoolboy and actually blushing redder and redder, Mies, who was more than fifteen years younger than Wright, obediently complied. The overdose of attention embarrassed him, but because he was an admirer of Wright, whose work he had long known, he was also pleased. A year later, when writing about his American colleague, Mies said, "The work of this great master presents an architectural world of unexpected force, clarity of language and disconcerting richness of form. . . . Here again, at long last, genuine organic architecture flowered." From Mies, who was not given to hyperbole, this was high praise.

It was the same evening, though no doubt not for the first time, that Wright in his after-dinner speech heralded architecture as the supreme art while relegating painting to little more than "the smearing of linseed oil and color" on a bit of "cloth." Throwing up his hands, he questioned how the two could be considered in the same breath — one so virile and life-giving, the other ephemeral and useless. The artists present were not amused.

As the years passed, the friendship between the two architects wavered. Wright, whose old age was characterized neither by tact nor restraint, sporadically struck out at Mies and the so-called International Style, both of which he claimed were littering the American landscape with glass boxes. Mies never responded. I'm sure he would have considered it beneath him to involve himself in a public altercation. In addition, he had far too much faith in his own work to feel pressured by criticism. He continued to admire Wright's architectural achievements, which characteristically he valued more than personal relationships.

Walter Gropius had loyally championed Mies after he arrived in America, and in honor of his seventieth birthday Gropius was feted by the Chicago architectural community in May 1953. One celebration took place at the Blackstone Hotel, where Mies made a warm speech introducing his old comrade, but I remember a briefer exchange between the two. At a luncheon for Gropius, the two men were seated next to each other and they were chatting politely. I was sitting nearby and at one point I heard Gropius say to Mies, "All that work and what have we got to show for it — the picture window?"

Mies had three daughters, but the only one I came to know well was the youngest, Waltraut, who was trained as an art historian. She had remained in Germany in the 1930s and 1940s, barely living through those terrible war years, and finally, when the fighting was over, he asked if I could help him bring her to America. He realized that at the start she wouldn't legally be able to earn a living but at least she had a better chance of emigrating if there was a volunteer job waiting for her at the Art Institute. And so, of course, I agreed to help. He assured me that if her work were not satisfactory, the museum would be under no obligation.

Eventually Waltraut arrived. Her very name frightened me. It conjured up some sort of towering Wagnerian figure, but the gentle, shy young woman Mies introduced to me could hardly have been less imposing. Pale and thin to the point of emaciation, she spoke so quietly that one could barely hear her excellent English. In all the years we worked together, I rarely saw her smile and I never heard her laugh.

Waltraut appeared to live in a perpetual state of anxiety, both at home with Mies and at the museum with me. When she died tragically young of cancer, I remember writing to him from New York, lamenting how we must have terrified her at first, how overpowering we must have seemed. She was a highly reliable if not always imaginative art historian who joined the Art Institute's staff as a research specialist. For her father, whom she in no way physically or temperamentally resembled, she retained a kind of breathless hero worship. She did, however, share with him one important characteristic — both were undeviating in their conscientious respect for any work they engaged in. My memories of Waltraut always include a glimpse of her gliding wraithlike through her father's living room, serving drinks to his friends but never interrupting or entering the conversation. She accepted the role of helpful handmaiden, while he on his part did not change his way of life one iota after she came to live with him.

One Saturday in 1950 Mies invited me to see the almost-completed house in Plano, Illinois, that he had designed for Dr. Edith Farnsworth. I'm afraid his motive for encouraging me to tag along was not entirely disinterested, for it seems that the lady had earlier unleashed a litany of complaints over the phone and he hoped my presence would deter her from further charges. According to her, the fireplace wasn't drawing properly and the space divisions in the one-room house weren't high enough to protect her from prying eyes. I never believed that these minor discrepancies were the basic problem: it was her deteriorating personal relationship with Mies. She, like many other women, had become emotionally involved with him, but gradually and as usual, he cooled off. Only Lora Marx was able to stay the course. I've always suspected that her long friendship with him must have depended on a mutual respect for total freedom. Even a hint of possessiveness was enough to drive Mies away. Years ago the sculptor Mary Callery was still indignant when she told me how after a close relationship and without the slightest explanation, Mies quietly walked out of her house, never to return. Arguments, recriminations, and psychological burrowing were not in his lexicon. Nor were complications that interfered with his work or the rhythm of his life.

While we were driving out to see Dr. Farnsworth, Mies prepared me for trouble ahead, but I was so amazed by the house itself that I scarcely heard her grievances. Here, sixty miles outside of Chicago, on an unremarkable site facing the Fox River, admittedly a not too impressive stream, floated a most unlikely structure. Later, when I asked Mies about the location, he said, "I don't feel site is that important. I am first interested in a good building." Indeed, I sometimes think he preferred a nondescript site, because it would not compete with the architecture. If he was not a stickler for site as such, he was extremely particular about securing adequate space around his architecture, feeling that "often the space between buildings is as important as the buildings themselves." In that respect, it was interesting to see how sensitively the Farnsworth House is related to each tree in its vicinity, and it is also wonderful to see how pure and eloquent the house itself is. It resembles a flawless modern Greek temple more than than a weekend haven for a hardworking middle-aged woman. There is no leeway for scattered possessions or casual housekeeping — the total integration of interior and exterior space is all that counts. The entire house is sheathed in shining glass, denying privacy unless the windows are covered. Mies preferred raw silk hangings, which would have been very costly to hang over all that glass.

As our visit progressed, Dr. Farnsworth grew increasingly truculent, yet her lengthening list of indictments elicited little more than amused indulgence from Mies, though he did assure her that, wherever possible, corrections would be made. His concessions were too vague to satisfy her. Finally, of course, the root problem surfaced — money. With the house costing considerably more than originally anticipated and with the once warm relationship unraveling, Dr. Farns-

The Farnsworth House, Plano, Illinois, in 1951, shortly after its completion. Edith Farnsworth's furnishings can be discerned inside. Photograph by Hedrich-Blessing.

worth was feeding on her own frustrations. When we left after an unhappy hour or two, I found myself feeling sorry for her. There she was, the duenna of an already famous landmark that only fractionally resembled the flexible hideaway she had earlier envisioned. Though she had seen and agreed to the original plans, she had not fully understood them, nor had she been able to anticipate the demands this architecture would exact from her. To make matters worse, bills were pouring in. She later told me that despite paying for the house, it was never hers. It always belonged to Mies, for it was his dream child. Dwindling funds prevented her from equipping the place with proper Miesian furniture, which explained why she was camping out on the day of our visit. Except for an occasional folding chair, there was little or nothing to sit on. Bedsheets were tacked up helter-skelter over the expanses of offending glass windows.

The story ends sadly. There were suits and countersuits, and years later Edith, after a long, brutal battle, emerged the loser, which I understand left her nearly bankrupt financially and emotionally. In 1968 Peter Palumbo, the London real estate developer and arts patron, offered to buy the house from Dr. Farnsworth, who moved out three years later. Since then, Lord Palumbo has returned the house to its initial pristine purity and endowed it with furniture designed by the architect. Edith Farnsworth died in 1977. Ironically, her name is remembered only as a corollary to a building that ultimately destroyed her.

After I moved to New York, I saw less of Mies, but in 1964 I returned to Chicago to interview him for *Saturday Review*. I knew he had long suffered from severe arthritis and finally undergone surgery to relieve the unbearable pain. I also knew that he was confined to a wheelchair because of the nature of the operation. I dreaded seeing that powerful presence incapacitated but I needn't have worried, for his agility in getting himself around in the chair was beautiful to watch. He had lost none of his independence or quiet authority.

In the office where the interview took place, Mies had hung an enlarged photograph of a drawing he made in 1921 for a Berlin skyscraper that was never built. It was as if he were reminding himself that forty-three years earlier he had hit his stride and during almost a half-century never swerved. The building, conceived as a high-rise glass structure, was a revolutionary idea for its time and an interesting foil for a nearby scale model of a horizontal modern museum he had recently designed for West Berlin. Both structures were characterized by the same uncompromising clarity, the same unrelenting attention to detail. Mies had known that the earlier skyscraper would never be built. "I realized at that time that Germany was not ready," he said. Fortunately, America was ready for him. And it is to the United States and especially to Chicago that one must go to appreciate the full measure of his achievement.

3
The Two Vincent van Goghs

Of all my curatorial memories, perhaps the most moving are those from the period I spent working with Vincent van Gogh's nephew in Holland. The first time we met, the stab of recognition was palpable, though at that point the nephew was considerably older than his famous uncle had been when he died. Still, the resemblance was uncanny — the same high cheekbones, the same tightly defined facial contours, the same tawny coloring. I was fresh from studying a procession of unforgettable self-portraits, and the two faces seemed to coalesce.

It was 1948, and I was in Amsterdam with Dan Rich and Theodore Rousseau, then curator of paintings at the Metropolitan Museum of Art. The two men were organizing the first important retrospective exhibition of Van Gogh's work to come to America, where it was to be shown at their museums. I accompanied them because of a supplementary explanatory show I was preparing for both institutions.

The retrospective was one of the first blockbuster surveys to form the vanguard of a ceaseless procession that eventually helped to popularize nineteenth-century French art. In Chicago, to our amazement, such hordes of visitors poured into the Art Institute for the Van Gogh show that the gallery floors suffered serious erosion. This was the period when stories about a severed ear circulated to a largely uninformed public more interested in Van Gogh's life than his art. That's why we felt an explanatory show was mandatory. No paintings in history are more autobiographical than Van Gogh's, and there is no doubt that his life influenced his art, but it was less his life than his art that I stressed. His paintings demanded to be seen as more than illustrations of a tragic life story. And so I grappled with his unconventional technique, with his astute draftsmanship and symbolic use of color. Very few words were used in the interpretative exhibition; the aim was to show rather than to tell. Being told rarely compensates for finding out. My hope was to illuminate the artist's work through visual comparisons, contrasts, analyses, and strategically placed questions encouraging the viewer to become more than a passive observer. Color charts, linear graphs, everyday objects, photographs, maps, original works of art, X-rays, and much more were included, often in dramatic setups.

The nephew was the son of Theo van Gogh, Vincent's devoted brother, who was four years younger than he. Leaving an infant son named Vincent, Theo died at the age of thirty-four, only six months after the painter committed suicide. Theo worked for a Paris branch of the Goupil art gallery, and he had done everything possible to promote the Post-Impressionists and especially his brother. Without Theo's symbiotic attachment, it is doubtful that Vincent could have persisted even as long as he did. Legend has it that only one painting was sold during the artist's life. It was not solely financial help that Theo provided: he and Vincent were in constant touch by almost daily correspondence that has become an invaluable addition to art history. These letters, which were translated, published, and widely read internationally, are documents that probe the psyche of art making.

The letters, as well as all Van Gogh's work and memorabilia, were saved from oblivion by three heroic relatives. First, of course, Theo preserved everything, and after his death, the task fell to Theo's young widow, Johanna van Gogh-Bonger. When she died in 1925, this trust was passed on to her son, the painter's namesake, Dr. Vincent Willem van Gogh, better known as V. W. van Gogh, or the Engineer. Though he never knew his uncle or his father (he was only a few months old when Theo died), he continued his mother's unbroken record of preservation. She was only twenty-nine when she was widowed, but nothing seemed to daunt her, including the meticulous preparation of Vincent and Theo's letters for publication. No one could have protected and yet made known the artist's work more diligently or with more integrity than her son, and this despite a busy professional life as a practicing engineer. Yet he found time to oversee every detail of countless loan exhibitions, each of which he normally accompanied. A quarter-century after my first visit with him, when I was again in Holland, he told me that during those twenty-five years he had traveled to the United States thirty-one times, not to mention innumerable trips to other parts of the globe. I've always suspected that the Engineer's enthusiasm for those large loan exhibitions was partly influenced by his zest for travel. For him, however, the prime reason to circulate the collection was more selfless — he wanted to assure his uncle an undisputed niche in history because of his art and despite his sensational life. He approved of the explanatory exhibition because it focused on the work. Yet his appetite for travel may have sometimes encouraged him to keep the show on the road longer than was healthy for the paintings. After all, canvas and pigment need rest no less than human beings. I hate to think of how many restorations the nonstop exhibition schedule must have necessitated. Now the collection is safely preserved, thanks to the Engineer, in its own museum in Amsterdam. There, the roles are reversed and the public travels to the paintings, which, if we want to preserve our heritage, should become a practice more frequently adopted.

The Engineer's itching foot spearheaded his expansive assemblage of train schedules acquired from all over the world. He showed them to us one evening, specifically pinpointing the routes between New York and Chicago. He'd already decided on the exact train he would take even though the exhibition was far more than a year away. As time went on, he augmented the train collection with plane schedules.

Remarkable was the Engineer's unyielding refusal to sell any of the paintings and drawings he had inherited. From the beginning, his intention was to see them safely installed in a national institution. In 1948 Holland was still recovering from the German occupation, and there were indications of austerity everywhere. Mrs. van Gogh, the Engineer's second wife and a charming woman, asked us timidly whether she would need evening dress for the American openings. She explained that during the war it was impossible to buy clothes or practically anything else and that since then there were more important replacements to make than evening gowns. During the occupation, the Engineer was tempted to sell some of the collection; his family was often in need of food. To make matters more difficult, he was hiding several imperiled Jews in his home, namely, the conductor of the Amsterdam Symphony Orchestra and his family. Only once did he capitulate and trade a Van Gogh painting for provisions at a time when it was virtually a life and death matter. He still felt guilty. Other than that, his protection of the collection was little less than saintly.

In Holland, our work for the exhibition centered on the three locations where concentrations of Van Gogh's paintings had been gathered — the Kröller-Muller Museum in Otterloo, the Stedelijk Museum in Amsterdam, which had many works on loan from the Engineer, and at his home in Laren, southeast of Amsterdam. Working at the Stedelijk was sheer joy and very nearly ruined us for a return to our impersonal lives in American museums. Every midmorning and midafternoon, around came a sparkling cart with tea, coffee, and appropriate tidbits. Everyone from the director to the shipping room men stopped work and chatted. Nothing could have been less bureaucratic. I particularly recall the head of the restoration department, who regaled me at these coffee breaks with his unorthodox theories about Vincent's compulsions, which he had neatly catalogued, and which, by the way, may have hit the mark more often than I cared to realize. He was full of abstruse Freudian explorations that seemed to project Vincent into our very midst. As for the director, Willem Sandberg, no one could have been more generous with his knowledge, contacts, and hospitality. At his home he and his wife overfed us and shared their friends, but above all he impressed us with his wide knowledge of contemporary art. Already in 1948 he had installed a large Calder mobile in the entrance of the museum, an object lesson to most of his American colleagues who scarcely knew the artist's name at that time. Some years later after he retired from the Stedelijk we met again in Israel, where he was advising the recently established art museum in Jerusalem and I was doing a story for *Saturday Review.* His understanding of the art of this century was prodigious; his eye was as open as his spirit.

At the Kröller-Muller Museum, it was no less delightful. That extraordinary museum, set in a fine park and designed by the Belgian architect Henry Van de Velde, is memorable not alone for its large cache of Van Goghs, but also for its extensive group of Mondrians, an artist little appreciated then. Because I was an aficionado, I was shocked when Ted Rousseau, the Metropolitan's curator of paintings, confessed he'd never heard of the artist and couldn't imagine any reason why he should have.

It is, however, from the Engineer's modest suburban home in Laren that my most striking memories spring. The house was filled with Vincent's work, and there were also several Gauguins and a few other Post-Impressionists. Over the large bed in the master bedroom hung a poetic canvas of a single blossoming almond tree. It became the first painting chosen for the exhibition and was promptly refused. No matter how often Dan and Ted repeated their request, the answer was always the same. Later I learned that the picture was painted in celebration of the Engineer's approaching birth, and after its completion Vincent fell ill and was unable to work for many weeks. By the time he recovered, the almond trees were no longer in flower and the variations on the motif that had been envisioned were never executed. Van Gogh died six months later, and *Branch of an Almond Tree in Blossom* stands alone as a poignant token of the artist's last spring. The painting eventually left the Engineer's home in 1973 to become part of the Rijksmuseum Vincent van Gogh in Amsterdam. The approximately two hundred paintings and five hundred drawings willed to the Engineer by his mother, plus illuminating memorabilia, are the lifeblood of this museum, which is strategically located between the

Rijksmuseum, with its outstanding old masters, notably Rembrandt, and the Stedelijk, famous for its modern collection.

The Engineer always talked to us freely about the paintings, but the very private *Branch of an Almond Tree in Blossom* was a forbidden subject, and so also were others he considered too personal for general conversation. For example, I quickly gathered that he didn't want to

Vincent Willem van Gogh at his house in Laren, about 1948–49, displaying the treasures he preserved with such integrity. *Branch of an Almond Tree in Blossom* (1890), painted to commemorate the Engineer's birth, is the largest canvas hanging on the wall. Note the negligible framing that the Engineer favored and museum officials deplored.

discuss his father's death in an asylum within six months of Vincent's suicide; we never learned the circumstances of that premature tragedy, but we did surmise that the painter was not the only psychologically disturbed member of the family. In addition, Mrs. van Gogh told me that the Engineer had earlier also suffered a severe "nervous break-down." Yet I always found him highly dependable. He could be stubborn, too. His paintings were all unframed except for natural wood strips. Ted and Dan repeatedly urged him to permit more orthodox frames, at least for our American exhibitions, and even persuaded me to work on him, but he was adamant. I was concerned that these narrow flat strips were not adequate protection for paintings often hastily and emotionally executed, some of which were already in doubtful condition.

From Vincent's letters to Theo, we know that a canvas in the Art Institute of Vincent's bedroom at Arles had been rolled and shipped off to Theo in such haste that the underpainting had not dried properly, forcing areas of pigment to lift and drop off, which explains why Van Gogh painted a second, almost identical version. Vincent's need for his brother's instant corroboration was only one symptom of his sense of isolation and self-doubt. It was Theo who kept him alive spiritually as well as economically. I've often pondered whether, in return, Vincent may not have reciprocated as Theo's intuitive alter ego.

Working so closely day after day with Van Gogh's paintings and drawings was an expansive but no less interior experience. Gradually I came to realize that his approach to these two media was surprisingly opposed. In his paintings, he drew in color with loaded brushstrokes; in his drawings, he depended on pen or pencil, but no matter the medium, his draftsmanship was as lucid as it was stabbing. I often thought that he might have said, as his colleague Degas did, "Drawing is not what you see, but what you must make others see." Color was his emotional release, but drawing was the bone and sinew of his vision. It gave structure to everything he touched, once his work matured, which happened with unusual rapidity after he moved to Paris.

There came a time at the Art Institute when we doubted one of our own Van Goghs, a still life of a magnified slice of melon. We had never questioned it until Dan became increasingly suspicious. After considerable study in the laboratory, we discovered that the underlying structure of the painting rested on false credentials that differed radically from the painter's canvases that we knew to be authentic. Comparisons by X-ray showed that the understructure of the work had not been drawn with Van Gogh's characteristic staccato brushstrokes, but had been suggested by more traditional lines and underpainting. What was missing were those decisive brushstrokes that drew as they painted. For Vincent, it was one integrated operation. Modern science thus corroborated Dan's doubts. The painting, by the way, was not a copy of a known Van Gogh, but a fake quite creditably conceived in his image. One should never be so blinded by Vincent's troubled emotions as to underestimate the strength of his technical powers.

One evening after we had gotten to know the Engineer and his wife better, we had dinner with them at home. It was there that he produced a group of metal (I think they were tin) boxes filled with Vincent's original letters to Theo. He asked us if we would care to read them since they were written in French. Many of the letters were illustrated with urgent small sketches that either clarified works in progress or underlined incidents in the artist's daily life. The yellowed wisps of paper, the strong personal calligraphy, the candid little drawings, all combined to intensify the sometimes despairing words. Vincent came to life with unbearable immediacy. The letters are not merely important art documents, but literature in their own right. I can think of only a few other important artists — Delacroix, Whistler, Noguchi, Klee — who wrote as evocative prose.

The overemphases on lurid stories depicting the artist and his brother as crude madmen in books and movies are cheap dramatizations proved false by the letters. There is no argument that Vincent was dangerously disoriented psychologically, but he was at the same time a man of knowledge, intelligence, sensitivity, and unbounded creativity. It wasn't all happenstance that he soared as an artist. The letters are proof that he knew what he was doing and that his frustrations were unendurable.

A few samples of the letters are shown in the Amsterdam museum, along with other memorabilia such as Japanese prints and mag-

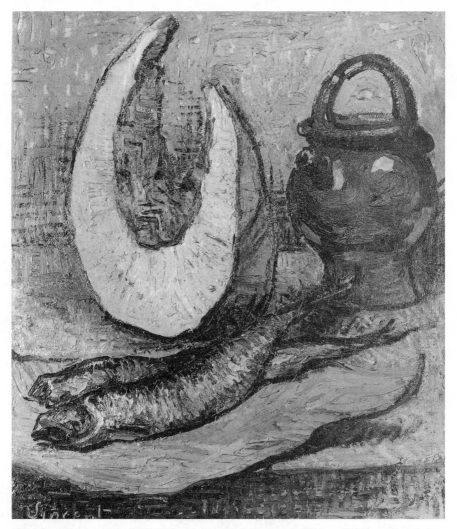

Unidentified artist. *Still Life: Melon, Fish, Jar,* n.d. This still life entered the Art Institute in 1926 as a work by Van Gogh as part of the impeccable Helen Birch Bartlett Memorial Collection, which also contained *La Grande Jatte,* Toulouse-Lautrec's *At the Moulin Rouge,* and the Van Gogh bedroom at Arles. The painting was not discredited until the 1950s.

azine illustrations that influenced Vincent's work, as well as every conceivable publication referring to him. The Engineer did more than give his collection of works by Van Gogh and many of his associates; he supervised and advised con amore on every facet of the museum.

The Dutch government in return financed the building. Vincent pervades it as a believable, literate, if harassed man, and only rarely as the over-romantic myth that popular fiction has made him, and this, to be sure, was how his nephew had always wanted him to be presented.

On our last visit together, when I visited the new museum in 1974, I found the Engineer little changed. At the age of eighty-four he was still vigorous and living in the Laren house, although his wife had died. He commuted to Amsterdam several days each week to work on various projects at the museum. At the moment, he was editing forty-two letters from Gauguin written to Vincent or Theo, none of them ever published before. He still found time for his own work, and during the week I spent in Amsterdam, he was off to Utrecht for a meeting of consulting engineers and subsequently to Lunteren for a conference of the Royal Institute of Engineers. The day before I left, while walking to lunch, we passed through a small square where he called my attention to a modest plaque. It was a memorial placed there by the city of Amsterdam to honor his son, who had been assassinated at that spot by the Nazis while he was serving in the Dutch underground.

4
Fernand Léger
Pioneering the Present

Early in 1952 I was organizing a Léger exhibition, a large retrospective to be held the following year at the Art Institute of Chicago, the San Francisco Museum of Art, and the Museum of Modern Art in New York. The show, to my considerable disappointment, was sparsely attended in all three cities. Léger's paintings were probably too austere for his time, and yet no one reflected his time more astutely. I've always looked on Léger as the folk artist of our scientific and mechanistic age, albeit a sophisticated one. He was likewise an optimistic devotee of mass production and an important forerunner of pop art. Calder, Stuart Davis, and Jean Hélion all told me at one time or another how much they owed to him, and Richard Lindner mentioned his indebtedness, too. If not always easy to take, Léger's work had nonetheless a profound influence on the art of this century. Like Buckminster Fuller, who perennially believed that the machine and modern invention are the ultimate way to a utopian life, Léger was dedicated to contemporary innovations, which may partly explain why his work was often denigrated by the art-conscious public. After all, it took years for most of us to recognize that gears and pistons had the potential to be aesthetic objects.

No artist looked less like an esthete than Léger, who was born on a farm in Normandy and could easily have passed as a farmer with his weathered skin, rugged features, bulbous nose, and heavy-set body. His preferred drink was wine, and red wine at that; he found white too bland.

Léger talked to me at length about why he wanted certain pictures in his exhibition, but he never insisted. He was an excellent and amiable self-critic, but visiting him caused me great anxiety. The only other artist who made me feel equally ill at ease was Edward Hopper, but for a different reason. Hopper's long silences unnerved me, but Léger, though far from garrulous, was outspoken and expressive. However, he refused to use even a word of English, and despite understanding everything he said, I faltered when responding to him. As an agile linguist, I invariably fail, and when I wanted to get across a complicated idea, I'd lapse into English. But perhaps the real reason for my intimidation was the extreme awe I felt for the man. I admired his self-confidence, his pragmatic, workman-like philosophy, his clear Gallic intelligence, his indifference to public opinion, his excellence as an artist. Like his work, he was supremely healthy and disciplined. I always felt inept in his presence.

In all honesty, it was Madame Léger who added sharply to my distress. She was *formidable* in the way the French mean it — oversized, overweight, and noisily aggressive. The former Nadia Khodossievitch was Léger's second wife — his first, Jeanne Lohy, died in 1950 — but she had been associated with him for many years before their wedding, both as his student and as an assistant in his school. They had gotten married only a few months before I arrived in Paris. Almost slavishly influenced by his work, Nadia painted what looked to me like bastard Légers, some of which I fear are occasionally pawned off today as the real thing. One Sunday when I was lunching with the Légers at their farmhouse outside Paris, Fernand took me into an empty room where he was working on the *Acrobats* series — wonderful, witty, joyous paintings that made up the last important group of works he produced before his death. Nearby in Nadia's studio, I was shocked to see how shamelessly she imitated him, though she was unable even to approximate his precision or cool classicism. Her works impressed me as overeasy vulgarizations. Léger was casual about his wife's plagiarism and the possibility that her work might be taken for his after his death. He shrugged when I dared say anything about it.

Nadia was particularly hard on me because I was an American and she, as an ardent disciple of the Soviet Union, had nothing but scorn for the United States. Léger told me half in amusement that his wife had been the youngest Russian commissar in history. Despite or perhaps because of this signal honor, she never failed to attack me, and I did everything in my power to avoid her. I must say I was craven where she was concerned, but fortunately I had to deal with her only rarely, because I worked almost exclusively with Léger at his studio.

Léger's studio was in Montparnasse, in 86, rue Notre-Dame-des-Champs, a building that had accommodated hundreds of artists since it was put up in the nineteenth century. The only way up to the studio was by navigating a spiraling oak staircase. I remember many visits when I pulled myself up those four or five flights of circular stairs, arriving breathless to find a bare, unembellished room that looked less like an artist's atelier than a mechanic's workshop. The milieu fit the man who once described "the electrician in his blue smock" as a "modern god, emperor-king, chief of us . . . all." Relatedly, Léger believed that "a work of art must bear comparison with any manufactured object." For him the no-nonsense power of mass production was the final arbiter. He said he used "the machine as others have used the nude or still life," meaning that he was the first modern French painter to incorporate the objects of his time as artists of other centuries had deployed theirs. Léger's contempt for Victorian furbelows and "deluxe decorative objects" was monumental.

Often stacked against the studio walls was a group of strikingly similar compositions that the artist was tackling; he tended to work in series. The long sequence of canvases devoted to the same idea added up to an almost stenographic report on what Léger considered important to retain, to emphasize, and to incorporate into his final painting, which, as a rule, he labeled *état définitif*. At times only the slightest modifications separated two versions and pointed up how minutely and

Fernand Léger in the window of his studio at 86, rue Notre-Dame-des-
Champs, whose steps Katharine found a torture to climb.
Photograph by Alexander Liberman.

deliberately he organized his material. Innumerable drawings, watercolors, and oil sketches usually preceded the *état définitif,* the earlier
works tending to be more naturalistic, the later ones more abstract
and simplified. When I was choosing works for inclusion in the exhibition, he usually wanted the final picture of a series to be selected.
Clearly, the first idea interested him much less than the last one.

Léger would let me spread the pictures around the room, and
sometimes while I studied them he continued painting. He allowed
nothing to disturb his routine, and explained to me that he kept work-
man's hours — up very early in the morning, to his studio rain or

shine, and there all day painting. He considered art to be an occupation like any other and thought of himself as a craftsman. Léger had little patience with the exigencies of mood or inspiration, nor did he worry too much about the physical well-being of his canvases. Dan Rich told me about an incident that occurred in 1935, while he was an associate curator of the Art Institute of Chicago and before I had joined the staff. Léger was on hand for an exhibition of his work when one of his paintings was damaged the day before the opening. There wasn't time to repair it. He asked for a stick of gum, chewed it thoroughly, and then proceeded to stuff it into a small hole in the canvas. With some hastily procured paint he covered the gum and presto! — the work was on the wall.

Léger made a lasting impression when he asked me to identify the subject of a brief sketch he had made. I said it looked like a snow-capped mountain. "Exactly!" he crowed. "But it's really a blow-up of

Léger in Chicago, 1945.

a woman's fingernail." An admirer of motion picture techniques, he believed in the power of enlarged and isolated fragments. By separating a detail from its original context, he claimed, one could totally transform its meaning. Once the sketch had served his purpose, Léger destroyed it. I still regret not rescuing that enlightening bit of pedagogy.

I spent part of May and June 1952 working with Léger in Paris, and he used to take me to the Closerie de Lilas, a Montparnasse restaurant a block or two from his studio. One day we were having aperitifs on the terrace before going in for lunch when I spotted a man bowing to me from a nearby table. It was Jean Dubuffet. Only recently he had given up his profession as a wine dealer and turned to full-time painting, so he was not yet a familiar figure in the Paris art world. I had been Dubuffet's guest for dinner the previous evening when he fed me costly truffles and told me how extravagant (Jean did everything extravagantly) his esteem for Léger was, though he scarcely knew him personally. So today we invited him to our table. The two men talked politely, Léger gruff but cordial, Dubuffet charming and modestly admiring. It all seems so long ago, while Jean was still stubbornly iconoclastic and before he had converted himself into a popular version of art stardom.

After Dubuffet left and we went into the restaurant for lunch, Léger discussed him. He knew his work only slightly but disliked it. "Too self-consciously naive," he told me, "too disorganized, but I respect him. He's authentic." No two men could have been more dissimilar in their work, their appearance, or their behavior — Léger was all of a piece, a positive, unwavering public figure, while Dubuffet was unpredictable, nihilistic, secretive, highly self-motivated, and bent on attracting publicity. Each artist has written persuasively about his own work, and to juxtapose their statements is to highlight the differences between them. "Truth in painting," said Léger, "is color at its fullest," whereas Dubuffet stated, "I don't find the function of assembling colors in pleasing arrangements very noble." Dubuffet also asserted, "I believe beauty is nowhere," while Léger consciously tried "with mechanical elements to create a beautiful object." "I believe very much in the values of savagery," observed Dubuffet. "I mean instinct, passion, mood, violence, madness." For Léger a true work of art must be "in perfect balance." If Dubuffet painted "landscapes of the brain, aiming to show the immaterial world that dwells in the mind of man," Léger frankly admitted, "I am most responsive to externals." Dubuffet's favorite words were *involuntary* and *ambiguous,* where Léger's were *order* and *clarity*. Curiously, the more that Dubuffet pursued primitivism, the more the beau monde pursued him. That both of them became outstanding twentieth-century artists only goes to prove how wide open are the mores of Western culture.

Léger the man never quite resembled the robust contours of his own image. There he was — hearty, three-dimensional, peasant-like, direct, and practical — yet always slightly baffling. A model of masculine virility and power, he was at the same time responsive to the more elusive innuendos of life, and he was extraordinarily thoughtful. He talked to me repeatedly about the American obsession with premature obsolescence, about our disregard for objects still useful and only beginning to show signs of wear. Automobiles, household utensils, machinery of all kinds, even people, once they reached maturity, he claimed, were ready for the ash heap in the United States. Surprisingly, he did not seem to connect this profligacy with the inherent nature of mass production. When he was in America as a war exile, he spent some time in the northeastern part of the country, renting a cottage near Lake Champlain, and there he made a series of drawings featuring broken bits of farm equipment often interlaced with isolated hands. This juxtaposition of discarded machinery and human skill was symbolic of the contrast between America and Europe in the forties. In Europe, then far less prosperous than the United States, those hands, he assured me, would have been busy restoring the discarded objects.

Léger was fluent if sparing in his use of words, and also very exact. For a man whose art grew so lucidly out of the twentieth century, he was surprisingly tied to the past. He talked to me as much about the mosaics of Ravenna and the classicism of Poussin as about the syncopated jazz of Chicago (on which he doted) and New York's gaudy window displays. Filled with a faith in the future that rarely deserted him, he enjoyed his years in America during World War II, not least because of the mass-produced vulgarity he found there. Modern folklore entranced him, the more blatant the better. To walk along Broadway with Léger was like watching a child at the circus. He always fastened on the most garish objects — bawdy postcards, unexpected juxtapositions of junk jewelry, and madcap hand-painted neckties popular in the 1940s were his particular favorites, and he incorporated them into several of his American paintings. In this respect, he was, indeed, the first genuine pop artist, but above all, it was the speed, color, and vitality of urban life that he pursued. He looked on the modern city as an electronic miracle, which may explain why his greatest painting is called *The City*.

I met Léger in 1941, when he was in America during the war years. I had first shown his work in 1936, and in the late 1930s, my gallery was fortunate enough to be consigned a group of works that had been consigned to a New York dealer about to go out of business. I sold a piece or two at what now seem ridiculously low prices — one fine watercolor went for eighty dollars. Considering, however, that the two Kandinsky paintings I had recently carried away from the Eddy auction were knocked down for a total of twenty-five dollars, the Léger figure was not so much shocking, but merely another indication of how meagerly contemporary art was accepted in those days, especially in the Midwest.

While Léger was still in France during the occupation, it was impossible to send him a check written on an American bank. One day in the fall of 1940, however, I read in the paper that he had escaped and landed in America. After some difficulty I reached him and sent the money to New York. He'd never heard of me or my gallery, but was delighted to receive an unexpected check from an unknown woman when he couldn't have been too flush. In any case, after a trip to the West Coast, he stopped off in Chicago and we met.

What I remember most are the hours we spent together on the South Side in black nightspots listening to jazz, and listening, to be sure, was only one aspect of frenzied interaction. Fernand would sit for hours, drinking it all in, visibly expanding and totally hypnotized by the enveloping smoke, the noise, the beat of the drums, the early-morning uninhibited interplay of drinkers and performers. He ceased to be an observer and became a participant. "This," he told me, "is *la verité,* an authentic folklore." Years later he mentioned that the chief reason he regretted missing the opening of his 1953 show in Chicago was because he had been looking forward to "imbibing Chicago jazz again."

Otherwise Léger seemed to have few regrets; he had always done pretty much what he wanted. He appreciated public approval, but when it was withheld, he rarely seemed disturbed. Life amused him. He accepted his associates, including his frequent feminine companions and even his explosive second wife, with a certain sanguine detachment. The only disappointment he ever mentioned to me was that he never received an important public mural commission. True, he did design several large architectural mosaics, but he had long yearned to paint imposing wall projects. He always thought big. The framed picture with its cramped, bourgeois connotations was never his ultimate goal. In many ways, he outpaced his period — witness how little his canvases have dated.

At least on the surface, Léger was without bitterness or venom, and though a professed Communist he was scarcely an ardent one. It was "the workingman" he championed more than any political system. Somehow he was convinced that the Soviet Union was the "blue collar's" true hope; yet at the same time he was an enthusiastic admirer of America — its newness, bigness, and daring. I've always felt that our government overreacted when it denied him entrance to our country and he could not attend his retrospective.

The Soviet Union also gave him a similar show, but the works were suddenly removed well before the exhibition had run its course. It's likely that Léger's work was too abstract for Moscow. For me, his least interesting series of paintings, *The Construction Workers,* resulted from his partisan politics. These versions of slightly overhappy workmen, which I first saw exhibited in Paris in 1951, not long after he completed them on his return from America, struck me as too naturalistic, too obviously message-oriented for his proverbially dispassionate brush. I much preferred *The Divers,* the series that germinated while Léger was waiting to escape to America. He was in Marseilles, saw the boys diving for coins, got the idea there, and executed the paintings in the United States. I was delighted to be able to acquire one (*Divers on Yellow Background*, done in 1941) for the museum in 1953.

Léger realized that his paintings, even when they borrowed from the past, were an integral outgrowth of our century. And if he glorified the machine, he did so deliberately, since for him modern technology was at once the hope of the future and the revelation of the present. His attitude toward the First World War, in which he was wounded, was typical: he was stimulated, actually excited by the shimmering machinery of death, so finely tuned, so impervious and triumphant. He suggested that only with exposure to this arsenal did he find his way as an artist. Technology even invaded his nudes, which became prototypes for well-tuned robots. Curiously, the always macho Léger produced female images that were far from feminine and often overpowering.

While working on the Léger exhibition, I asked the artist to list the ten works he felt were landmarks in his development and indispensable to the show. He chose ten, with the proviso that one had been lost since 1913, when it had been shipped to the United States. Léger gave me a faded photograph of a tall, vertical painting done during 1910–11, but he wasn't even sure of the correct title, muttering something about "Three Figures" or "Three Personages." He urged me to search for the picture, saying, "If you find it, I will always be your loving servant," though we both realized that the odds against locating a picture after a forty-year lapse were minimal. I tracked down the other nine paintings on Léger's list, but this early work was nowhere to be found. Whenever I visited a Léger collector, whether public or private, I produced the dog-eared illustration, but without success. The picture seemed lost, and eventually Léger and I gave up hope.

At that time in 1952, I was also working on the "Chicago and Vicinity Exhibition," which encompassed reviewing the activity of every artist within a hundred miles of us. In my travels for the show, I went up to Milwaukee to look at the work of a painter named Joseph Friebert, who was teaching at Milwaukee State Teachers College (now the University of Wisconsin, Milwaukee). I arrived in a pelting downpour, and I was steered to a rear entrance where I could avoid the rain. Friebert met me at the back door of the school, and led me up a dark rear stairway that was the shortest way to his studio. On the dimly lit landing hung a big painting so dirty I could hardly make it out. When I asked Friebert what the picture was, he said, "I don't know. It's been there forever, and nobody knows where it came from." I stared at the canvas, covered with years of grime, and knew that a minor miracle had occurred. "This is the picture!" I gasped. "This is the early Léger!" At first Friebert thought I was crazy, but then he got someone to help him take down the painting and carry it into a room where there was more light. It was the picture — filthy but marvelous, and eighty-some miles from Chicago all these years.

Three Figures, as the painting was temporarily titled, had at some point entered the collection of the Milwaukee Art Institute (now the Milwaukee Art Museum). No doubt inspired by the epochal Armory Show, Gimbel's department store sponsored a traveling exhibition of Cubist paintings in 1913–14. The Milwaukee Art Institute was the last stop on the tour, and perhaps the department store made a gift of the painting to the museum after the show ended. After it was donated, the picture was relegated to storage. In the early teens, Léger was hardly known in America, and certainly not in the Midwest. The painting remained in the storeroom until the head of the art department at Teachers College borrowed it. Just how it finally ended up as a neglected and anonymous item in a musty back stairway has never been satisfactorily explained, but the picture's history is an acrid commentary on sealed eyes and sealed minds. How ironic that the two institutions involved were related to education of the eye and mind.

I was enchanted by my discovery, and immediately wired Léger that the search was over, but I was appalled by the condition of the painting. Its varnish badly discolored, its luminosity hidden under layers of dirt, the canvas was almost impossible to decipher, and even when we moved into better light I could find only two of the three figures. The picture was brought to Chicago, and I watched its progress every step of the way. After it was cleaned, all three emerged as mechanized forms in a complex assemblage of cylinders and cones, a combination not unusual from a pioneer of Cubism. The heads, recalling

Fernand Léger, *Essai pour trois portraits*, 1910–11. At Léger's behest, Katharine searched fruitlessly throughout the United States and Europe. She found it by accident — and less than a hundred miles from Chicago.

the strong broad planes of wood sculpture, were unexpectedly individualized, yet Léger insisted that they were not portraits. (The Milwaukee Art Museum stands by *Study for Three Portraits* as the true title of the painting.) The carefully knit composition seems to coil upward, impelled by a kind of tonal counterpoint. Léger was jubilant when he learned of his favorite's "resurrection," but, alas, he was never to see it again. Léger had been denounced on the floor of the United States Congress by the red-baiting Representative George Dondero of Michigan and was prohibited from entering the United States throughout the McCarthy era. At the Art Institute we pulled every string we could, but Léger could not attend the opening of his retrospective nor the installation of his murals for the General Assembly Building of the United Nations. At least the painting turned up in time to be included in our exhibition.

Through organizing the Léger show, I met the Baroness Gourgaud, whom I found unforgettable. She owned eleven Légers, several of them important paintings that I knew only through reproductions, so I wrote to her asking if I could come to see them. She not only agreed, but sent her car and chauffeur to pick me up at my hotel in Paris. I was driven through the countryside for an hour or two, eventually arriving a Louis XIII château set in its own parklike private landscape in Yerres, not far from Fontainebleau. It was all quite correct — until I entered the house. The chauffeur led me through a back entrance, then a dark empty hall, and finally into the main salon, a vast and once stately room now in the oddest state of abandonment. A wicker chair or two, a shabby table, and several outstanding paintings by, among others, Cézanne, Picasso, and Léger, only made that cavernous space seem more deserted. Because all the windows were covered with makeshift shrouds, the light was eerie. I don't believe I was ever in a more unloved room.

I remember a fine classical Picasso harlequin haphazardly displayed on a freestanding easel that had been pushed into a corner. There was also what I imagined to be a portrait of the baroness as a young woman, painted by Jean Lurçat. She was very beautiful, so I was hardly prepared for the incongruous apparition that soon entered the room — an old hag of a woman gaudily rouged and powdered who at first sight appeared more a caricature than a person. I felt I was looking at a clown's chalk mask daubed with stylized circles of red, but once we talked together (she avoided all English), I found her quite interesting. She was nothing if not frank, telling me that her husband, Baron Napoleon Gourgaud, now long dead, had married her for her wealth. The baron had expensive avocations — not only was he the art collector in the family, but as an explorer and a direct descendant of General Gaspard Gourgaud, the loyal aide-de-camp who had accompanied Napoleon to Saint Helena, he was an avid purchaser of memorabilia having to do with Bonaparte's campaigns and last days. But it was only after his wedding in 1917 that the baron could enjoy such interests with the nonchalance he wished. In the early 1920s he began buying paintings and in 1926 he purchased Napoleon's last home on French soil, which the baroness subsidized and later vigilantly maintained as a museum. With marriage, Baron Gourgaud's freedoms were not limited to money. The baroness described his infidelities involving both men and women with dispassionate sangfroid, even showing me the secret entrance reserved for these assignations.

What genuinely fascinated me about Baroness Gourgaud was her description of the war years when she remained incarcerated in the château during the entire German occupation. She claimed that the estate was under constant surveillance, and she was safe only if secluded in a hidden area of the house. "Why?" I asked. "Because I'm American," she replied. My first reaction was one of extreme annoyance because she had forced me to speak French for several days when in fact we were both Americans. She had been Miss Eva Gebhard, distantly connected to the Vanderbilts by marriage, and had spent her early life in New York. For the rest of my visit, we lapsed into comfortable English. As the day wore on, I realized how solitary she was, how totally alone. She had no children, and in addition she seemed to trust no one, especially not her three servants, whom she described as "hostile, dishonest, and abusive." Whether she was paranoid or senile I do not know, but my visit was periodically punctuated by her raucous fights with one or another of her entourage. However, when she talked alone with me, she was entirely lucid and engagingly perceptive.

At lunch the bickering intensified, and the rather informally cos-
tumed butler who served us was far from courteous, but the food —
at least mine — was delectable, a perfect cheese soufflé, excellent wine,
a fresh salad. The baroness, however, consumed only mounds of what
looked like ordinary grass without a drop of salad dressing to disguise
it. She informed me that this was a healthful diet she followed religiously, which may have accounted for her gaunt appearance. During
the meal she talked with suppressed passion about the home she loved
the most — obviously not the château in Yerres, nor her elegant house
on lower Fifth Avenue where I once subsequently visited her, but a
camp-like place on an unspoiled island near Bordeaux. She longed for
its freedom and told me that she spent as much time there as possible.
The island is now best known for its nudist colony and may well have
boasted one during her time, which I'm sure would not have dis-
pleased her. The Baroness Gourgaud always struck me as a renegade
from that era when the parents of presentable young American girls
parted with their riches in exchange for a titled European son-in-law.
I gathered that her solitude had not been limited to the German occupation.

Late in the afternoon it was time for me to leave, but the baroness
tried to postpone the moment when she would again be left alone
with her "staff." She suddenly appeared rejuvenated and persuaded
me to pick berries with her in the garden, which was better looked after than the house. Then she produced a camera and took two pictures of me; one she sent me as a gift and the other she eventually
pasted in her guestbook. I noticed that the signature above mine was
Clare Booth Luce's. "We're both converts to Catholicism," the baroness
explained, "and that's a strong tie."

She lent two splendid paintings to the Léger exhibition, the more
important a 1924 canvas called *La Lecture*. It is one of the artist's
most uncompromising compositions: not so much as an extraneous
dot interferes with its classical severity. Léger, who was originally
trained as an architect, designed this work, of two women holding
books but staring impenetrably ahead, with structural precision. The
baroness was unlike most owners of imposing collections, because she
didn't identify with hers. I suspect that she had very little affection for

Katharine on the grounds at La Grange, the Baroness Gourgaud's estate in Yerres, France, 1952. This was the snapshot the baroness insisted on taking.

the paintings, never displaying the usual possessive enthusiasm. In addition, she made no pretense to being an art authority. I found her a refreshing anomaly. However, when I asked if she would consider leaving *La Lecture* to the Art Institute if only because I was so enamored of the picture, she said indulgently, "I'd like to, but the collection meant a great deal to my husband, and he would want it to remain in France. He chose each work with care and knew most of the artists personally." She implied that everything was intended for the Louvre.

The Léger trail also led me to Gerald Murphy, that urbane epicure who was the model for Dick Diver in F. Scott Fitzgerald's *Tender Is the Night*. By the time I met Murphy, he had long ago made his reluctant departure from Europe and two of his three children were dead. He was in New York, heading Mark Cross Company, the family business. Because he was a close friend of Léger (and also of Picasso, Stravinsky, Hemingway, Dos Passos, and many other luminaries), I wrote to him about the projected exhibition, and he invited me to visit him in his office, saying he had something important to show me. On my next trip to New York, I encountered a gracious if reserved gentleman who warmed up once we started discussing Léger. He unlocked a cabinet and lovingly unwound layers of tissue paper to reveal a sketchbook Leger had filled while on the Murphys' yacht.

Later Gerald Murphy wrote me a letter telling me about the cruise and the sketchbook. "In 1934," he wrote, "we started from Antibes aboard our schooner the 'Weatherbird.' Fernand and Jeanne were with us. During the first day out, the sea was smooth and Fernand, who had never been aboard a sailing vessel, was fascinated with the rigging and all the contrivances on board. He had brought the

Fernand Léger, *La Lecture*, 1924. Katharine's determination to have *La Lecture* in the Léger exhibition led her to the Baroness Eva Gourgaud, a collector as unforgettable as her paintings.

notebook and a few watercolors with him and he spent the entire day making sketches. He had never worked under such conditions and it stimulated him enormously. The second day out the weather turned bad as we encountered mistral. Very much to his surprise, he did not feel the rough sea as he expected and persisted in his work. He made quite a joke of his being able to remain at his post while some of the rest of us were unable to do so. It was for this reason that he wrote on the cover of the notebook, 'À Sara et Gerald de leur mousse fidèl'" (To Sara and Gerald from their faithful cabin boy). The sketchbook offers an unfamiliar glimpse of Léger, one of the few instances when his work was even faintly autobiographical. It includes studies of riggings and shipboard activities, but the two images with the most panache are faceless likenesses of the Murphys. They are seen in sun clothes and only from the rear, yet they emerge as individual personalities, accurately and affectionately recorded.

Mr. Murphy produced a small package, a gift for Léger that he asked me to deliver when I next went to Paris. His nostalgia for the beautiful lost years moved me, though he himself was a model of aloof decorum. Yet in that elegant Manhattan office, the past seemed to haunt him. During the years in France he had painted intermittently and Léger once confided that he considered Murphy an accomplished artist who had never received the exposure he deserved. Fortunately, a few years before Murphy died in 1964, his work was shown at the Dallas Museum for Contemporary Arts, and again in 1974 at the Museum of Modern Art. If he was influenced by Léger, and I believe he was, it was only peripherally. His specialty was cool compositions combining prosaic and typically American objects like razors, watches, and fountain pens in arbitrary organizations. When Fernand talked about Murphy and the golden days they spent together, he too was openly nostalgic, the only time I observed this artist, who lived so securely in the present, reverting wistfully to the past.

5
Stuart Davis
and the Jazz Connection

Stuart Davis was the American Léger — a daring artist who understood the American urban landscape and the meaning of America, though he used French methods to interpret them. More than any other American artist of his time, Davis was enamored of jazz, so it makes perfect sense that two of the European painters he admired and studied — Mondrian and Léger — were also riveted by the same music. During our century, the influence of jazz, never as a literal presence but often evident in spirit, has become almost as dominant a refrain as the machine. As a strong component of modern painting, the phenomenon of jazz should never be minimized. It was a language curiously sympathetic to the adventurous experiments of early-twentieth-century art, because both were concerned with liberated methods and liberated emotions.

Léger and Mondrian, the two established European artists who were most mesmerized by American jazz, came under its power only after being in this country. Mondrian was introduced to it when he lived in New York during the last years of his life. His late paintings owe their rhythmic syncopation to jazz. It has always amazed me that an artist who eliminated every possible nonessential from his work was able to embrace a new vocabulary without in any way altering his objectives or his primary methods. Nothing changed fundamentally, yet somehow the paintings were Americanized — or, better, they were repaced. In the end, it was not jazz that took over Mondrian; it was Mondrian who took over jazz and adjusted it to his will. No matter whether the work was titled *Composition* or *Broadway Boogie-Woogie,* the same total clarity prevailed. As the painter Hedda Sterne once observed, "Early on Mondrian must have undergone some kind of epiphany." Perhaps that is the only explanation for this ability to turn basic principles into abstract visual organizations that are marvels of related tensions. Léger, on the other hand, was made for jazz. The minute he'd arrive in Chicago, he was off to a smoke-filled, all-night session in some South Side joint. He was transported by the direct assault of the music and its stabbing juxtapositions, not unlike paintings he had created long before he ever heard the sound of a wailing horn.

Stuart Davis named his son after the drummer George Wettling and the pianist Earl Hines. Earl was born in 1952 and, after decades as a Greenwich Village resident, Stuart and his wife, Roselle, moved to a larger apartment and adjoining studio on the Upper West Side. I was visiting Stuart in his studio on West 67th Street two or three years before he died, when young Earl bounced in from school. He couldn't have been more than nine or ten, energetic and demanding, and after a while Stuart weakly scooted him out of the studio. After Earl left, Stuart, who often reminded me of an unflinching bulldog, sighed and said he was too old and impatient to raise a child. He adored this boy, but he was exhausted at the thought of him. Stuart also explained the origin of Earl's name and what jazz had meant to him during his entire adult life. "Jazz," he said, "was the only thing that corresponded to an authentic art in America. Mondrian also felt its impact: I talked to him about this several times. He responded to the basic rhythms of jazz in a direct physical way; they even made him want to dance. For me — I had jazz all my life — I almost breathed it like the air. I think all my paintings, at least in part, come from this influence, though I never tried to paint a jazz scene. . . . It was the *tradition* of jazz music that affected me."

Even the briefest of glances at a canvas like *Hot Still-Scape for Six Colors — Seventh Avenue Style* of 1940 (Museum of Fine Arts, Boston) demonstrates how much jazz remained a living component of his work. In the mid-1980s, long after Davis's death in 1964, I was asked to annotate his journals, which Stuart's widow had given to the Fogg Art Museum at Harvard University. Reading through them, I was repeatedly impressed by the role jazz had played in his grammar of seeing.

That afternoon visit remains in my memory. Stuart was old and ill; he was scrunched down in a large chair with one leg elevated on a

Stuart Davis, playing a record, early 1950s. The artist was a lifelong devotee of jazz.

stool. He claimed it was gout. Nonetheless, he was drinking (whiskey, as I recall) with considerable gusto. There was a late work on the easel and another, somewhat earlier one, standing nearby on the floor. The easel painting, if I remember correctly, was the superb *Schwitzki's Syntax* (1961; Yale University Art Gallery), one of the *Champion* series. The earlier canvas dealt with somewhat the same subject. He said that at the moment he didn't want either of them sold, because on the days he wasn't well enough to paint he sat there comparing, studying, eliminating, and solving almost imperceptible problems. Like Léger, who worked toward the painting he would mark *état définitif,* Davis liked to keep as much of a series in front of him as he could until he completed the last one in the sequence. Both men developed an idea, often with numerous preliminary sketches, and continued to recast it until it became a tremendously overpowering final picture.

Davis relied on what he called the "structural continuities" between his paintings to brace and inspire him. He told me that he had "no sense of guilt" when he reused designs and motifs he had conceived years before. "The past for me is equal to the present," he said, "because thoughts I had long ago and those I have now remain equally valid — or at least the ones that were really valid, remain valid." Yet as he grew older and weaker, his visual logic grew tougher and his work became stronger: the late paintings are incandescent.

Davis never worked quickly, although I only observed him toward the end of his life, after I moved to New York in 1959 and he was an old man, drinking himself into a fog and not terribly well. Our acquaintance actually began by letter in 1938. When I had my gallery, I wrote to Davis about having a show. Neither of us had a cent, but because I was interested in his work, he agreed, and a mutual friend paid the shipping charges to make an exhibition possible in February 1939. Stuart chose the pictures, and the show was superb. I couldn't sell one thing. After the show closed, he wrote me a furious letter, typewritten and single-spaced, absolutely crucifying me. He told me he had lost his teeth and didn't have enough money to get them fixed. He was depending on the show, but instead it was the plaything of some dilettante who couldn't sell his work. I was devastated, and perhaps that was the reason I never tried to meet him until many years later. I certainly remained embarrassed. By the time we met, he'd completely forgotten the letter. I never did.

Davis wrote frenetically day after day and year after year in his private notebooks, admonishing, advising, explaining, directing, analyzing, and berating, but always repeating himself ad nauseum. He may have been drunk from time to time, but he nonetheless provided invaluable data on his work. He had contempt for most of his American colleagues, but overwhelming admiration for European groundbreakers like Léger, Matisse, Picasso, and Seurat, readily admitting the influence of the first three on his own work. A man of superior intelligence, he investigated the most intransigent problems of technique and meaning. Often he seemed to be arguing with himself about politics, color, words, museums, society at large, his own work, and jazz; he never wrote a syllable about his family or personal life. For him, art was more than a profession. It was the only air he breathed.

Why would this artist have found the time day after day and year after year to write reams of repetitious statements in what often approximated a secret language? Words for him were not just visual components of his paintings. Like jazz, they also carried wry and multiple meanings that changed so often that one was never quite sure of a final interpretation. It was as if Davis was consciously evolving a hidden language that only the most persevering detective could untangle. As the years passed, the same word (sometimes one of his own invention) assumed different meanings. Decoding him requires a touch of prescience, but there was usually a raison d'être for each alteration and verbal inversion. The more I perused those pages, the more paranoid they seemed, and yet there was much that was brilliant. Take Davis's very personal conception of drawing, which had nothing to do with conventional draftsmanship: lines resulted from the tangible intersection of different colors. In short, color was the lifeblood of his art, providing boundaries, edges, and definition.

Scattered among the pages of Davis's journals are about one hundred drawings, some of them hasty sketches and diagrams, others full-scale works that were designs for important paintings. The condition of the drawings, and of the predominantly handwritten pages in the original notebooks, was nothing less than shocking. I used photocopies, which, after some time, produced an unpleasant allergy. As a result, for the next few months, whenever I was making notes on the papers, I had to wear surgical gloves and an unlined rubber rain-coat. Several summers ago, when I was on Cape Cod, the newly appointed director of the Fogg Art Museum, who is no longer there, called on me. (During the mid- and late 1980s, the Fogg's directorship seemed to change with the season.) In any case, he told me that he was a great admirer of Stuart Davis and that the Fogg Museum had only recently bought one of his major drawings for a sizable sum — $30,000, as I remember. Some years earlier, in my report on the papers, I had urged Harvard to waste no time in restoring the drawings, which were rapidly disintegrating. The new director didn't even know that they existed, and nothing had been done to preserve them. This is the same hall of learning, by the way, that mishandled a group of murals by Mark Rothko. Those paintings eventually had to be removed from view on account of premature deterioration. For some years, they were installed in an area where food was served, an obvious danger to large, unprotected murals.

The titles of many of Davis's paintings can seem irrational, but in fact they were usually related to his own immediate experiences — an advertisement he'd seen, a place he'd visited, an idea that had engaged him. All his paintings, he said, "affirmed an urban continuity," and New York City and Philadelphia, where he was born, figured heavily into Davis's art, but not always in a conscious way. As Davis himself noted, "You're born with a genetic tape that has a coded prescription for your behavior throughout your entire life — and never forget that it's in code." As his health faltered toward the end of his life, Stuart's handwriting became larger and larger. Sometimes only a few words filled an entire sheet. Leaping from a page in outsized letters was my name, "K. Kuh." I was afraid to read on — Stuart could be a caustic observer. It seems that in 1956 I had written him from the Art Institute for data on the title of the painting *Ready-to-Wear* (1955), a canvas the museum had recently acquired. I made a habit of questioning living artists about the work we received by them, hoping to benefit our archives. In that way, we found out all kinds of revealing data — that an early portrait by Kokoschka was a likeness of his tailor, for whom

Stuart Davis, *Ready-to-Wear*, 1955. Stuart Davis was never timorous, and *Ready-to-Wear* is no exception. It is a high-voltage painting in which fragments of forms and objects, all conveyed in clean, light color, are interlocked in a pulsing, integrated design.

he had painted it in return for a tuxedo; that an interior by Chagall was an imaginary scene of his own birth; that de Kooning's brilliant *Excavation* was inspired by a grade-B movie of peasants digging up the earth. Davis, it seems, was annoyed with me and wrote that "even K. Kuh" had bothered him for the meaning of a title! At the time I wondered if Duchamp's conception of the "ready-made" had affected Davis in any way, or, more likely, whether the title of the picture came only from popular American business argot. I was at least happy that he included that qualifying "even."

I shouldn't have been surprised at Stuart's irritation. Only a year before, in response to a request for an explanation of the painting I was showing in the Venice Biennale, he rapped my knuckles, replying,

> Since a painting is only a drawing after all, it is a mistake to look for identifications among its elements that are alien to its reality. I refer to the demand, occasionally made by some people, for the name, meaning, and credentials of certain shapes in the painting. Such identification is not impossible, but the odds are heavily against it. In a way it is like asking a New York traveler in Europe whether he knows a friend of yours in Bolivia.

Thinking back, I find Stuart Davis a complex enigma whose work and life deserve a full-scale study that has yet to be satisfactorily done. There have been essays galore, festooned with the usual array of footnotes, but any discussion that is at once scholarly, probing, and encompassing is lacking. Somehow his philosophy of art, life, and language have never been fully deciphered, and most helpful would be a reliable translation of the secret vocabulary that played such a large visual role in his paintings. His notebooks supply elliptical clues, but he was dogmatically wary of art historians and museum personnel. Regulation art history never failed to exasperate him. He was digging for the union of meaning and method, a combination, to be sure, that involves most serious artists.

6
Constantin Brancusi
Elision and Re-vision

What is the legacy of Constantin Brancusi? Between Michelangelo and Brancusi — a period of roughly four hundred years — no other sculptors except Bernini and Rodin have had such conclusive impact. Moreover, it is reassuring that this progression showed a certain continuity, with Rodin borrowing from Michelangelo and Brancusi from Rodin, in whose studio he actually worked. However, after two months in the master's atelier, he departed, making a famous remark by way of explanation: "Nothing can grow in the shadow of the great trees."

I am wondering whether, contrary to popular opinion, Brancusi was less the beginning of an era than the triumphant culmination of one — an unusual situation, since today we are accustomed to thinking of endings as slightly anticlimactic. It is the new we demand — the different, the cataclysmic, as represented by individual artists and even by successive steps in their careers. Not so Brancusi. He pursued his own course with scarcely a nod to transient fashions. Although he introduced

the most subtle elisions and condensations, he adhered to acknowledged concepts of form. Isamu Noguchi, who was an apprentice in
Brancusi's Paris studio for six months in 1927, learned direct carving,
new subtleties of polishing, and a fidelity to materials that were unique
to Brancusi, but he also said that the older artist exemplified the acceptance of "art in its most aesthetically pure form, without reference
to social issues." Noguchi further observed, "What Brancusi does . . .
is to take the essence of nature and distill it." And indeed, Brancusi did
have a special way of seeing human and animal life in terms of their
origins. With him ovoids modulated by fleeting variations repeatedly
evoke the idea of genesis.

Brancusi was more concerned with positive than with negative
form and in this respect he looked to the past. At times he was interested in implied motion as reflected on highly polished surfaces, but
he did not foretell tangible movement nor the dedication to space,
which a bit later were to become keynotes of modern mobiles and
welded metal sculpture. He was nonetheless a true pioneer, if only because of his ability to define the most complicated aspects of life with
the most simplified means. His interests centered on the secrets of reproduction and replenishment, themes that, in the hands of a lesser
artist, could have become mawkish or pretentious. He was able to
sublimate all nonessentials and concentrate on basic meanings. For
him it was not a case of the emperor's clothes; he envisioned no ameliorating addenda but, on the contrary, pared away familiar details to
expose generic realities.

The industrial age was rarely his mentor, for methods and materials seem to have engrossed him less than the mysteries of living organisms. He was involved not alone with the physical core of life, but
also with its psychic ramifications. His was an inner-directed, almost
Oriental focus. In the 1930s Brancusi visited India at the invitation of
the Maharajah of Indore, an important patron of modern art who was
an ardent admirer of his, but the sculptor's work had little relation to
the subcontinent's explosive styles. He was closer to the urbanity of
China. Yet there is no reason to believe that he was directly influenced
by the art of any Eastern country; it is more likely that he merely operated on a somewhat similar wavelength.

I remember being taken to visit Brancusi in the summer of 1952 by the French writer and dealer Henri-Pierre Roché, who had known the artist since his early years in Paris. I was in Europe working on the Léger retrospective, and also looking for what we could buy. I had heard that we could purchase some sculpture directly from Brancusi, although I felt that because he was not young, the museum had waited too long already. *The Seal* (1924–36; Solomon R. Guggenheim Museum), of white marble, was available. I hungered after a polished brass *Princess X* (1916; Musée National d'Art Moderne), but Brancusi did not want to sell it. However, Roché had three fine pieces for sale, none of which I was able to obtain. Even though I came away with nothing for the museum, that invitation to the Impasse Ronsin before Montparnasse was razed for development was a treasured event. There was that fantastic studio — one large room filled with turntables on which were sculptures, hidden under cheesecloth. There was that small man in coveralls who leaped about somewhat like a sturdy monkey removing the cloths and connecting the turntables to an electric circuit, thus making the figures rotate slowly in a kind of rhythmic euphoria. Several versions of *Bird in Space* and *Mlle Pogany,* shining *Ledas* and *White Negresses,* all enhanced one another and yet retained their uniqueness. There was a *Turtle,* too, no version of which I had seen before. Brancusi explained that this latest sculpture of his was extremely recalcitrant, even refusing to be photographed, so he had indulgently given in. This remark was more than evasive repartee. Brancusi himself was a gifted photographer who had obsessively recorded his own work since 1914, and regarded the process as an artistic necessity; he also created a number of self-portraits with his camera, while hardly ever permitting anyone else to make an image of him.

Brancusi always reveled in having awestruck, attentive women around him, and as he fed me mint-flavored cough drops from a glass container, I examined the furniture — all carved by him from wood and resembling the chunky permanence of a peasant environment. Here supple sculpture mingled comfortably with stocky tools, a bunk bed, and tables, giving graphic evidence of the artist's duality. Today the studio has been reconstructed as part of the Musée National d'Art Moderne in Paris, the city where he spent most of his adult life. The

Constantin Brancusi, *Leda,* c. 1920. This version of *Leda* was the sculpture that Duchamp made sure came to the Art Institute as a consolation prize to Katharine for losing the Arensberg collection.

sculpture and the furniture are all there, but the total effect is a disastrous misrepresentation, recalling a sterile period room or, worse, a frozen habitat. The radiant sculpture is not rotating. There are no mint lozenges, and of course the shadow of that enigmatic figure in coveralls has vanished.

It is scarcely surprising that from time to time Brancusi looked back to his peasant origins. He was born into poverty, the child of a family of shepherds, in the small Romanian town of Hobitza. At the age of eleven he permanently left home. From then on he supported himself and determined his own direction. Brancusi once stated that his life had "been a sucession of marvelous events," and perhaps the first was this early, brave departure. One senses, however, that these "events" were more often the result of internal revelations. In any case, when carving from wood, Brancusi often reverted to indigenous memories. The furniture, the puzzling bases and pedestals, the deliberately primitive wood sculpture (some of the best of which belongs to the Guggenheim Museum), all show the same delight in the immediacy of the material. The wood is never camouflaged; it is starkly and robustly revealed.

Some years ago, a friend lent me a book of documentary photographs on peasant life in Romania. And there, in farmhouse interiors, were the prototypes of Brancusi's furniture, while in the village cemeteries were wooden grave monuments that pointed the way to his sometimes heroic, sometimes witty sculpture of the same material. Still, there is a massive difference. Brancusi's wood carvings, whether utilitarian or purely aesthetic, were designed with intentional multiplicity. A stool can be sat on, but it can also be seen as a latent animal or a living force. Pedestals often double as independent sculptures. Take, for example, the wood carving *Adam and Eve* (1921) in the collection of the Guggenheim Museum, where Adam acts at once as a base for and an integral element in the overall composition. Eve, conceived in interlocking curved planes, and Adam, more roughly hewn and more angular, become symbols of male and female opposed and yet conjoined. The masculine form supports the feminine, while together they produce an evolving synthesis.

With Brancusi there are always double entendres. The swelling *Torso of a Girl* (1922) turns into a vessel, each aspect emerging as a compressed abstraction. The many *Birds in Space* are in fact birds in flight or, better, they are flight itself — their upward-thrusting forms the closest approach to dematerialization that the sculptor ever intended. Perhaps the most sensuous of all Brancusi's works is *Princess X*, combining as it does both male and female reproductive organs in a single sinuous shape. Strongly phallic and also possessed of suggestive ellipses, the sculpture was banned as pornographic by the Salon des Artistes Indépendants of 1920. Four versions exist — one in marble, the others in bronze. Just what the title refers to is obscure, but less obscure is the artist's intention. The figure, again encompassing the origins of life, fuses the two sexes in composite interaction.

Brancusi pursued the same theme relentlessly. Once he had found a form, or shall we say an idea, that absorbed him, he doggedly returned to it, altering, refining, and reseeing until he had extracted its total potential. Typical was his long involvement with the portrait of Margit Pogany, a young Hungarian painter in Paris whom he found especially beautiful. Some six different versions, covering a period of approximately twenty-three years (from about 1910 to 1933), suggest how persistently he stalked a favorite subject. He executed his busts of *Mlle Pogany* in a variety of marbles and in polished bronze, but though the material may have affected certain aspects of the work, it never became a basic motivation. At times he included arms, at times various hairdressings, at times he twisted the long neck and oval head until the image assumed a rotating, three-dimensional ambience. Slowly the sculpture evolved into an almost metaphysical presence. In each version, Brancusi extracted certain underlying characteristics from his sitter — her elegance, her strange inward gaze. He emphasized the large egg-shaped eyes until eventually these great spheroids took over the entire face.

He grappled with *The Kiss* in the same way, strengthening the sculpture by patient readjustments. Again he made several versions, each touched by a poignancy that even a blocklike stone design could not dispel. Unexpected flashes of humor are threaded through Brancusi's work; his wit is always terse, often affectionate and, at times, bitingly satirical. One need only refer to his *Portrait of Nancy Cunard* (1928–32), its shining metal surface reflecting the viewer's likeness in a featureless face topped by a precarious chignon. To see oneself so frankly mirrored in another is provocative on both levels. Far more devastating is Brancusi's wood carving, *The Chief* (1925). Here a small head crowned with rusty iron is identified by a single feature — a gaping, babbling mouth. Sidney Geist, the Brancusi scholar, states that the work represents the pope, rather than a military or political head of state, but for me it encapsulates all the aspects of arrogant power.

That Brancusi adhered to strong philosophic convictions is clear, but nowhere clearer than in his renowned *Endless Column*, which, pushing up above the earth, acts as a curiously exultant testament to

Constantin Brancusi, *Self-portrait in the studio,* c. 1955. Perhaps his last
self-portrait, this image shows Brancusi's relationship to his vocation.
Old and unable to work, he sits at the portal of the studio he no longer
enters as an active artist. Unvanquished, he grasps a tool in his right hand,
a reminder of the hours of labor he lavished on the creation of
one of the most exquisite bodies of work in the history
of sculpture.

freedom from worldly ties. The column, rising ninety-six feet into the air, recalls the statuary in the cemeteries of Romanian villages, and its first purpose was to commemorate the dead who had fallen during World War I. Yet, modulated by elusive differentiations, *Endless Column* (1937) ascends in nodes, sheds its literal references, and appears to be limitless. Both its title and austere repetitions reinforce the idea of an unbroken, continuing experience. It is fitting that the finished work can be seen only in Romania, in the town of Târgu Jiu, where Brancusi ran away to as a child shortly after leaving home.

At the end of his life, Brancusi was approached by Barnet Hodes, a Chicago lawyer and art collector acting for several other local businessmen and art lovers, who proposed that an even taller cast of *Endless Column* — in gleaming stainless steel — could be installed on the Lake Shore of Chicago. In June 1956, the sculptor agreed to the plan, provided that he could supervise the work in person and nothing would be done without his full approval. Discussions and correspondence continued over the next five or six months. By then, fatally ill, Brancusi was too sick to travel.

Hoping to salvage the project, I and Al Arenberg, another Chicago collector and a good friend of the museum, paid a call on Brancusi. We reassured him that his slightest specifications would be followed religiously and supervised by any sculptor he designated, though we had a suggestion of our own. Both of us felt that Isamu Noguchi was the right artist to direct the project. Noguchi, of course, had been Brancusi's assistant thirty years before, and he also happened to be in Paris at the same time, working on the garden he had designed for UNESCO. Furthermore, Noguchi was enthusiastic about being commissioned to oversee the erection of *Endless Column*. But Brancusi was not. When we mentioned Noguchi's name, Brancusi did not answer. He merely shook his head, and turned his face to the wall. Regardless of what promises were made, he continued to shake his head no. He was too ill to speak, but a sculpture without his personal imprint could not be his. Finally, recognizing that Brancusi would never permit anyone else, no matter how distinguished or close to him in approach, to supervise his work, I turned to Al and said, "He is not interested." For the first time, Brancusi nodded yes, and we left him in peace. This was to be my last visit with Brancusi. He died on March 16, 1957.

We should have understood how little Brancusi left to chance in his work, and as for "specifications" — these were merely clues to final decisions. As Sidney Geist put it,

> *Endless Column,* in its ever-increasing dimensions, was not a subject of random enlargement by Brancusi. Rather, its significance seems to have changed with the occasion that called it forth and with each change in dimension. We can only imagine the special poetry of the unrealized final *Column* — thirteen times as tall as the previous one [in Târgu Jiu], in polished chrome steel, set on the . . . lake front. This luminous image would have probably not looked dense enough to appear as a link between heaven and earth. In its seemingly transparent skin, it would have been the agent of their fusion, dissolving in its own reflections of the water below and the sky above.

Brancusi's influence on our century has been both direct and indirect. Such sculptors as Arp, Henry Moore, Noguchi, and Barbara Hepworth obviously are in debt to him, but more important is his indefinable impact on all of us who hope to understand the art of our period. His devotion to primary forces, his ability to clear away nonessentials and discover and even invent forms in their purest manifestations, set him apart. If his intention was not necessarily to break new ground, his vision was so penetrating that he was able to make the past seem new.

7
Three Encounters with Bernard Berenson

My first visit to I Tatti some sixty-eight years ago is etched in my memory. That house filled with early Italian paintings, several of which to be sure no longer carry their original Berenson attributions, that astounding library of volumes on art and history from all times and places, those carefully designed gardens, together combined to overwhelm me. I was just out of college and only recently embarked on graduate studies in art history. Central to my memories was our host, Bernard Berenson, a small man of sharp reactions and seemingly very much to the manor born, which, of course, he was not.

He was an impecunious Jew born in Lithuania in 1865 and an immigrant to Boston ten years later, but his ambition, probing mind, cosmopolitan wit, and erudition projected him beyond the realm of a mere art historian. He was a product both of Harvard University and of his own unique capabilities. During his entire life (he lived to be ninety-four), he kept his eye on the main chance. He knew precisely where he was going and how to get there. Despite his size, Berenson was a towering personality and curiously attractive. Even when he was in his nineties, I was flattered if he so much as held my hand. He could also be biting and at times ruthless, but there was always something seductive about him. He commanded and demanded attention. His large wife, Mary, another American expatriate, was a formidable physical presence, but not as intimidating as her tiny husband.

My parents and I had been invited to I Tatti for lunch thanks to Louis Levy, a New York lawyer and an early beau of my mother's, who had given us a letter of introduction. He became friendly with Berenson while working on a legal problem that involved the art historian. There were several such cases over the years owing to Berenson's not always judicious habit of mixing money with attributions, but of these I know only through hearsay. However, I do know that as an acknowledged authority on Italian art, Berenson was in a position to make lucrative discoveries. His word carried weight and if, for example, he might have elevated a Luini to a Leonardo or a fine copy to an authentic original, large sums could change hands.

There were other visitors at I Tatti that day, but Berenson and his wide-ranging interests impressed me most. Politics, history, literature, and all the arts were his territory, not to mention gossip, which he turned into sociology. He even took time off to lead me to the library where he showed me his own new methods of cross-indexing and a recent book on Botticelli, whom he considered an artist waiting in the wings for more substantial research. It was a project, he suggested, that I might consider. He himself was an admirer of the painter and observed how at that time (the mid-1920s) Botticelli was too often viewed as a charming mythologist. Berenson saw him as a tough symbolist who exposed contemporary problems in a deceptively graceful vein.

As we left after luncheon, Berenson accompanied us to the door. He sent greetings to Louis Levy and then turned to my mother and asked, "Tell me, how did you cop this beautiful man?" My mother, who considered herself quite good-looking, was crushed, my father, always unself-conscious about his appearance, amused. It was an extra hard blow for her because she had long been a Berenson fan, partly because of the paintings he had acquired for the Isabella Stewart

Gardner Museum in Boston. When I was growing up, Mother made sure to take me there whenever she could to see them. Because Mrs. Gardner was still alive at the time, the museum was open to the public only a few days each year. My mother even tried to arrange our periodic Boston visits for consultations with a polio specialist (I had had polio, became paralyzed, and was still suffering from the after-effects) to coincide with the museum's schedule. We always stayed at the Copley Plaza Hotel and my mother had learned that on precisely the same day of every week at precisely the same time John Singer Sargent joined Isabella Gardner for lunch, and they sat at the exact same table. For this historic event, we purposely ate lunch early in order to assure ourselves front-row seats, and, just to make sure, my mother would tip the maître d' heavily to obtain a table nearby. Sargent was handsome and elegant, Mrs. Gardner severely bent and dressed in what always looked to me like layers of cheesecloth. Since I have become equally old and bent, I understand her costume better. She just wanted something soft and unrevealing to hide behind. Their conversation appeared more sporadic than spirited, but there was a quiet forbearance between them that signified a long friendship. I was riveted, convinced I was witnessing living if not altogether sparkling history.

Berenson's books on art, however, were what most intrigued my mother. Here at last was a scholar who knew how to write graceful prose on a subject too often weighed down with pretentious technicalities. He dared to reevaluate art history not alone for his colleagues, but for a larger audience of the interested lay public. His whole approach was humanistic; his methods of attribution, it is true, were sometimes dubious but more often enlightening. Knowledge didn't clutter his vision — on the contrary, he used it to intensify his emotional responses. I haven't read any of his books for decades, and I'm not sure how I'd react today. He wrote a great deal about form, "plastic form," as he put it, which may explain why twentieth-century art and its emphasis on space eluded his understanding.

Many years pass. It is 1951, and I am now a curator at the Art Institute of Chicago, in Venice with Dan Rich to see a comprehensive Tiepolo show. Over the years I had occasionally visited I Tatti again, but this time in Venice was to be the longest single period I was able to observe Berenson. By chance, we were stopping at the same hotel where he customarily stayed. Mary Berenson had died and was replaced by Nicky Mariano, a woman I always found very simpática. Long his valued assistant, she was an ideal companion for Berenson, who, now quite old, was extremely demanding.

I recall all too vividly occasional dinners together in the hotel's formal dining room. The windows all opened on the Grand Canal, but the moment we entered Berenson insisted that every one of them be tightly closed. It was summer; the room became suffocating. Many of the guests were British, and no sooner did they appear in their usual

Bernard Berenson and Nicky Mariano in one of the gardens
in the Villa I Tatti in the late 1940s.

"dressed for dinner" raiment than our contingent arrived. Because Berenson was something of a celebrity in Italy, his word was law. Nicky tried to calm him, to persuade him to be more reasonable, but he was inflexible where his health was concerned. The slightest breeze he found life-threatening. When he sat down, every waiter was expected to hover over his table. I also remember him sending the food back because it was not up to expectations. The dining room performance also highlighted his need for center stage, a spot he appropriated as his due.

Nevertheless, we both happily paid him court, both at table and in his suite, which was even more hot and airless. There we would have aperitifs before dinner. While I went mad from the heat, he and Dan discussed every nuance of the Tiepolo show. Large retrospective exhibitions can be as illuminating as they are exhausting. The artist, encapsulated on the wall, evolves before our eyes. Years contract to highlight the peaks and continuity of a lifetime. The quality of a retrospective depends on two sources: the artist and the persons responsible for the show. What is included and excluded and how the works are organized all contribute. Emphasis can be thematic or chronological, but in order to succeed the exhibition must do more than be inclusive. It must encompass in a single experience the entire meaning of an artist's work.

For me the Tiepolo show was another step in my education. Just as I'd neglected Baroque art until Carlos Mérida turned it into living history for me in Mexico, so too had I given short shrift to the eighteenth century. I'd miscalculated the drama of the former for decadence, and I underrated the eighteenth century, including even its greatest stars — Watteau, Fragonard, Gainsborough, and Tiepolo — as too artificial. Because of sustained immersion in the exhibition, as well as the influence of Berenson as mentor, I came to realize that it was the very artificiality that gave life to Tiepolo's paintings. Though superficially naturalistic, his volatile figures, hovering in abstract space, encourage even the most prosaic visitor to soar. Lighter than air and yet unexpectedly substantial, they swoop, float, and dip. Nothing defies them. These idealized heralds challenge stability as they confirm the freedom of the human spirit.

Here I refer to the work of Giambattista Tiepolo (1696–1770), though the exhibition also included the paintings of one of his sons, Giandomenico, who at times was influenced by his father and at times by Italian contemporary life. He tended more toward the colloquial and, though a fine painter, probably never received the acclaim he merited because of comparison with his illustrious father. It was Giambattista who epitomized his century and the Venice in which he lived by escaping from the real world into a utopia of eternal grace. Technically he was extraordinary. One of the great draftsmen of all time, he was able to create form and yet distill it into space and flux. Observing Berenson at the Tiepolo exhibition made me realize that he, unlike many art historians of our century, never allowed his emotions to be dimmed by scholarship. It was not his habit to split hairs.

He could be cruel, too. One day in 1956 when Dan and I were leaving the Uffizi in Florence, we heard someone calling us. It was Nicky, who led us to a large limousine where Berenson was perched on pillows and covered with blankets, even though it was summer. He was ninety-one, but as sharp as ever. After a brief chat through an open window, he invited us to I Tatti the next day. Meanwhile, he leaned out of the window and jabbed at an Italian decoration Dan was wearing on his lapel. Berenson could scarcely conceal his disgust. "What in the world are you doing with that thing? Get rid of it!" he commanded. For the remainder of the trip, the ribbon disappeared. I must admit that Dan was often a pushover for medals, and Berenson knew only too well how to humiliate him.

The next day we went to I Tatti. He hadn't changed much since our visit in Venice, nor had Nicky, and I Tatti still remained as alluring as I'd found it some thirty years earlier when I was in my gullible twenties. It was clear that everything in that mesmerizing establishment still rotated around a single figure. I returned only once after Berenson's death, but the magic had vanished. He left the place to Harvard University as a graduate center for the study of Italian art, yet without his presence I Tatti, though still beautiful and unquestionably useful, was no longer the aesthetic and intellectual Shangri-la he had created.

Katharine and Dan at a restaurant in Rome, about 1954. The image is
rare because it documents one of the few instances in which
their personal relationship is apparent.

We were in Italy in 1956 because the Art Institute was responsible
for the American Pavilion at the Venice Biennale; I had organized the
exhibition and Dan was a commissioner. Not unnaturally the subject
of "modern art" came up, and Berenson stated that any painter after
Degas, whom he respected for his draftsmanship, was unacceptable.
He brushed aside Picasso, Matisse, Mondrian, and indeed every important innovator of our period. He preferred the Italian painter Renato Guttuso, whom he enjoyed as a conversationalist, despite the
artist's strong Communist bias. But more likely it was Michelangelo's
influence on Guttoso's work that tipped the scale. As for the acknowledged masters of twentieth-century art, Berenson seemed to have not
the least understanding. Could it have been old age that blinded him
to the present? I've always been sad that this man who responded so
profoundly to art of the past was unable to participate in his own
world. Now that I'm approaching ninety myself, I stop to question

Bernard Berenson and Harry S. Truman in the summer of 1956, on the same day that Katharine and Dan visited I Tatti.

why I find the art of the first half of our century so much more excit-ing than that of the last half. But in the end, no matter how bleary my eyes, I stand by this judgment.

Earlier on the day that we visited I Tatti, Harry Truman had been there. Berenson reported a most pleasant interchange of ideas. There are not many art historians who become "musts" on a VIP's itinerary, but as time went on this small man born in Lithuania and educated in the United States emerged as one of Italy's proudest living monu-ments. From what Berenson told us, he and Truman evidently en-joyed a lively conversation, but of one thing I am sure: it was not art they discussed. In that area, I don't believe Truman ever got beyond *Saturday Evening Post* covers.

We too had enjoyed a brief encounter with the former president in Florence. On this long weekend respite from Venice and preparations at the American Biennale pavilion, we stayed with the Henry Cliffords in their handsome villa outside of Florence. At that time Henry was a curator of paintings at the Philadelphia Museum of Art. There were various other guests, among them Frances Perkins, the secretary of labor under Roosevelt, and Truman. She invited us to an evening party in honor of the Trumans, to be given by an American living in Florence. It was an informal and very small gathering. I was fascinated by Truman's joie de vivre; he seemed released, like a boy out of school. No guilts from the past, no regrets or other emotional baggage, were evident. He exuded optimism and a kind of modest self-confidence. I recall having the temerity to urge him to play the piano, which he did with more energy than skill. And then, fortified by champagne, I asked him to describe his most memorable White House experience. He claimed that it was leading his only child, Margaret, "down the aisle. That was my most nerve-wracking experience," he said. Bess Truman, in a dark blue lace dress, remained inconspicuous the whole evening, but as it grew late she looked across the room and caught her husband's eye. He nodded and said, "Yes, Mother, it's time to go." It was all so very gemütlich, yet it was this man who had changed world history forever by his decision to drop the atomic bomb.

Despite his Italian adoption, Berenson remained American. Many of my museum colleagues in the United States had worked under him as assistants at I Tatti. Some remained devoted; others found the experience restrictive and Berenson too autocratic, but there is no doubt that his approach to art reached far beyond the boundaries of his villa. His way of life intermixed art with all aspects of living. There were no dividing barriers. Americans came to pay homage most often. Many of them stayed both faithful to and in awe of him as they arranged periodic pilgrimages to I Tatti. In return, I think these American connections were important for Berenson and made for a healthy exchange. He needed the Americans' freer attitudes almost as much as they appreciated his way of life and grasp of art. He also liked to be kept informed of the latest American gossip.

What makes the saga of Berenson enigmatic is how unquestioningly he was accepted by most of the top American museum professionals of my day. Though they knew of occasional legal episodes and had heard rumors about problematic deals, I don't believe I ever encountered one of them who was not proud to know him or who openly doubted his authority. About matters of connoisseurship he was quoted widely. How often I heard a director or curator claim as a clincher, "B.B. thinks it's authentic." I Tatti was a beautiful luxury, but I can't remember worrying about the source of its sustenance. Now, as I look back, I realize that the term "conflict of interest" plainly does apply. Because Berenson himself was inventing new art-historical methods, he felt free to use them in unconventional, even questionable enterprises.

On the same day that Truman stopped by, another American luminary appeared. While Dan and I were still there, Judge Learned Hand and his wife, Frances, were announced. Berenson had been sitting next to me, clutching my hand, and I was feeling very pleased. As soon the Hands walked in, he dropped my hand and rushed forward. The two old men embraced warmly and immediately entered into a private tête-à-tête. They had been close friends since the 1920s. Judge Hand, who was seven years younger, was so highly respected in the United States that any mention of his name precipitated the question, "Why isn't he on the Supreme Court?" According to the late Judge Henry Friendly, whose appointment Hand recommended to the Second District Federal Court of Appeals, it was chiefly politics that interfered. Friendly described him as one of the greatest legal minds in American history and found it scandalous that he never served on the highest court of the land. Judge Friendly, who was likewise denied a seat there, though long considered more than qualified, explained his own predicament to me. "I am too conservative for the Democrats and too liberal for the Republicans." He was, by the way, a Republican. In those days the denial of the highly qualified was almost as hotly debated as is the acceptance of the underqualified today.

Later at tea the conversation became more general and the two friends discussed everything from world politics to mutual acquaintances. When it came time for them to part, Judge Hand said, "B.B., I'm afraid this is our last good-bye. We're getting on, you know." Then the two old men put their arms around each other and kissed. Berenson died first, in 1959, Learned Hand two years later at the age of eighty-nine. We drove the Hands back to their hotel in Florence. The judge was visibly moved.

8
Mark Rothko
A Portrait in Dark and Light

One February morning in 1970, I was reading the newspaper when the telephone rang. It was the painter Theodoros Stamos with the news that Mark Rothko had killed himself. I was immediately stabbed by a nameless guilt, almost as if I and other friends might somehow have prevented this death. We knew he was gnawed by ambivalence and doubt, especially where his work and family were concerned, but circumstances forced us to stand by helplessly as we watched his anxieties engulf him. He had intimated to me a desire to end it all, but I believe I was the sole friend he burdened with this confession.

Only a few weeks earlier at a small party in my apartment, Rothko, looking wan and depressed, followed me into the kitchen where I was mixing drinks. That night, on doctor's orders, he was on the wagon, an unusual regime for him and one that probably increased his dejection. He was, at that point, so completely caught up in himself that he was scarcely aware of the festivities around him. What he wanted to know was when I had last seen his wife, Mell, from whom he was separated, and how she and their six-year-old son, Christopher (who was always called Topher), were getting along — this despite his own uninterrupted contact with them. He had, no doubt, talked with Mell within the previous hour or two, as he phoned her constantly.

After Rothko left his family and began to camp out at his studio on East 69th Street, he called me periodically with this same question, which to be sure, was merely a plea that I keep in touch with his wife. He was unnerved by worry about Topher and Mell. From time to time, she drank heavily — as did Mark — and, though he phoned her each day, he also counted on mutual friends to look after her, partly to calm his own fears and even more to ease his conscience. He, after all, was the one who had done the leaving.

That evening in the kitchen I found myself asking him why he didn't go home. The ties were obviously still strong. Despite occasional philandering, Mark had always impressed me as a confirmed family man. He agreed that part of him wanted to go back, but at age sixty-six he realized that the past, with its many bitter confrontations, could no longer be bridged. "It just wouldn't work," he claimed. And then he said, "I've been thinking they both would be better off with me out of the way." Then, citing the examples of Pollock, Gorky, and Ad Reinhardt, he wondered aloud whether it was only death that could guarantee an artist's reputation.

He wanted above all to assure his name a permanent slot in history, an ambition that developed into a fixation. As he grew sick and old and less resilient, he became more involved in the search for fame than in his previous commitment to painting. It is true that he was no longer tormented by the anger that devoured him earlier when his work was ignored; instead, it was fear that nagged at him, fear of becoming the forgotten man, and this at the very time when at last he was covered with honors. During his late years, at once repelled and yet tempted by the idea of death, he produced darkly opaque, brooding canvases that reflected his despair. Many critics find this an oversimplified equation, and it was probably only a partial explanation for the blackout. They point to the murals commissioned by Dominique and John de Menil for the space now known as the Rothko Chapel in Houston, which, though dark, are based on a hidden radiance more related to religious passion than to personal mood. I believe that with those murals he was also trying to prove he no longer needed luminosity to accomplish his ends. And whether subconsciously or not, Rothko was competing with his colleagues Franz Kline, Clyfford Still, and Reinhardt, who found the dark of the moon as persuasive as the light of the sun.

I have never known anyone as worried about his reputation or as aware of each nuance of New York's fluctuating art scene as Rothko, who felt he was in total competition with every artist who had ever lived or was still living. He viewed each new art movement as a potential threat and, like a Hollywood star, protected his turf with every available safeguard. He resented it when museums showed younger artists prominently, carrying on as if each appearance of a new painter on the walls of the Museum of Modern Art was a dagger plunged directly into his back. As he told another artist, "When young painters come to me and praise my work, I am certain that they are really assaulting me. Beneath their praise I feel their envy and jealousy . . . by praising me, they actually try to destroy my influence over them."

For me, it is less painful to call up earlier memories when Rothko, every inch the iconoclast, immersed himself exuberantly in his painting and also in his various biases, which concentrated on museums, critics, dealers, exhibitions, European influences, and the New York art scene — all subjects on which he was unregenerately outspoken. In those years when he was an inveterate crusader, his color was optimistic, and shot through with pulsing light. Nothing stimulated him more than a righteous fight against what he considered the commercialization of art, but as he became more successful, he too was threatened by the evils he had earlier denounced. The conflict left him despondent, unsure, and guilt-ridden. He was always rebelling against something; exactly what mattered less than the process itself. Whether it was the venality of art dealers, the condescension of museum curators, the timidity of collectors, the indifference of the public, or the pomposity of critics, he never lost a chance to blast away. However, his own wings were clipped after he was accepted by the same art establishment he had excoriated. Earlier, when he had been so caught up in the paintings themselves during the process of evolving a visual vocabulary, he was less vulnerable. Success depleted him, and at the same time the fragile relationship between ethics and art no longer absorbed him.

Mark, a heavy-set, largish man, looking more like a professor than a painter, was a warm, articulate companion. To share lunch with him at one of his favorite Chinese restaurants was usually a lengthy pleasure filled with good conversation and a sense of unrushed well-being. As a friend, he was both loyal and affectionate, his personality, like his paintings, enveloping you in its amplitude. I first got to know him in the early fifties, when I was planning a one-person show of his recent work at the Art Institute of Chicago for 1954. Though he had participated previously in "Fifteen Americans," an exhibition curated by Dorothy Miller at the Museum of Modern Art in 1952 and a survey of his early works had been organized at the San Francisco Museum of Art, the Chicago show was the first solo exhibition of his abstract paintings to be seen at a top American museum.

In a cramped studio on West 53rd Street, Rothko shifted immense canvases around so that I could see them isolated, one at a time. He realized that these luminous paintings were emotional experiences to be savored separately, though he felt they sometimes enhanced each other when properly spaced in a homogeneous one-man survey; he often refused to participate in group exhibitions where a work of his might be sandwiched between antipathetic neighbors. One of the first things Rothko ever said to me was how his canvases suffered immeasurably when they were seen on a wall next to "ordinary" paintings. By ordinary, he meant work by other people. As time went on, Mark became more uncompromising. He dictated to various institutions precisely how his work should be installed, but his strictures were already being enforced when I met him.

In connection with the 1954 Chicago exhibition, which was relatively small and comprised only recent work, he wrote to me on how to avoid certain pitfalls:

> Since my pictures are large, colorful and unframed, and
> since museum walls are usually immense and formidable,
> there is the danger that the pictures relate themselves

Mark Rothko, 1952. This was the Rothko that Katharine first knew — ebullient, open, and full of life. Photograph by Kay Bell Reynal.

as decorative areas to the walls. This would be a distortion of their meaning, since the pictures are the opposite of what is decorative; and have been painted in a scale of normal living rather than an institutional scale. I have on occasion dealt with this problem by tending to crowd the show rather than making it spare. By saturating the room with the feeling of the work, the walls are defeated and the poignancy of each single work for me becomes more visible.

I also hang the largest pictures so that they must first be encountered at close quarters, so that the first experience is within the picture. This may well give the observer a key to the ideal relationship between himself and the rest of the pictures. I also hang the pictures low rather than high, particularly in the case of the largest ones, and often as close to the floor as is feasible for that is the way they are painted.

Before I visited the New York studio, I was already an admirer of Mark's, but that day turned me into a fan. All afternoon we reviewed the paintings; that procession of transcendental abstract canvases took my breath away. No artist ever looked less like his work than this overweight, untidy man with his high bald pate, bifocal spectacles, rumpled suit, and shirt half untucked, but when he talked, some of the magic came through. He was surprisingly expressive, selecting the mot juste with infallible intuition. His sonorous voice always reminded me of certain resonant Hebraic chants. It rang with the same mellow inflections.

During the first months after I moved to New York, Mark helped me through a lonely period by appearing unexpectedly and taking me to small neighborhood bars where we spent hours arguing about art and the state of the world. He still found most painters of the past (Turner and Rembrandt excepted) slightly distasteful, even denouncing Piero della Francesca for producing nothing more than "tinted drawings." Indeed, he deplored the entire Renaissance, though he did admire Fra Angelico, if only because of his radiant spiritual fervor. Mark talked about his visit to the convent of San Marco in Florence, where he was entranced by each single painting in its own contained cell. The isolation of the individual frescoes was a tender and solitary experience, an ideal version of how he wanted his own work seen. Other than these exceptions, he felt that the day of bowing to Europe was over, adamant that the wave of the future must come from America. He was also convinced that his own destiny was to be a pioneer in the development of an internationally recognized American art movement.

At that time, brush-offs only made him more militant. I recall walking along 54th Street with him and passing the Whitney Museum of American Art, which was then located in a building next to the Museum of Modern Art. After examining a small display window, he told me he had smashed it a few days earlier because of some altercation with a member of the staff. In addition, he swore that under no condition would he ever allow a painting of his to enter the museum's permanent collection. But years later, giving in to repeated demands, he permitted the Whitney to acquire one of his major works. By this time, the fight had gone out of him, and establishment mores seemed more important than keeping the faith.

Both Rothkos provided me with warm friendship when I most needed it, accepting me almost as a member of the family. I look back with nostalgia on Christmas parties when Mell and Mark stuffed their friends with drinks, turkey, and kindness. These gatherings were initiated after success had arrived and the Rothkos were living in their own capacious town house on East 95th Street. At the last Christmas party, in 1969, after Mark had left, Mell made a gallant effort, but the house was shrouded in sadness. Less than eight months later, both Rothkos were dead.

Mell, who was born Mary Alice Beistle in 1922, was still in her forties when she died unexpectedly of high blood pressure. She was already worried about the handling of her husband's estate and the eventual disposition of his paintings. I recall a May evening in 1970 when we were walking along East 95th Street on our way to dinner with Linda and Giorgio Cavallon, and she confided her fears to me: "There's some pretty odd hanky-panky going on, and I don't know what to do." I urged her to consult a lawyer immediately. It was little more than two months later that Mell died early one morning in that lonely house.

Among the guests who usually attended the Rothkos' parties were always a sprinkling of artists. As a rule, Philip Guston, Robert Motherwell, Helen Frankenthaler, Paul Burlin, Herbert Ferber, and invariably Theodoros Stamos were invited, and art historians, critics, curators, and dealers made appearances more infrequently. There were also neighbors, art students, musicians, and writers, the most memorable of whom was the poet Stanley Kunitz. Stanley and Mark were at home with each other. Moreover, Rothko respected Kunitz's sensitive understanding of the visual arts — no one spoke more persuasively for the painters of the New York School than he did. Stanley was especially perceptive about Mark's work, which no doubt buttressed their relationship, but the friendship went far deeper. They shared a similar Russian-Jewish-American background, a strong political liberalism, and a kind of conversational rhythm and poetry that made the interplay of their personalities a pleasure to witness.

During the last year or two of Mark's life, when he was besieged by doubts and by a bourgeois concern with taxes, renown, and financial security, he dreaded being alone. He had always been gregarious, but his need for people became exorbitant. In doubt about his work and his future, he used people indiscriminately to fill the vacuum. No party or art opening was too banal to attend. He ran away from himself with grim determination. He phoned his friends incessantly, especially Stanley, who, like the rest of us, felt impotent. None of us were able to cope with Rothko's increasing paranoia or his constant demand for company. I remember toward the end calling Stanley to discuss once more whether there was anything we might do. He was out, so I talked to his wife, the artist Elise Asher, who seemed certain that we could no longer reach Mark. Elise turned out to be right. I was still naive enough to think that an able psychiatrist might be the answer and broached the subject with Mark, but he was dead set against it. He found the very thought alarming. This artist, who was inextricably bonded to his paintings, could not or would not face the possibility of a destabilizing procedure that might jeopardize what he had carefully created over the years, an image he nurtured as much for his own needs as for the public's. He didn't want a refurbished psyche: the idea frightened him.

When I first got to know the Rothkos they were living in a small apartment on the West Side not far from the 53rd Street studio. Their daughter Kate, who was born in 1950, was a willful small child who baffled her father. Mell, much younger than Mark, was better able to handle her. Keeping house, cooking, working, and looking after Kate made for a hectic schedule, yet somehow it panned out. Mell always impressed me as well organized and practical, but scarcely a connoisseur of art. In order to augment the family income, she illustrated children's books and commercial catalogues, while Mark taught at Brooklyn College, a job he was shortly to give up after a tempestuous confrontation with the chairman of the art department. He was willing, he said, to teach painting, but when it came to lecturing on art history, he rebelled, arguing that this was not his domain. Mell backed him and continued with her own work until the sale of Mark's paintings could support them.

Those were relatively happy years for the Rothkos, who were obviously strongly attracted to each other and, though money was tight, in control of their lives. I cannot forget an episode that involved the early days with Mell and with one of Mark's so-called Surrealist paintings. I say "so-called" because I've never looked on these works as authentically Surrealist. Filled with opaque symbolism, they are watered-down romantic fantasies lacking the bite, erotic drive, and naked exhibitionism that fueled the European movement. Mark was, of course, exposed to the thinking of Europeans like Max Ernst and André Masson when they and several of their colleagues lived in New York during the war, but what brushed off on him was more foam than form. The bulk of Rothko's amorphous compositions are pastiches of various Surrealist influences, with obvious borrowings from Ernst. Contrary to what many critics think, for me the paintings of the mid-1940s are milestones only in that they helped to free him from his earlier awkward city scenes while at the same time presaging his future color exuberance.

In any event, during the early 1960s, the trustees of the San Francisco Museum of Art asked me to advise them on their permanent collection, and said that they did not envision buying any further works by Rothko for it. Since the trustees had decided that there was room for only one Rothko in San Francisco, I advised the museum to trade a large painting from 1944 called *Slow Swirl at the Edge of the Sea* for a later, totally abstract canvas that I felt better represented the artist's unique contribution. For this he never forgave me, explaining repeatedly that *Slow Swirl* was a favorite of his, if only because he identified it with Mell. It was painted during the period immediately before they married and thus was filled with warm memories. Until Mark's death, it hung in the Rothkos' living room, and whenever I went to the house, Mark would say, "Don't you see what a mistake you made?" I would always answer, "But I still don't think so." Diane Waldman, the art historian who organized the 1978 Rothko retrospective at the Guggenheim Museum, even suggested that the picture, which now belongs to the Museum of Modern Art, "may, in fact, be a symbolic portrait of the couple." This I find very unlikely. Mark discussed the painting with me frequently and never alluded to such an idea. I think that such a literal interpretation might have offended him, but only the other day I noticed a more recent Rothko catalogue that included the same proposal, echoed thereafter as historical fact in a newspaper review.

I've often wondered whether it wasn't success that destroyed the Rothkos — first Mell, who gradually began drinking as Mark's fortunes escalated. Troubled and confused, she suddenly found herself superfluous. This woman, who had been the central cog in the family, was now displaced by the turn of events she had fostered. In the early 1950s, before prosperity arrived, whenever I was in New York and visited the Rothkos, we used to have dinner in a tiny kitchen where the stove was so near at hand that Mell could conveniently cook and serve without getting up. Later, over nightcaps in the small living room, Mark would produce his most recent painting, preferably large, which he had brought home from the studio for our private viewing. Hauling the canvas up the narrow staircase that led to the apartment was not easy, but for him it was worth the effort if only to savor it in uncluttered surroundings and in the company of appreciative eyes.

Mark had firmly established convictions about how his canvases should be shown, and he was especially enamored of the installation at the Phillips Collection in Washington, D.C. There, in a special Rothko room, originally featuring only three sumptuous paintings (a fourth was later added), the visitor is encouraged to sit down and enjoy them at leisure. Light in the gallery is reduced, a condition Mark mandated, insisting that brutal luminosity could destroy the subtle interaction of

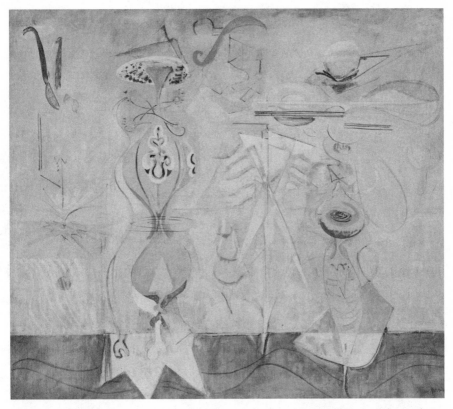

Mark Rothko, *Slow Swirl at the Edge of the Sea,* 1944. *Slow Swirl* was the cause of a stubborn argument between Katharine and the artist. Katharine was not convinced of the painting's importance, and Rothko never ceased to hope that he could change her mind.

his color. He also preferred the viewer to "experience" each painting slowly as it gradually emerged from muted surroundings. He would have agreed with Pissarro, who once observed that "the eye of the passerby is too hasty and sees only the surface." Rothko, who realized that looking was not necessarily seeing, deliberately subjected his viewer to delaying tactics. Why he was ever called an "action painter" is puzzling, and no one denied the allegation more vehemently than he. Quite the contrary, he claimed it was not action he pursued but meditation. Similarly, Mark opposed impressive architectural settings for his canvases, favoring intimate spaces so that the work itself would never be overpowered. He intended his pictures to be studied in close proximity, the observer deliberately forced to bathe in a sea of hypnotic color. Persuaded that paintings of normal size might appear to be little more than circumscribed rectangular objects, he opted for extremely large canvases that could not be absorbed at a glance. Yet when I asked him about the importance of scale, Rothko attempted to elude categorization about the matter, telling me, "The pictures have no size. They are exactly the right size for the idea." Then he admonished me to forget about size when I looked at a picture. "Size," he said, "only has to do with real estate." Mark insisted that his paintings were made to be seen in "normally scaled surroundings," immersion being the operative concept for him: "They were not conceived to be viewed from a distance." Characteristically, his most revealing comments were made to a fellow artist, as when he explained to Alfred Jensen that he used large canvases because "I wanted to paint my own size. I wanted to recognize myself in my work."

I have seen occasional very small paintings by Rothko that are suprisingly successful in their vision and values. They are not preliminary sketches or hasty afterthoughts, but thoroughly considered compositions that possessed much of the intensity of his larger works. He made only a few of these as gifts for old friends. One December day in the early 1960s when Mark was visiting me, he pulled three little paintings on wood out of a shopping bag. Lining them up on my sofa, he told me to make my choice and consider it a Christmas present. They were each splendid in a different way, and I was torn, but finally after several hours I made my decision. He watched me intently, as if I were Solomon deciding the fate of his children. With him no occasion that concerned his work was casual.

As an artist Rothko was curiously defensive. He protected his paintings and in a way himself (for the two were indivisible) from any hint of unfair competition, actually setting up ground rules that provided formidable shelters. In this capacity, he supervised the final design of the Rothko Chapel in Houston, which I must confess has always impressed me as a bit truncated, even architecturally pedestrian. In addition, the Tate Gallery in London faithfully followed his wishes in the installation of a series of paintings he gave that museum. Unhappily, he did not live to see either group installed.

Mark's esteem for Turner, whom he characterized as a giant who not merely pre-dated the Impressionists but outpaced them, explains in part why he donated his works to the British gallery, which boasts the largest extant concentration of Turner's paintings. He often told me he felt a strong kinship, a sense of continuity, as if his own color discoveries grew logically from those of the English artist, yet Rothko's series was never originally intended for the Tate. He had been commissioned to make the murals for The Four Seasons restaurant, which was about to open in the Seagram Building. Mark worked on the paintings over a long period, producing more than were needed so that he could have freedom in his final choices. In any case the denouement was dramatic. One evening, in a state of high emotion, he phoned to say that he was returning the advance down payment (a quite substantial sum) since under no circumstances would he permit the paintings to be installed in The Four Seasons. He had visited the recently completed restaurant for the first time at the dinner hour and come away traumatized by the experience. He urged me to go with him and see for myself, which I did. When he was working on the project, his imagination plus a dash of wishful thinking projected an idyllic setting in which captivated diners, lost in reverie, communed with the murals. I'm afraid it never entered his head that the works would be forced to compete with a noisy crowd of conspicuous consumers. For him to allow his murals to become background decorations was intolerable. I must say I agreed. Now they hang in their own gallery at the Tate, where Mark would be pleased with the subdued light and reverential quiet.

Rothko sent copious directives to the Tate proposing how the paintings might be displayed for the optimal benefit of the viewer, and it was the viewer who concerned him. How best to involve, embrace, and emotionally reach this hypothetical outsider was his ultimate target. Light, space, color of walls, even the location of benches for contemplation all played a part. He also spent considerable time planning for the setting of his celebrated murals in the chapel built for them in Houston. There, he reversed the usual architect-artist relationship. Instead of acquiescing to any possible "master builder," he insisted that the architecture follow the dictates of his paintings. Originally Philip

Johnson was the architect, and Rothko found his design too grandiose, too threatening. He worried that it might upstage the murals, but later Johnson withdrew from the project. The final result is a building so modest as to be inconsequential.

Rothko's relationship with Yale University, which he had attended on a scholarship, was likewise intransigent. The school once offered him a special citation that he turned down because he wanted nothing less than an honorary doctorate. Why, Mark demanded, shouldn't art be on a par with literature, science, and other academic studies? Some years later, toward the end of his life, Yale capitulated, awarding him an honorary Ph.D., and thus, in his eyes, acknowledging the significance of painting as a profession.

Rothko's relationships with other artists could also be troubled. Because he could never judge himself objectively, he no sooner arrived at his destination than he saw himself displaced. He pitted his energies against both the real and the irrational, often confusing the two. For example, immediately after the Metropolitan's much publicized exhibition "New York Painting and Sculpture: 1940–1970" opened in 1969, Mark called me. What did I think of the show? More important — what did I think of his room? Not so many years earlier, his pulse would have raced with delight at the thought of an entire gallery devoted to him at New York's most illustrious museum. But this time he was wounded: other younger artists were given more space and more thoughtful representation — his birthright had been denied. It is true that Rothko was not seen at his best, yet he was already widely accepted as a pivotal figure in American art and scarcely needed further endorsement.

What most upset him was the room devoted to Ad Reinhardt, who, though younger, was recently deceased and had rather suddenly been accepted as a germinal figure. Mark felt Ad's work was selected with considerably more care and discrimination than his, a bitter pill in light of his intimacy at that time with Rita Reinhardt, Ad's widow, who had become Mark's closest companion since he'd left home. There was something poignant about this artist who, riddled with doubts, was vulnerable to every peripheral incident that touched his life. He could never dispassionately remove himself from even the most casual competition. He was also disturbed that several of the pop and minimalist artists, for whom he had nothing but scorn, had been elevated to top billing. Their rather obvious irony and brutal techniques appalled him, even alarmed him; he felt supplanted. Of these younger men, the only one he occasionally admired was Jasper Johns, chiefly because of his drawing, which Mark found both "sensitive and skillful."

As a rule, Rothko was loath to admit which contempories he esteemed or had affected him. When I asked him which artists he liked best, he snapped, "Nobody's business. I'm not an art critic." But he could deliver scathing opinions, and invariably the mention of Barnett Newman's *Stations of the Cross* infuriated him. He repudiated both the paintings and their overall title, which he considered an unacceptable affectation. Yet he had his enthusiasms and could be warm and open when you least expected it. Long before Louise Nevelson became a popular figure, he would say, "No matter what she does, she's an artist." I can't imagine higher praise from Mark, for there was no word more hallowed than "artist" in his lexicon. On Milton Avery, however, he lavished his warmest and most unstinting praise and at a time when he was little recognized. Mark claimed him as a leading influence on his own work and as a cherished friend. When Avery died in 1965, Mark delivered the eulogy. Avery's unconventional surging and at times palpitating areas of color sparked a strong response in Rothko as did the older artist's daring disregard of traditional compositional principles. He was touched and in a sense liberated by Avery's frank lyricism, which in the forties and fifties was rare.

Rothko also loved Matisse, another incomparable colorist. He was such a favorite that, in 1954, Mark dedicated a wonderfully emotive painting suffused with color surprises to the French master. This was an unusual gesture for Rothko since, after the mid-forties, he rarely identified his pictures with anything other than a date or number. Over lunch one day, I was amazed to hear him state (a bit pretentiously) that Rembrandt's paintings were the works from the past most akin to his. When I appeared somewhat dubious and asked him how he'd reached this conclusion, he agreed it was not that their paintings were visually similar, but because he and Rembrandt were motivated by the same principle. What he was after, Mark said, was "a maximum of poignancy," and this he also found to be true of Rembrandt.

When I was still working at the Art Institute, Rothko wrote me that since one or perhaps both of his older brothers and their wives were planning to change trains in Chicago, he wanted them to visit the museum and see the painting we had purchased from his 1954 show. Rothko explained that his brothers were not very appreciative of his work, but he hoped that seeing a canvas prominently displayed in an important museum might win them over. And so they came. I don't know whether they were impressed, but I do know he was right. They had no idea what he was after. I was touched by how eagerly he longed for their approval. This was the only time in the years I knew Mark that he mentioned his Russian family — he never referred to his childhood in Russia or his early years in the United States. Later, after he died, I met his brothers again when the Rothko Chapel was dedicated in Houston in 1971. Now fame, time, and perhaps death had made his art more palatable.

At some point in 1965 or 1966, when I was planning a business trip to Chicago, Mark asked me to visit Kate, who was then a freshman at the University of Chicago. Little more than fifteen, she must surely have been one of the youngest members of her class, and though she was very bright, she was not emotionally ready for college life. Mark, who was ambitious for her, wanted her to achieve, to shine, but he didn't, alas, know how to communicate with her. A lonely child, Kate was often hostile to her father's friends and work, both of which kept him away from her. When I saw her in Chicago, she was overwhelmed with homesickness. She felt exiled and urged me to make her parents understand how desperately she wanted to return to New York. I think my affection for her dates from that brief encounter, for it was only then that I recognized her as an unsure child struggling to find a place for herself in her father's life. I communicated all of this to Mark, who asked, "You mean she's suffering?" Let it be said that, after my report, he brought her home immediately.

After her father's death, Kate grew to identify with him closely, even learning to speak Russian. While still in her teens she first resolved to fight to protect his work, hoping to find him, at least posthumously.

Her need may explain why she was able to persist and triumph in a remarkable but agonizing lawsuit, replete with duplicity on the part of the Marlborough Gallery and the executors of Rothko's estate. Soon enough, it became all too clear that the "hanky-panky" Mell had feared was in fact operating to the serious detriment of Rothko's artistic legacy. The suit, which Kate initiated in 1971 (after she turned twenty-one) and which took six years to be decided, split a sizable slice of the New York art world into two separate camps.

What divided the art world were opposing reactions to the conduct of the executors, all of whom had been intimate friends of the painter and were active figures in New York's cultural life. To many observers they seemed, at best, self-serving and insensitive. Two of them — Theodoros Stamos and Rothko's accountant, Bernard Reis — in cooperating with the machinations of Marlborough and its director, Frank Lloyd, feathered their own nests by becoming commercially associated with the gallery. Typical were the actions of a good friend of Rothko's who traveled across the country to testify against Kate while at the same time accepting a generous payment from the opposition.

Barely of age, Kate stuck to her convictions with fortitude and won the case. As I look back, I'm perplexed by how unrealistically Rothko prepared for the final disposition of his work, which led to the defrauding of his estate. His abdication reflects how torn he was between his antipathy for art dealers and yet his need of them. The hero of this cause célèbre was not Rothko, but his daughter. Day after day she quietly sat in the rear of the courtroom absorbing every detail with a kind of fatalistic composure. One evening a powerful New York lawyer not directly involved in the case called me to say that if I were really Kate's friend, I should advise her to drop the whole ugly business. He claimed that her chances of succeeding against insurmountable odds were more than doubtful. I never passed his message along.

As I look back, it was Mark's Museum of Modern Art exhibition in 1961 that radically changed his point of view. Until then, though he was occasionally skeptical and often pugnacious, he fundamentally believed in himself and more expressly in what he was doing; he knew his own worth. During the fifties he created his greatest paintings, those radiant life-giving canvases electrified by pulsating color mutations.

He deliberately dematerialized all form and turned color into his sole activating force. And it was then, too, that his ecstatic paintings became more than pictures on the wall — they were emotional events of epic proportions. For me, Rothko was at his most eloquent between 1949 and 1960, after he had found his own way, yet before his color was swallowed in darkness. During those years, he experimented ceaselessly, each painting a new adventure. He left little to chance, studying how the intensity, texture, and overall area of certain colors interacted. Something of a magician, he broke all the rules, causing color that normally recedes to advance and vice versa. In the artist's own words, "two characteristics exist in my paintings; either their surfaces are expansive and push outward in all directions, or their surfaces contract and rush inward in all directions. Between these two poles you can find everything I want to say."

Mark's exhibition at the Modern was of inestimable importance to him. One must remember how influential the museum was at that time, when it was still almost the only institution that avant-garde artists, both European and American, looked to for approval. Mark had long wanted an exhibition there, but when it finally happened, he allowed innumerable minor details to bog him down. He even worried about which floor was preferable, claiming that certain areas of the building had more panache than others. The most rewarding result of the exhibition was a belated public recognition of Rothko as a leading American artist, though many art enthusiasts had long known this. The most alarming outcome, however, was the abrupt interruption of his work and a drastic shift in his outlook.

All artists spend months preparing for comprehensive retrospectives; such exhibitions can be as revealing to the painter as to the public. Rothko testified that the experience was not a mere gathering of pictures, but an "aggregate of the forces ruling my life." But even after the show opened, he remained its captive. He stopped working, and no day passed without his attendance at the museum, where he hovered over his canvases, avidly reacting to each stray comment. How the public responded to his paintings began to assume greater significance than how he himself confronted the process of painting.

Some years later, during a disastrous summer the Rothkos spent

Rothko on his birthday, September 25, 1960—and a few months away
from his self-consuming retrospective at the Museum of Modern Art.
Photograph by Regina Bogat.

in Provincetown, a sad little incident highlighted how fully this alienation had taken over. One night after a birthday party in Provincetown
for Stanley Kunitz, I drove home to Wellfleet with the historian Richard
Hofstadter, who was shocked by Rothko's confession to him that even
the thought of pigment and brush was repugnant. Mark told him he
continued to paint only because he was driven by habit and conscience

and, I might add, by a continual search for acceptance that had goaded him from the beginning. Hofstadter, who was already fatally ill and under pressure to finish a book, found Mark's admission little less than sacrilegious. That summer of 1968, when Rothko was so desperately unhappy, he was recuperating from an aneurysm, which curtailed his activities. He did, however, paint in Provincetown, but chiefly small acrylics on paper that I've never considered entirely successful. They are a bit heavy-handed: the supramundane glow is gone.

In New York some months later, Rothko appeared uninvited one evening at Hedda Sterne's house while she and I were having dinner. That night, after too much solitary drinking, his defenses were down and his loneliness palpable. He was rich, he was famous, but he was also vulnerable. Even before we had finished our coffee, he insisted that we accompany him to his studio to see the acrylics. These he began shoving at us with such compulsive speed that many ended up on the floor. Our fleeting impression was of an occasional triumph interspersed with perfunctory repetitions of the past. When we left him to go home, we were both pierced by his overwhelming solitude.

To have witnessed Rothko's headlong abandon as he fed us picture after picture in tumultuous succession was unsettling. He, who had always demanded a rigorously controlled milieu for viewing his work, appeared now to have dispensed even with elementary caution. Because this was the first time I had seen him less than deferential toward his paintings, I still doubt if he was entirely happy with them. Paper proved to be a less resilient ground than canvas for his color; it lacked the give, the absorbency of fabric.

The profusion of acrylic works on paper that Rothko turned out that summer did not take up all of his time, and to avoid any possibility of solitude he arranged for several young artists to visit his studio each week for informal discussions. The idea backfired when they occasionally disagreed with one of Mark's cherished theories or dared to question his work. Whether they ceased coming of their own volition or because Rothko canceled the meetings, I never learned, but I do know that the visits stopped abruptly. At that point Mark no longer wanted an interchange of ideas, only an adoring audience. I cannot help but think back to earlier, more robust years when he and Stanley Kunitz investigated the meanings of art with such intensity that conflicts only heightened their gratification.

The Rothkos were happier in Provincetown ten years earlier, when they lived in a cottage on Bradford Street near the center of that over-active town. Because of the noise, automobile fumes, and tumultuous traffic, I suggested they move to Wellfleet or Truro, where they could find authentic country surroundings, but Mark was horrified at the idea. He didn't want to commune with nature — he needed people. He didn't want to sit with a book under a tree, he was a city person. In Provincetown each morning, he would saunter up and down Com-mercial Street looking for an occasional acquaintance to chat with, for unlike many artists, he was never reclusive. It was sometimes difficult to relate this man to his own silent, disembodied works.

There were other worries, too. As the years passed, Rothko felt more and more locked into his own aesthetic doctrines. The fact that he was never an able draftsman was a handicap he had earlier turned into an advantage. I think this lack of skill forced him to explore other potentials — in his case, the multiple possibilities of color. It is, how-ever, interesting that Rembrandt and Matisse, two of the artists who most dazzled him, were both brilliant draftsmen. Mark made color the core of his work, coaxing it into a visual dialogue in which viewer and painting were inexplicably enmeshed. Yet there came a time when he found himself imprisoned by his own brainchild. I've never been sure whether it was lack of confidence in himself or insecurity about his draftsmanship that stood in the way of further experimentation. Though Mark rarely talked openly about his growing sense of entrapment, he alluded to it ambiguously, sometimes questioning what drove him on, or why he persisted. He admitted that he had lost his zest for easel paintings, finding them inadequate and episodic. All that really mat-tered now, he said, were public commissions provocative enough to rivet his prolonged concentration, though even these were unsatisfac-tory unless Mark was in total control of the project, a condition rarely feasible when architects were involved.

Once he finished the Houston series for the Menils, he was stymied; the future was a question mark. He worked on the chapel paintings with such oneness of purpose that he was virtually burned out when they were completed late in 1967. He sank all his energies into them, and now, quite suddenly, he seemed to have lost his raison d'être. At that point Rothko had said in paint what he had to say, and anything further was either superfluous or repetitive, yet he persisted. While the series was under way, Mark thought of nothing else, even renting an old carriage house on East 69th Street and converting it into an exact mock-up that duplicated three walls of the interior of the projected but as yet unbuilt chapel. In order to control the light he installed an adjustable parachute over the skylight.

Periodically, as paintings were completed — there are fourteen in the chapel, but he made four more — he called his close friends and invited them over, one at a time, to share the event with him. And sharing it was, for you would enter the somber studio and see nothing but vast black canvases, or at least what appeared at first glance to be black. Then slowly as you sat there with Mark beside you, the color emerged, predominantly dark, dark red burning through dense overlays of pigment. He wanted to make these paintings, which relied both on color and carefully adjusted texture, breathe with a mysterious incorporeal life. It took time not only to see but to understand them. Meanwhile, the artist waited for your reaction. I can almost hear him asking that inevitable question, "Well, what do you think?" I always found surprising the singularly reverent message these nonobjective canvases managed to convey, despite their prosaic milieu of a carriage house shrouded in a parachute. Mark himself readily agreed that most of his paintings, if not strictly religious, were related to realms of the spirit and conceived as contemplative experiences. For me they reverberate with Hebraic fervency, though formal religion did not play a role in Rothko's life.

Throughout the best years of Mark's life and right up to the end, he railed at art dealers and most of all at the Marlborough Gallery. He never missed an opportunity to flay that establishment, and I joined him in righteous denunciations for reasons of my own. Early on in my tenure as art critic of *Saturday Review,* Frank Lloyd tried to bribe me. He offered to put me clandestinely on his payroll if I would cover the gallery's shows and award them good reviews. My contempt was unbounded, and I never had anything to do with Marlborough, or Lloyd, again. To my enormous astonishment, I learned after Mark died that, at the same time he was repudiating the gallery to me, he was involved in arranging an elaborate agreement with it. Anxious for my respect and fearing my disillusionment, he was ashamed to admit the dishonesties he had engaged in, and which he had lied about — mainly, that he never had any relationship with Frank Lloyd. I was dumbfounded to discover that the morning following his suicide — could this have been a factor? — a representative of Marlborough was to meet with him at his studio on East 69th Street to go over business details. I have no doubt that Mark's duality tormented him as much as it confused and disturbed me.

The evening following Mark's suicide, I happened to attend a small dinner where the painter Jack Tworkov mentioned he had unexpectedly met Rothko on the street the previous day. Coincidentally, both men were coming from checkups with their doctors, and Rothko reported that his had been good, that he was definitely on the mend. Yet within a few hours he ended his life, which can only suggest that his despondency stemmed from wounds deeper than ill health. He was unable and unwilling to accept the future.

Rothko's wish was to create a body of work that was inherently tragic, work confronting the reality that life had no answer, for all the artist's striving to discover one by plumbing the depths of existence and himself. Each painting was not what counted; it was the cumulative expression. He saw the verities of life in dramatic perspective, but also through misanthropic eyes. He regarded death, which seemed devised chiefly to derail his assault on posterity, as his most thoroughgoing adversary. Divided by dichotomies, he was torn between the personal and the cosmic, the worldly and the transcendental, and doomed to disappointment. It was never lack of ambition that defeated Mark, but the physical limitations of paint and brush. His means undercut his aspirations, but could any artist have met his demands? He set himself an impossible task and then grieved when he couldn't force canvas and paint to embrace the whole of life. He consciously remodeled his persona by reiterating precisely what he expected of his work. Most artists are more concerned with self-discovery than reinvention; few of them are so deliberately involved in both processes.

Rothko's unrequited desire was to remain alive only through his work, but it was his suicide — and subsequent litigation over his paintings — that spread his name around the world. Torrents of words poured out, in books, magazines, and newspapers. Behind this deluge, the painter dissolved in a mist of romantic jargon. Ironically, the fame he yearned for finally arrived via a turn of events he would have despised.

9
Alfred Jensen
Competing with the Sun

During the 1950s, when Abstract Expressionism was flourishing and Manhattan was becoming the fulcrum of the art world, artists seemed to be irrevocably divided into cliques and rivalries. Those in the realist camp, like Ben Shahn and Reginald Marsh, never went near Barnett Newman or Willem de Kooning, and many of the established Abstract Expressionists either feared up-and-coming painters as envious usurpers or dismissed them as desultory lightweights. The lines were drawn in the bars, cafeterias, and studios, and they were not usually crossed. Therefore it came as an enormous surprise when I learned, albeit thirty years after the fact, that Alfred Jensen, the creator of geometric paintings based on ancient hieroglyphics and laboriously researched numerology, had shared a secret friendship with Mark Rothko, who worked intuitively and shied away from overt symbolism. However, this period of closeness lasted only during the early and mid-fifties, when Jensen posed no threat to Rothko, either as a competitor or an opponent. He was an unknown and sometimes pallid abstractionist who had not yet formulated his own style, whereas Rothko was already an ascending figure who had found his signature image and was engaged in exploring its permutations.

The relationship was so important to Jensen that he kept records of his meetings with Rothko, very few of which remain. He jotted down notes compulsively in halting, often illegible English, and later destroyed them with equal compulsion. Just why Jensen was driven to accumulate Rothko's verdicts on art and life is not entirely clear, but I believe it had to do with his unbounded admiration for the man, his work, and what Jensen considered his "superior erudition." There is no doubt that their private get-togethers helped Jensen to sharpen his own thinking and finally to free himself from the shibboleths that had initially united the two men. For Al, these were years of growth and gnawing doubt, disorientation, and deprivation. His association with Rothko was more than reassuring — it was life-giving. That this highly accomplished, intelligent artist chose him as a confidential friend was in itself, Al felt, a solid proof of his own worth during a period when few others were eager to confirm it. But perhaps more important was his conviction that he and Mark shared basic moral values about art and its social responsibilities. Even after their friendship was over, no other artist ever took Rothko's place in Al's hierarchy. For Rothko, on the other hand, the relationship was more equivocal and of considerably less importance; he was the docent who justified his own theories as he guided his devotee. When this mix ceased to work, so too did the friendship.

Jensen treasured what he found reassuring, those observations relating to his own enthusiasms, doubts, and questions. Most notably, he always maintained that a few casual words of Mark's set his painting career in orbit. On a visit to Al's studio, after seeing his current, rather hesitant Abstract Expressionist paintings, Mark turned to a group of unrelated color diagrams tacked up on the wall. For some years, Al had been investigating Goethe's optical theories and was enthralled by his abstruse treatise of 1810, *Zür Farbenlehre*, which he read as an "artistic Bible." Goethe claimed that color was not a fixed entity or solely a physical response, confined to light striking objects and entering our eyes. Rather, the sensation of color was also shaped by perception — by how the brain processes information. Color, Goethe argued, depends on the context in which it is seen — it has a reciprocal relation to the color next to it or the degree of brightness or darkness around it, and painters from Turner to Hans Hofmann have agreed with him. Goethe made diagrams as visual equivalents of his words, and Al's own diagrams were attempts to reconstruct various color experiments from this book. They were not necessarily intended as sketches or preliminary studies for paintings. Jensen characterized them as a form of metaphysical research, but overlooked their power. Not Rothko, who pointed out, "Jensen, these are your real paintings." And, after that, they were, or so Jensen always claimed.

The two men remained friends for about seven or eight years. They met in March 1952, at the opening of the "Fifteen Americans" show at the Museum of Modern Art, shortly after Jensen settled permanently in New York. They were the same age — both were born in 1903 — and both were fascinated by wayward feedbacks from society and art, but temperamentally they were worlds apart. Mark was totally involved in and with himself; Al was more objective. Mark was intuitive and repudiated the past; Al turned to established theorums and ancient civilizations. Mark, above all, pursued a secure niche in history, while Jensen, not necessarily averse to such future success, concentrated on the past, on elucidating the relationships of legendary solar number systems of Mexico and China. Rothko dug deeply into himself. Jensen, no less investigative, was concerned with the enigmas of cultural and cosmic forces. Both were involved with color, but, for Rothko, it was an individualistic tool, whereas for Jensen, it evolved into a concomitant of basic principles. Mark, who was beginning to make his stand as an influential American painter, feared the future, especially in the form of young and developing artists. Al, still struggling for the smallest particle of recognition, had all he could do to concentrate on achieving a toehold in the present.

Yet both artists were vulnerable, dedicated, and flawed by personal frailty. Their friendship blossomed at a time when Jensen was overcome with loneliness and financial worries. Born in Guatemala City to a Danish father and Polish-German mother, he had had to support himself since the age of fourteen, eking out a living as a seaman and a laborer. In 1927, while studying at Hans Hofmann's summer school in Capri, he met and began a lasting affair with Saidie Adler May, a well-to-do woman considerably older than himself. May was originally from Baltimore, but the twenty-four years she and Jensen spent together were peripatetic. Traveling constantly in search of art, they rarely settled down for any appreciable length of time. The relationship was never a frivolous affair for Jensen — he was genuinely devoted and dependent, for Saidie May was at once his lover, mother, companion, and benefactor. He in turn became her invaluable advisor, spearheading the avant-garde collection of modern art that she eventually left to the Baltimore Museum of Art.

After May died in 1951, Al gravitated to New York, and though he was already forty-eight, he had yet to find his own direction as a painter. He admired the New York School but, with the exception of Rothko, its members confronted him with a brick wall of indifference, even antagonism. He was excluded, alone, and very much an outsider. Many New York artists looked on Jensen as an interloper who for years had been supported in high style by a rich divorcée. He had lived in the best hotels, traveled widely, and hobnobbed with important European artists in his search for contemporary works. The Abstract Expressionists considered him a dilettante and, even worse, a theoretician who was trying to break into their private domain. Jensen remembered an encounter in the Cedar Street Tavern with Franz Kline and Earl Kerkam, both of whom attacked him unmercifully. Whether they were as outspoken as he reported was less important than the sense of unmitigated hostility he retained from the incident. Jensen said that as soon as Kerkam laid eyes on him, he began to scold him about his inability to become a real part of the New York art scene, growling, "The trouble with you, Jensen, is that you talk. All one can say is that the verbal is your meat. You say things, but you don't exist." Kline, he recalled, concurred with Kerkam's estimate.

Milton Avery's widow, Sally, once told me that Jensen had often complained to her about the drastic change that took place in his life once Mrs. May was no longer on the scene. VIPs in the art and museum world dropped him abruptly when it was clear that, without her, he was useless to them. Where he had once been courted as her art advisor and constant companion, he now became a virtual outcast, money-less and powerless.

The sculptor Lila Katzen met Jensen in the early fifties at a New York art gallery, right after getting off the train from Baltimore, where she then lived. She was carrying her suitcase and, though she had never set eyes on Al before, he started a conversation. "You are from Baltimore," he told her. At first she thought he was psychic, but later realized he had probably read the label on her suitcase. He was still grieving for Mrs. May, and he reacted emotionally to any mention of Baltimore, which the two had frequently visited. Insisting that Katzen come to his studio immediately and see his work, he steered her to a taxi. "Lo and behold," she said, "we stopped at a fancy building on East 57th Street. He explained that Saidie May had left him just enough to as-sure his studio expenses for a year or two because she was sure that the only way he could develop fully as an artist was to be on his own." To be sure, there were times when he resented the posthumous discipline and yearned for the earlier security and luxury. (To the end of his life Al remembered Saidie May with undiminished affection. When he was dying, he murmured something about looking forward to joining her.)

"We took the elevator to what seemed to me a gargantuan apart-ment," Lila continued. "The place was completely empty — no furni-ture, no paintings; it was like walking into an uninhabited apartment. I got pretty nervous at this point and asked him where he kept his paintings. He told me he'd bring them out. 'I'd offer you a glass of water,' he said, 'but I've only got ice cubes, not glasses.'

"He scurried away into the bowels of the apartment and finally, with the help of an enormous dolly, wheeled in a large painting on ma-sonite. The pigment, built up with heavy brushstrokes, was inches thick. His work at that time was based mainly on ambiguous color marks — somewhat like Abstract Expressionism. He then proceeded to unfold various unstretched pieces of canvas and attach them to the white wall. Everything in that apartment was dead white. What I saw was a series of configurations that reminded me of mysterious charts. Then he ex-plained the painting on masonite in terms of these configurations. Af-ter he showed me other works on masonite with similar accompanying charts, he asked me what I thought. I told him I didn't understand the ones on masonite, but that the small configurations were what counted. Years later, I bumped into Jensen at the Pace Gallery during an exhibition of his work. I reminded him that we'd met before and that probably he didn't remember me, but he said, 'Oh, yes, I do. You're the lady who changed my life.'"

Al may have been offered the same advice by other visitors, but he always claimed that it was Rothko who had set him on his course. Mark, after all, was an internationally respected painter, whereas Lila was still an art student when she saw his work. It is hardly surprising that Jensen chose to identify himself with the established artist rather than with the young neophyte. But it is worth mentioning that, in Katzen's story, the "mysterious charts" were already serving as studies for the finished paintings, which may indicate that Rothko had offered his pronouncement before Katzen's visit.

Katzen's memories are corroborated by the painter Sideo Fromboluti and several other artists who also recall being unceremoniously hijacked to Al's studio. In the years when he was diligently searching for himself as a painter, he turned to fellow artists for help. Through communication with them he hoped to unearth a possible resolution of his dilemma, a procedure he would eventually find futile. Then, in an about-face, he repudiated easy socializing and withdrew more and more into himself.

Fromboluti described meeting Jensen in the early 1950s at the Artists' Gallery on Lexington Avenue. Al almost immediately kidnapped him to his studio, which was in the same large apartment that had impressed Lila. Sideo reported that the East Side neighborhood and the stylish building replete with doorman and elevator operator amazed him no less than the vast living room, empty except for a large rack stuffed with paintings. Sideo suggested a bite to eat, but there was nothing but a bottle of whiskey in the refrigerator. Ensconced on an orange crate, Fromboluti viewed the paintings, recalling some thirty-five years later that "they seemed to depend on pure strips of color interspersed with abstract forms." The two men drank steadily as Jensen held forth on his own work and on Mondrian, whom, at that time, he esteemed. Tacked up on the wall were the same color charts that Rothko and Katzen had admired.

The two painters, who became good friends, saw each other frequently and were usually joined by Sideo's wife, the painter Nora Speyer.
At one point, Al told them, "I intend to work for six years. If I haven't
made it by then, I'm planning to commit suicide." Some time later,
when he was well into his fifties and still in difficult straits, he informed
Fromboluti and Speyer that he had accepted a job as a messenger boy.
Nora and Sideo, filled with compassion, arranged an evening party of
friends who were teaching art in various academic institutions and
might be able to help Jensen obtain a post at one of them. Al arrived
late, shortly after 11:30, for on that very day in 1958, he had in fact
sold a painting to Henry Luce III, who would later have a Christmas
card reproduced from it. It was at this auspicious moment that Al decided against both a messenger-boy career and scheduled suicide. He
felt he was launched. Luce, who became a generous patron, remained
Al's friend until the painter's death. Sideo and Nora, who were considerably younger than Al, were somewhat disillusioned by Al's change of
plans. They had always looked on him as a suffering idealist. But money
was never a motivating force for Jensen. Once his livelihood was assured, he lost interest in it, and, unlike Rothko, he did not allow tax
shelters or Wall Street investments to harass him.

Jensen's friendships with Katzen and Fromboluti were a consistent element in the pattern of his life in the 1950s. Because he was
snubbed by the most prominent members of the New York School,
the painters of his own generation, Al reached out to younger artists,
who were intrigued by his bravado and insight. He went to "Happen-
ings," frequented the co-op galleries, and his circle of acquaintances
grew to include Allan Kaprow, Claes Oldenburg, George Segal, and Sam
Francis, the last introducing him to many people in the upper eche-
lons of the European art world. Jasper Johns and Robert Rauschenberg became admirers, and Al was convinced that Johns got one of his
biggest ideas from him. He maintained that the younger artist was indebted to Jensen's thickly painted color disks for the central image
and sensuous surfaces of his early target paintings.

But it was Rothko's friendship that Jensen welcomed with deferential gratitude. Their relationship was private: the two men shared
few acquaintances, and it was not until after Jensen's death in 1981

that I learned their paths had ever crossed. Then, Al's widow, the artist
Regina Bogat, told me of her husband's quiet friendship with Rothko.
Rothko always had a penchant for hidden, one-to-one relationships,
and he was able to dominate Jensen enough to make him keep their

Alfred Jensen in his studio in New Jersey, painting *The Sun Rises Twice,
Per I–IV* (1973), now in the collection of the Hirshhorn Museum and
Sculpture Garden. Photograph by Regina Bogat.

connection to himself. According to Jensen, Mark preferred not to acknowledge Jensen to any of his colleagues. In retrospect, Al was always bitter about this barrier at the very period he most needed an entry into the New York art world. I sometimes wonder if Rothko's hidden friendship with him may have related to the contempt many of Mark's fellow artists felt for Jensen. And evidently Mark wouldn't defy their opinion and stand up for Al.

There came a day when the friendship dissolved, ostensibly because of a trivial episode. Al was preparing for an exhibition at the Tanager Gallery, and he asked Mark to help him select the show. According to Regina Bogat, Rothko separated the paintings into three sections, saying, "This group will please the collectors, this group the critics, and this the artists." Al chose the last. Later he proudly told this story to a friend, which incensed Mark, who felt that every artist in New York would henceforth be after him for similar advice. It's hard to believe that the friendship broke up over such a minor event, and it was probably not the threat of importuning artists that so annoyed Rothko. He was irate at the possibility of his closeness with the much-despised Jensen being spread all over town.

Milton and Sally Avery, who knew both men well, never met Al at Rothko's home during the years of the friendship, nor did I. Mark neither mentioned nor introduced Al to any of us. Sally recounts how Jensen frequently sought them out in Washington Square, near their apartment in Greenwich Village, where they often walked after Milton finished painting about 3:30 each afternoon. Weather permitting, the Averys would settle down on a bench and friends might join them for informal chats. The Averys were known for providing a generous focus and welcoming ears for fellow artists. "Someone," Sally said, "would always drop by."

From time to time, Jensen also joined the Averys on their bench, often after seeing Rothko. Al reported the discussions in considerable detail, describing stormy disagreements that increased as time went on. As a rule, they concerned Jensen's paintings, for when Al dropped all vestiges of Abstract Expressionism, Rothko became disgruntled. He had started out as a charitable counselor, only to discover that his disciple was defying his authority. Jensen told the Averys, who were among the few to receive such confidences, that the friendship broke up because Mark disapproved of his new work, which Al claimed was based on carefully researched ancient numerical calendar systems, an approach that was totally counter to everything Rothko believed in. And no one was capable of being more severely judgmental than Mark.

Very likely, the relationship foundered both because of the exhibition contretemps and even more because of basic aesthetic disagreements. In his notes of a conversation dated July 23, 1956, Al quotes Rothko as saying, "Your own tendency, Jensen, is toward the heroic. You proclaim in a loud boisterous voice; you exaggerate pompously and tend to dramatize, while in my work I always stress the quality of intimacy. . . . I want my art to assert its purpose and meaning in quiet understatement." Earlier in the year, Jensen had written that the time had come for him to "take into consideration that specific thing which is me." He also decided that his future rested on dealing with "my psyche and evolutionary process of thinking," a process diametrically opposed to Rothko's intuitive methods. In any case, Jensen became disgusted with Rothko's reactions and terminated their relationship. In his anger, he stuffed most of the laboriously recorded conversations into the incinerator, and only a few pages of his transcriptions survive.

This was not the only time Jensen terminated a friendship over aesthetic differences. A year or two before his marriage to Regina in 1963, Fromboluti and Speyer visited his studio to see a large new painting "completely divided into color squares" that Jensen explained was "part of his own genealogy" and related to major influences from his birthplace in Guatemala. The squares were red, blue, and yellow with seven additional green ones, which he said represented "dragon's teeth." For some time Fromboluti had felt that "Al was so self-hypnotized, he was impossible to reach anymore." Communication was blocked, but it did not impede Al from accompanying them to Sideo's studio on 22nd Street later that evening. There he exploded in angry denunciations. "You're still using Matisse space and that's outdated!" he shouted. "You're still using Mondrian space, and it's outdated too!" Jensen was so enraged, Sideo reported, that it was no longer possible for them to remain friends.

Because of the different nationalities of his parents and being

born in Central America, Jensen became a linguist as a natural outcome of his early life. When he was seven, his mother died, and he was
shipped off to school in Denmark, where he remained until he signed
on as a ship's cabin boy at the age of fourteen. For the next eight
years, he was an intermittent seaman, but later, shifting from country
to country, he supported himself as a cowboy, farmer, and lumber sales-
man. He could speak French, Spanish, German, Danish, and English
and, whenever possible, he studied art, including stints in Paris with
Despiau, Friesz, and Dufresne, and with Hofmann in Germany and
Capri. Then he met Saidie May, and not until some two decades later
did he cease his wanderings and concentrate on his own painting.

I recall first meeting Al and Saidie May in Chicago on one of
their transcontinental trips. Twenty-five years older than he, she was a
bouncy enthusiast with an open mind and eye. He was serious, ardent,
and modest. Although for a moment I wondered if he wasn't perhaps
a gigolo, I quickly realized that it was he who was her mentor. Having
at that time recently discovered Jean Dubuffet well before this artist
had become an international figure, he was advising his companion to
splurge a bit. During this early visit, when I was at the Art Institute, he
showed me photographs of two paintings by Dubuffet that May was
considering and, in a flow of passionate, if broken, English, expatiated
on the French artist. Once he settled on a project, no one could have
been more persuasively supportive and, at that time, his project was
Dubuffet. On the surface, he appeared mild, but he became intensely
excited when describing the work of contemporary artists he admired.
Later he would speak of his own paintings with the same shining eyes.

I sometimes question whether late starters are always handicapped.
Al's restless treks in search of important works by other artists may
have proved a valuable preparation for his own future role as a painter.
Eventually he was not influenced by any of them. He advised Saidie
May to buy works by such artists as Gabo, Giacometti, Klee, Kandinsky,
Masson, Miró, and Pevsner, and, whenever possible, arranged personal
meetings with these men. After his own painting direction was on
course, he never looked back, but, during his years with Mrs. May, both
of them exploited their relationships with the artists they collected by
visiting their studios and trying out various experimental techniques

they observed there. They made Constructivist sculpture à la Gabo, Surrealist sketches right out of Miró and Masson, and even dabbled with Matisse-like interiors. Nor did they limit themselves to the European avant-garde. In 1943 they acquired from Peggy Guggenheim's New York gallery, Art of This Century, the first paintings by William Baziotes and Robert Motherwell to be sold publicly. Only with considerable difficulty was Jensen later to slough off all these influences and start from scratch. For him, the years spent buying paintings and sculpture were not unlike a protracted art school education.

Both he and Saidie May always insisted they were artists, but because of their emphasis on collecting I regarded them more as viewers than doers. They rarely mentioned their own paintings and, since they had no permanent single address, it would have been difficult for either of them to develop a serious body of work. I was, however, impressed by their zest for the newest in art, though I was never sure which attracted them more, the lure of travel or assembling a collection.

In 1947, when I was traveling through the country selecting pieces for the museum's "Abstract and Surrealist Art in America" show, I visited Saidie May and Al Jensen in the Park Manor Hotel in San Diego, where they were temporarily staying. In some notes I made, I described her as "painting watercolors and gouaches furiously. Her colors are explosive and her work is primitive. She seems influenced at the moment by Dubuffet. In fact, she has just bought a large painting by him which she gave to the San Diego Museum and they promptly returned. Too experimental. Incidentally the only good modern art in that museum are gifts from Saidie May. Her own work is interesting, much more so than I expected, but technically it isn't up to snuff. Jensen's paintings (all gouaches) have a degree of strength, but nothing more."

Traumatized by Saidie May's death and by his uprooted life, Jensen spent his first years in New York suffering from a sense of acute alienation. Well past fifty, he felt he had failed as an artist, painting because he had to paint, "a desperate man who feels himself incomplete." Interestingly, his sense of hopelessness and irresolution helped bind him to Rothko. Mark told Al that they had misery in common — one reason he was attracted to Jensen was that he too was "a man of despair."

Not that despair was an all-bad thing in Rothko's universe. Despair, Rothko felt, was a useful commodity for artists to possess, because it was "the only way one can expose one's inner self with honesty" and thus reveal one's art.

Later, in the happier days of 1968, I unexpectedly encountered Al, whom I had not seen in some years, in Yucatan on a street in Mérida. For a man in his middle sixties, he impressed me as looking remarkably fit. He was carrying a little girl and was accompanied by his attractive young wife. Some kind of carnival punctuated by the usual noise and dust was going on, and later we watched it from the balcony of my hotel room. Al had changed; now he was a family man, clearly enchanted by his three-year-old daughter, Anna. But, even more, he seemed intensely involved with his own paintings, insisting that I come to see them as soon as we returned to New York. Since he and I were both enthralled by Mayan archaeology, we talked of little else, and that was when he first told me of his consuming interest in Mayan hieroglyphics as they related to numbers, art, and especially to his own work. But, as Regina observed, her husband "was never interested in numerology per se or the occult. He steered away from both. People tried to relate his work to the kabala, but that was not what he was after." What *did* preoccupy Jensen was the system of magic squares common to both ancient China and the Middle East; he believed that numbers could be manipulated to re-create early religious beliefs. He studied the *I Ching*, the early book of divination that told fortunes according to numbers and is the foundation of Taoist and Confucian philosophies of life. "Al even made an *I Ching* board," Regina remembered. "When Anna's cat died, she consulted it. 'Why did my cat have to die?' she asked. And her reading was, 'You must learn how to give things up.'"

Jensen depended heavily on books, possibly to compensate for his abbreviated formal education, but also because of his searching mind. His library, both erudite and eclectic, covered the history, archaeology, art, religion, science, and philosophy of China, with a similar concentration on Latin America from Mexico south to the Andes. Another important group of books underlined his interest in classical Greece, with emphasis on art, the Delphic mysteries, mathematics, philosophy, and mythology. In addition, he amassed a survey of science. Because of his fluency in five languages, his library included untranslated and often recondite works, which he consulted conscientiously. He immersed himself in the intricacies of certain civilizations, as well as in the complexities of early and modern science.

He read voluminously, almost as if words were his salvation, and he firmly believed that his paintings were based on the findings of earlier revelations. His notebooks, bursting with diagrams of extraordinary intensity, coordinate specific colors with numbers in frenetic juxtapositions. At one point, he even took his findings to two noted pre-Columbian scholars, hoping that they would substantiate his theories, but neither responded with much more than bemusement. He also wrote to a scientist friend about his color theories, which were based on pigmentation. His friend replied that there was no such thing as his color theory because color was measured through light waves. But Al was not a man to be daunted by such details.

Most critics who have written seriously about Jensen accept his scientific equations as the basis for his work, but I have always been doubtful. The wonderful hypnotic diagrams, just as Rothko and Katzen observed, are his art. They combine dense structures with his obsessive need to equate visual experiences with calendrical mysteries of the past, especially those of the Chinese and the Maya. Jensen grappled with the solar number systems of these two civilizations, but just how authentically scientific his studies were is problematic. He improvised his own brand of science, as any creative artist must, but it was less theory or historical disciplines than Jensen's unconscious that determined his vision. But, at the same time, his dependence on Goethe's color theories permeated his thinking for well over twenty years and cannot be discounted.

Rather than pseudo-science, "the impasto and the geometry were Al," says Regina Bogat. "His whole being was in the paint itself and the geometric shapes." And that is precisely what I saw on several occasions when I visited the Jensens after they moved from Chinatown to Glen Ridge, New Jersey, in 1972. There they settled into a pleasant suburban street in a comfortable house, with the third floor reserved for Al's studio. Though the dimensions of that space were adequate, they were shattered by the onslaught of his paintings, especially the multipaneled ones. I remember climbing the two flights of stairs and suddenly finding myself under siege from the blinding power of those compositions. The intermix of rich surface irregularities, compulsive repetitions, and blazing color turned the top floor of that conventional house into a maelstrom. The upper-middle-class setting always seemed an anomaly to me, and Al, short, compact, and deadly serious, was also difficult to identify with his own artistic explosions. His scholarly pursuits may have been a conscious effort to temper his emotions, to keep him from flying apart. (Sam Francis once said to Al, "You talk like an academic and paint like a madman.") They were rationalizations that gave credence to his compulsions and were as much motivations as justifications. His scholarship was never academic, though he convinced himself it was.

To discuss his paintings with him was quite different from discussing the work of other artists with them. With Al, one spent little or no time on aesthetics or past and present art influences. Unlike Rothko, it was never Rembrandt, Turner, or Matisse he invoked, but rather Pythagoras and Faraday; nor did he dwell on such soul-searching vagaries as self-expression or private moods. His vocabulary was full of electromagnetics, prism machines, protons, electrons, and numbers, numbers, numbers. A frequently reproduced photograph of Jensen shows him sitting on the floor of his studio with a plethora of numbered color charts behind him.

However, he did tell me once that, for him, numbers and colors acting together could become more than cosmic abstract symbols: they could also imply human values. As his two children, Anna and Peter, named after his parents, grew older, he occasionally incorporated them in his work, not in an anecdotal sense but nonetheless in humanistic terms. One of his best-known paintings is a four-panel (192-inch wide) composition showing a girl and boy surrounded by a checkerboard of symbolic colors. The figures are almost submerged in row upon row of numbers, which are labeled "Ancient Calendar Year" and "Solar Calendar Year." The girl has two words attached to her — "boredom" and "Pleasure", and the boy "Work" and "justification." I am not sure that these designations necessarily reflected Jensen's attitude toward

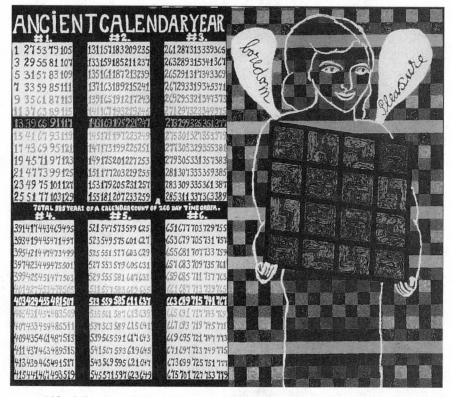

Alfred Jensen, *Girl and Boy and Numbers,* 1978. Panels I and II.

the sexes, though I am told that they did, but only toward the end of his life when, cocoonlike, he turned inward on himself. At that point, it was exclusively his work that concerned him; he was hostile to family intrusions. The painting, dated 1978, when Anna was thirteen and Peter eight, is titled *Girl and Boy and Numbers.* Each child is holding a magic square, the girl's with even numbers and the boy's with odd numbers, consistent with the designations for male and female in Chinese philosophy. Executed on four panels, the painting is a disturbing compound of ritualistic codes from the past and moralistic present-day values, each buttressing the other yet leaving the viewer sorely at sea.

Gradually I learned to see Jensen's paintings from my own perspective, free of theoretical jargon. But it was not until his posthumous retrospective exhibition at the Guggenheim Museum in 1985 that the full impact of his work hit me. In that beautiful space, his great

Alfred Jensen, *Girl and Boy and Numbers,* 1978. Panels III and IV.

compositions soared less as evocations of scientific and ancient discoveries than as living forces. These works are not about anything — they are. And, to a degree, this immediacy is Al's only holdover from Abstract Expressionism.

At best, his paintings are strident, assertive, enigmatic, and overwhelmingly demanding. They are also intimidating. And despite all scientific theories, they are far from readily accountable. Often incorporating words within his compositions, as in *Girl and Boy and Numbers,* Jensen may have hoped to provide his viewer with helpful clues. Not unlike a conjuror, he combined geometric shapes, impasto paint, color, words, and a jungle of numbers to achieve a mystifying art that needs no identifying signature; it is totally his.

Every possible mathematical parallel Jensen could wrench from his magic squares were victories attesting to the validity of past cultures and the inventiveness of his own adaptations. Just why he was so consumed by these numerical interlockings has never ceased to puzzle me. Undeniably the long tradition of the magic square, in its varied manifestations, offered him a basic underpinning for his paintings — the grids, the numbers deployed within them, the symmetry of odd and even, the symbolism of irreconcilable dualities evolving into oneness. We think of yin-yang, female-male, dark-light, of systems that have engaged and eluded man for some three thousand years. This was the poetry that drove Jensen, and it was poetry more than science that possessed him. I can still relive my anxiety in that third-floor studio when I was torn between the eloquence of Al's torrent of explanatory words and the paintings themselves beating at me with savage vigor. Though he insisted these works were not occult, for me they seemed closer to automatism than to any preconceived solution.

He once observed, "The dark of the universe and the light of the sun are both sources of energy." And, to be sure, it was energy he was after — he wanted his canvases to approximate the processes of nature and actually germinate a new kind of potency. He was not an orthodox abstract painter but an artist in pursuit of certain intangibles that he hoped to make visible. When he was seventy-four, he explained:

> Modern number abstractions have not meant much to me nor have mystical associations of number. Ancient calendar systems, the edge of the sun reappearing have been a source of my concrete and symbolic number structures. I follow Pythagoras, who said, "Let the true principle be known, the beginning is the half of the whole."

> My use of numbers is governed by the duality and opposition of odd and even number structures.

He went on to recount an illuminating anecdote:

> One afternoon during the year 1921, I was walking down a street in San Diego, California. I suddenly saw

the edge of a young man's face, a nose. I called out to the owner of the profile, "Karl, remember that I drew your portrait in 1915, when we were children in school?" "Of course, I remember, Alfred," he answered, "and I still keep the portrait as a remembrance of our school days." That was 6,000 miles away and six years ago, in Horsholm, Denmark.

The edge of things, a profile coupled with a past event, has always made me leap like an inspired diver off a board.

Edge events have occupied me for years — the edge of color as it is observed in a prism.

Jensen may have purposely exaggerated the physical properties and presence of his paintings in order to assure them greater authority. He was dealing with the past, but on his own twentieth-century terms. Moreover, he was not reacting against established art movements or joining new ones. He was his own man, making his own rules. Once he found his way, he was no longer concerned with the so-called art scene that tormented Rothko to the end. Al deliberately chose to absent himself and live in the nondescript serenity of an undemanding suburb.

Despite his elaborate historical-philosophical-scientific pronouncements, his paintings were never *representations* of any system, no matter how much they were infused with lofty allusions. Premises from the past were his self-articulated points of departure; they were the framework for his compositions, but they were not the end result. With nothing less than solar action as his lodestar, he was engaged in the herculean task of creating a new form of energy merely through the interaction of paint on canvas. One is reminded of an apocryphal statement by Turner — "I do not imitate nature, I improve on it." The only other twentieth-century artist whom I can recall with such an overweening ambition to rival the forces of nature was Clyfford Still. He and Jensen did not hope to reveal themselves, nor the look of nature; for them, such revelations were irrelevant. What they wanted was to invent an equivalent natural power solely through the auspices of art. This was their target, even if they chose different techniques to achieve it. They were nothing if not magisterial.

Al often claimed he was the bridge between Abstract Expressionism and pop art, but that was not true. Even when he borrowed superficially from the Abstract Expressionists, he was never probing for his own volatile feelings as they were for theirs, nor was he related to pop art, with its emphasis on irony, mass production, and denial of the unique. Both Rothko and Jensen hailed their own work as supremely unique, and both of them frankly espoused the legitimacy of paint itself, whereas the pop artists, always faithful to Duchamp, denied its value. Why should a painting look like a painting if by looking like an aggrandized advertisement or comic strip it could spark a wry attack on present-day society? Though Jensen's paintings have at times been identified with Constructivism because of their seeming geometric precision, they were in no way related to this movement. Geometry per se was inconsequential; his work was never minimal or pure. His heavy impasto paint, with its low bas-relief projections, originally stemmed from early advice he received at one of the various art schools he briefly attended. According to Regina Bogat, he was convinced that "very thick paint would meld together and in time become like glass, whereas thin pigment might soak into the canvas," lose its physical power, and disappear. Al was after permanence and presence.

How Al found his way back to 2200 B.C., when the earliest known magic square was said to have originated in China (subsequently spreading to the Middle East and finally to Europe), is not a matter of record, but I think Mayan hieroglyphics showed him the way. He once described his childhood as a time when he "drank in Mayan culture with my Indian nurse's milk." His memories also included myriad small squares of land on which Indian peasants rotated their crops from time immemorial. Whether or not this was a rationalization is scarcely important, since Jensen was convinced that these geometric divisions were the start of his long involvement with the grid. His birthplace in Guatemala retained a strong hold on him during his entire life. He remained a citizen of that country to the end, despite the fact that his wife and children were Americans.

Slowly, as he grew older, Al began to relate Goethe's color theories to Mayan number symbols, all of which he believed led him back to China and the magic square. This may seem a rather circuitous route, but every step of the way was facilitated by the mileposts of an expanding library. For example, J. Eric Thompson's *Maya Hieroglyphic Writing* was an electrifying experience that sent him investigating the Mayan calendar system and in turn other more ancient systems. Nor was it always books that served as the initial impetus; Al had to have noticed the artifacts he encountered during his extensive travels. He was seduced by these many disparate elements, eventually combining them into cohesive sequences that became the basis of his art.

Toward the end of their lives, both Rothko and Jensen disintegrated psychologically and physically, but unlike Mark, Al was able to produce some of his strongest work. For Mark, it was a period of unresolved questions multiplied by the loss of his once intense appetite for painting. He had always embraced a sense of romantic desolation like a badge of honor, but when the fiction turned to fact, he collapsed. With Al, even the reality of cancer did not deter him. He only became more intent on his work and on sweeping everything else aside, no matter the consequences. Mark had long maintained that "great art" could not be conceived without suffering. He actually loved to suffer or, at least, to think he did. He prepared for it conversationally all his life, but when sickness came, it engulfed him in deep depression.

Al continued to paint in his studio until his physical condition prevented him from lifting a brush. During those last years, he grew querulous and ingrown. He had always lived in an imaginary world of his own creation, but toward the end it took over and became the real one. Normal, outside activities, including family life, were burdens he could no longer cope with. When I visited him before he died, I was saddened to see how his warm relationship with his children had deteriorated into sharp irritation. However, once we left them behind and climbed the stairs to the studio, he became his old self, truly the master of all he surveyed. It is rather touching that at this time, when Jensen was participating as little as possible in family activities, he still continued to tend his rose garden. Al would rise at five o'clock and immerse himself in the backyard. In suburban New Jersey, he made no friends except for the volunteer who took care of the roses in Freeman Gardens, a small nearby park, but their contacts were restricted chiefly to elementary horticulture. Al also occasionally chatted with the manager of the local bank who, along with the Jensens' cleaning lady, appeared to be the only resident of Glen Ridge who knew that he was an artist, even though, by that time, he was having important exhibitions in New York, as well as internationally. I've often questioned how his neighbors would have reacted to that supercharged galaxy of canvases he was churning out in their midst.

Jensen considered friendship a luxury he couldn't afford. He wanted above all in those later years to be left alone with his passions, and his passions were painting and reading. Except for his roses, he had only one other mild hobby — baseball. Regina was a Mets fan and, through her, he began to learn about the game, solely via the radio. He only attended a game once, when a friend gave Peter several box seats. Already in his late sixties when Peter was born, Al was not about to become the proverbial American dad who fed his son hot dogs and applauded home runs at Shea Stadium, but he did master the intricacies of the game.

Though he was a loner, Al always had women in his life, the most important of whom were Saidie May, Regina Bogat, and, during the decade between these two, Lillian Picard. Lil, as she was called, had been a German art journalist who, along with her husband, immigrated to New York during the Nazi period. When I telephoned her in 1987 and tried several times to talk with her about the years of her friendship with Al, she was already in her late eighties and refused to see me. Though the breakup of their relationship had taken place a quarter-century before, she was still bitter. She had scarcely a kind word for Jensen, calling him an "unbalanced, uneducated peasant," though she did seem to respect his work. I can only surmise that the end of their friendship was acrimonious, and no doubt resulted from his marriage to Regina, but there is little question that Lil Picard provided Al with emotional support and understanding during what were likely the most trying years of his life.

Far more disastrous was his break with Rothko, which had occurred several years earlier. After her marriage, Regina could not help but observe how sorely Al missed the old friendship and, having known Mark well herself, she phoned him secretly one day and urged him to take the initiative and give the once warm association a second chance. Mark listened patiently, but he never responded. A year or two before Mark died, Sideo Fromboluti asked him casually if he'd seen Al recently. The friendship had ended just ten years earlier, but Rothko went blank at the mention of Jensen's name.

When Al learned of Rothko's suicide, "The news fell into his being like a stone falls into a lake," said Regina, "and later he followed the reports of the Rothko lawsuit avidly." They affirmed his dread of art dealers, whom he believed would clean out his studio and leave him without a history of his creative development. In fact, Mark had been Al's instructor in this aspect of his career as well. When Jensen was still struggling and worried about money, Rothko admonished him that no matter how destitute he was, he had to hold on to as much of his work as possible. Rothko even explained how to store his canvases at minimal expense. "It does not matter whether society cares for your paintings," Mark told him. "That is immaterial. The important point is that you keep them until your death." Later, when Jensen was beginning to sell, he complained to Rothko about his dealer, Martha Jackson. Al was sure she was cheating him, and one day when Rothko showed up at Jensen's studio, he found Al pounding nails into little wooden figures that were stand-ins for Jackson. Rothko suggested that he would be better off with "modern voodoo" — that is, a good lawyer. Mark's advice was gospel for Al, who did seek legal help. His attorney commandeered the gallery's books, detached Al from there, and recovered most of his paintings.

It was not Al's habit to go gently through life. I always marvel that our friendship remained intact during the many years we knew each other. As a young artist, he even quarreled with that most amiable of men, Hans Hofmann. In 1927, he led a brief insurrection among the students, mainly because he disapproved of Hofmann's practice of painting on his pupils' canvases. Following the revolt, Jensen left the school and, for some time afterward, denigrated both the institution and its founder. Years later in New York, he ran into Hans who, never one to bear a grudge, had just seen Al's mammoth composition *Das Bild der Sonne* exhibited in an uptown branch of the Hanover Bank. The older man told him, "You light up 57th Street," and so he did. I can recall very few paintings that compete with the intensity of solar light as successfully as does this eye-shattering substitute for the sun.

Of all the losses Jensen sustained, with the exception of Saidie May, it was Rothko he missed the most. And though there was no contact between them, Al always hoped that Mark at least visited his exhibitions. He, in turn, rarely missed one of Rothko's. What he thought of Mark's late work he never said, other than that it had "presence," something he claimed also for his own paintings. He had inherited the term from Rothko. Precisely what they both meant by the word is anyone's guess, but I think it had to do with a certain inherent life force, a uniqueness as differentiated from run-of-the-mill works of art. The idea of a "presence" suggested a personal statement, not merely a momentary impression. It presupposed substance, permanence, and the strong conviction of the artist. With Rothko, his paintings represented his own expansive presence. He needed a large arena; his persona could not be pinched. With Jensen, the word meant something else — by sheer physicality, each of his startling compositions assumed an independent power. They could not be ignored, and indeed they compensated for the many earlier years when this small, zealous man struggled to be heard. Rothko's personal presence in his own paintings was infinitely more subtle: he was in search of "poignancy," his own complicated emotional reactions and those of a larger world around him.

Once when Al was having a show at the Graham Gallery in New York, Joan Washburn, who was then the manager, casually mentioned that Rothko had been in to see the exhibition. Jensen, who bowed to no other artist, was inordinately pleased.

10
Clyfford Still
Art's Angry Man

Clyfford Still was an outspoken man periodically tormented by repressed fury. He was far from easy to get along with. Most dealers, museum personnel, and colleagues eventually bowed out or more likely were booted out by him. He chose to isolate himself from an art world he despised, yet he and I remained friends without a break in our long association. No doubt my unbounded admiration for his paintings was largely responsible for such staying power. This often happened to me with artists. I appeared to them more as an understanding eye and ear than as a critic with an agenda of my own. And that probably explains why, among the artists I associated with, the ones I knew best were those whose work I found most interesting.

At times Still's writings on art were a bit unhinged, as when he insisted that the Armory Show was a dumping ground for the "sterile conclusions of Western European decadence" and termed Cézanne, Picasso, Kandinsky, and Monet "monotonous." But in conversation — art was all he ever talked about with me — he was more lucid. Indeed,

I found him a perceptive critic of his own work and that of other twentieth-century artists, unless he was under some special pressure, either real or imagined. Then he could become irrationally judgmental, as when in 1959 he castigated his New York School contemporaries with the wrath of Jehovah and insisted on having his words reprinted in his Metropolitan Museum of Art catalogue twenty years later:

> The men and their work and their agents [dealers] became as one, and no borrowed images, political illustration, Bauhaus sterilities, symbols of potency, pseudoreligious titles, nor any concealment behind that most faceless of apologies, "Art," should hide the puerility and meanness of their purpose and games. And they are all amply worthy of the contempt and hatred they secretly exchange with one another even unto their deaths.

Though he wrote with venom about Abstract Expressionism (a movement he helped to found), he discussed his peers more rationally and analyzed them with considerable insight. I was often amazed at how judiciously he spoke and yet how paranoid were his writings.

When Still rejected New York and what he considered its fraudulent art scene, he broke all ties and moved to a small rural retreat in Westminster, Maryland, northwest of Baltimore. On my first visit there some time in the early 1960s, Clyff, even before allowing me to drop my overnight bag at the house, steered me to a barn that he'd transformed into a spotless, unfurnished space where, from time to time, he hung a few works in order to isolate and study them. That day he had installed three very large recent paintings, their color high-pitched and their presence overwhelming.

They were immensely open, free, shot through with light and endless space. His work had always impressed me as competing with rather than interpreting nature. Earlier it had seemed more cataclysmic but now, away from New York, a certain optimism had taken over. On that visit, I stayed overnight but never again. My room, in fact, every room, was stacked and packed with rolled canvases. I had nightmares imagining that in the dark I might inadvertently injure a painting or two.

I once described Still's paintings as "living organisms," their surging pigment gashed to expose bottomless voids and suspended solids. He was able to create a cosmos of his own. His individual canvases are less revealing than groups of them, a reality he understood when he gave thirty-one paintings to the Albright-Knox Art Gallery in Buffalo and twenty-eight to the San Francisco Museum of Art, hoping that these concentrations would act as counterparts to the world of natural phenomena. He hated good taste, he hated anything easy to label or to absorb at first glance. He felt, and probably justifiably, that he was the first to experiment with many of the New York School's most radical discoveries, though he was rarely given credit for it. This failure of other artists, namely Barnett Newman and Robert Motherwell, to acknowledge his primacy rankled enormously, and it was a source of everlasting bitterness. Differing from Mark Rothko, whose place in future history was a consuming preoccupation, Still had no doubt that his name would endure.

Too many artists — and Still was one of them — who have received public acclaim during their lives become fixated on this problem of permanent posthumous fame. The same men and women who clawed their way to acceptance, become, after finally attaining it, equally or more zealous of projecting it into the future. For these artists there seems no end to it all — no rest or relief from the ceaseless struggle to outwit history. In the long run, I doubt that it can be accomplished, but the attempts have been widespread. Not only Rothko and Still, but Duchamp, Noguchi, and Dubuffet were similarly preoccupied. One need only refer to his *Box in a Valise* (1941) and *The Green Box* (1934) to realize how ardently Duchamp was bent on preserving his name. Equally telling are his frequent reconstructions of individual pieces that were either lost or damaged. *Box in a Valise* recapitulated in miniature many of his more memorable works, while *The Green Box* preserved in facsimile each idea that paved the way for *The Large Glass* (1915–23). In addition, Duchamp made every effort to see that his small body of work was concentrated in the hands of one collector — Walter Arensberg. Duchamp told me that he felt his work had more

Clyfford Still, *1957-D No. 1*, 1957. Typically expansive in scale, *1957-D No. 1* belongs to the Albright-Knox Gallery of Art, one of the two American museums to which Still donated important groups of his paintings.

meaning as a sequential group than if it had been dispersed, and he hoped that the entire undivided group would eventually be given to a reputable museum. He may have appeared to nonchalantly halt his career in midstream, but he never for one moment left his past unprotected. And if proof of Noguchi's urge toward controlling his artistic fate is needed, the large museum in Long Island City that he dedicated solely to his own work should suffice. Perhaps Dubuffet was the one most concerned with his place in art's hierarchy. He was a great believer in publicity and wangled it wherever possible. Dazzled by the printed word, he organized a procession of books and catalogues about himself that at times poured over my desk in such profusion as to become stultifying. He always appeared to me as the consummate devotee of modern hype and self-promotion.

To return to Clyfford Still, at one time he and Mark Rothko were extremely close friends. Their relationship, which started in 1943, held profound significance for both of them, but ended abruptly at

Clyfford Still at his show at the San Francisco Museum of Art in honor of his donation of paintings to the institution, 1976. The painting in the background is from 1945; it was called *Self-Portrait* until 1979, when Still changed the name to *Untitled*.

least a decade before Mark's death. Rothko, who was less influenced by Still's paintings than by his thinking, was a late bloomer. He was composing rather conventional city scenes when Still had already embarked on radical nonobjective canvases. It was Clyff's uncompromising independence, coupled with his freedom from orthodoxy, that stiffened Mark's resolve to let himself go, to experiment, to find his own way. Mark was not a courageous man, because he cared too much about what other people thought, but Clyff had inner strength to spare. He imparted enough to his friend so that for a time Mark had the mettle to do what he needed to do. Clyff had helped Mark become something better than himself, and Mark was always grateful for it.

I never heard Rothko say an unkind word about the other artist, but I cannot report the same of Still. He was rancorous, and while recognizing the depth of their friendship, after the break he looked back with animus. I wasn't able to find out precisely why they split up, and despite Clyff's claim that he could no longer tolerate Mark's involvement with the New York art scene and its "corrupt art market," I have always wondered if that was the true explanation. There is no doubt that Still was deeply disappointed when his friend gave in to the "contaminations" of success — after Mark died and his business dealings with the Marlborough Gallery came out into the open, I began to sympathize with Clyff's point of view a little more — but it can't be denied that Still was a hard taskmaster who balked at any compromise.

When Clyff abandoned New York in 1961 and settled in Maryland, or perhaps even earlier, the friendship ended. It was, I imagine, Still's choice, for whenever I visited him, Mark sent wistful greetings and always added, "Look carefully, so you can tell me what he's doing." After I got back to New York, he always questioned me in detail about Still's recent work, for after he settled in Maryland, his paintings were seldom exhibited. Rothko yearned to reinstate their friendship, but Still was uncooperative. Mark reminded me of a little boy on these occasions, peppering me with one question — "What did he say about me? What did he say?" One time he was so persistent that I broke my silence: "He said that you're living an evil, untrue life." After Mark's death, in pondering how and why he had deceived us about his involvement with the art market, I realized that one reason Mark was bent on seeming ethical in front of me was not only because he wanted to retain my good opinion, but that he did not want me to disillusion Clyff.

Toward the end of his life, Mark talked about Clyff and kept telling me that he wanted to see him. He asked me to take Clyff that message, and I agreed. I went to Maryland to see Clyff and told him how depressed and sick Mark was, how much their old friendship meant to him, and how even a brief call would make a difference, but I wasn't able to get through. He refused to visit or telephone; Rothko had to approach him personally and make his feelings known. "It's up to him," Still said. "He has to come to me."

I'm afraid it was too late by then; Rothko was seriously ill and, in addition, I'm not sure that he fully understood the exact nature of their difficulties. If he did, he never told me, though we discussed Still more often than any other artist. By some strange coincidence, a few hours after Theodoros Stamos called to tell me that Mark had killed himself, Still phoned from Maryland. I naturally thought he wanted to discuss the tragedy, but, as it turned out, he had heard nothing. I filled him in and shall never forget his response. "I'm not surprised," he said. "He lost his way a long time ago."

I went at least once each year to visit Still. In 1966 he and his wife, Patricia, settled in a white-columned house in the nearby town of New Windsor. Located next to a funeral parlor, the new larger home offered more space, but it was rapidly filled to capacity with multiple rolled canvases, each identified by Pat with a small sketch of the original. Since the paintings were not titled (only dated), this arduous practice was necessary. Again the entire house was taken over, with only a cramped section of the kitchen reserved for sociability. I worried about the danger of fire, but Clyff claimed that the paintings were safer with him than in storage. I always suspected he was too attached to be separated from them.

A visit made in late 1969 stands out, partly because I had decided that day to emancipate myself from his abstemiousness when it came to eating and drinking, and partly because I'd been commissioned by *Vogue* magazine to write an article on Clyff, so this was chiefly a business trip. Blindly opposed to critics, he had limited the field to me — otherwise I'm sure *Vogue* would have looked elsewhere. Clyff always met me at the airport, well over an hour's drive from his house. A frugal man, he allowed himself only one luxury that I ever observed: he always drove a large, comfortable, conventional car, which in retrospect was probably a Cadillac. On each visit we stopped for lunch at the same small wayside restaurant, and each time I'd swallow my tongue when he'd say, "You don't want a drink, I'm sure, and the codfish balls are a specialty here — I always take them." This time I had geared myself in advance to declare my independence. Yes, I did want a Bloody Mary, and no, I didn't want those miserable codfish balls. He was surprised but indulgent.

When we arrived at his house that day, a small sports car with the top down was parked there. Clyff explained that it belonged to a photographer sent by *Vogue* to illustrate the article. I was vaguely introduced to Mr. Somebody-or-Other, sportily gotten up in a brown corduroy jacket. He was obviously British, as was his young assistant, and he amazed me with his agility. Because the canvases he photographed were very large and the rooms crowded with rolled ones, he often worked from the top of an extension ladder, Clyff having installed the unstretched, unframed paintings flat on the floor. As I took notes, the young man took pictures. It was dark and we were all parched before Pat invited us into the kitchen for "a drink," which turned out to be weak tea and limp graham crackers. Subsequently, I was picked up by friends with whom I stayed in Baltimore. Some months later, when the article appeared in *Vogue,* I was amused to see that the photographer, who was given star credit, was Lord Snowden. No one could have behaved more professionally, and indeed he had been a professional photographer before he married Princess Margaret. Actually, Snowden was most deferential to Clyff, but he wasn't noticeably interested in the photographer. Still was much too involved in his own work to be concerned with the peerage.

When Thomas B. Hess became head of the department of twentieth-century art at the Metropolitan Museum in 1978, he promptly scheduled a long overdue retrospective exhibition of Still's work, but because of Hess's premature death later that year, the project was not without complications. Though Clyff, whose standards were high and implacable, was extremely demanding, the museum made every effort to smooth his way. The director, Philippe de Montebello, was both understanding and flexible. There were innumerable small altercations, and I heard about most of them because my apartment was so close to the Metropolitan that Clyff could almost use it as a way station. But by far the most serious problem was his health. He'd been diagnosed as having a stomach tumor and advised to undergo immediate

treatment. Because he felt it imperative to plan and oversee every detail of the exhibition, he insisted on delaying any surgery until after the
show opened in November of 1979. Even in a life-or-death emergency,
the paintings came first. "They are my way of growing and thinking,"
he explained, "they're my autobiography." He told me his quest was
"self-discovery," and claimed that "art is the only aristocracy left where
a man takes full responsibility." He went on to say, "I never wanted
color to be color. I never wanted texture to be texture, or images to
become shapes. I wanted them all to fuse into a living spirit."

The Metropolitan arranged a small opening luncheon in Clyff's
honor. Except for members of the museum's staff and board, I recognized just a handful of guests from the contemporary art world, pre-
sumably because Clyff had vetted — and vetoed — the invitation list.
The only important artist present other than Clyff was Saul Steinberg,
who I doubt was a close friend. Possibly because his forte was draftsmanship, he had never presented Still with competitive or philosophical dilemmas.

There were a few brief speeches by various dignitaries and then
Clyff rose, his face drawn and white but still handsome in its stern clarity. Around his neck and shoulders he had draped a tan wool scarf,
which he never removed during the entire proceedings. He must have
been in agony, and his voice was so weak I could hear little of what he
said. The show was too large and not always the best possible selection,
but for me it was a landmark experience and, let me add, an engulfing
one. No decorative concession or easy solution softened the impact.
Because Still was reaching out to a new dimension, his work was not
uniformly resolved. As far as he was concerned, even the modulations
of matte to shiny blacks could project entire spatial sequences. And
it was space he pursued through sweeping color, texture, and yawning
voids.

Clyff never recovered his health. He called me one day to say that
he was coming to New York to consult a doctor. Would I drop by his
daughter's apartment to see him? I was shocked by his appearance.
Very thin, weak, and obviously in pain, he nonetheless directed our
conversation toward the usual art pros and cons with the same vigor
and anger of the past, his eyes boiling, his body failing. He mentioned

nothing about his condition, though I could see he was suffering. When I rose to leave, he insisted on accompanying me to the elevator. There he shook my hand and said quietly, "This is good-bye." Less than two weeks later, he died.

Clyff forfeited everything for his work. He was one of the few artists I knew who could have made a fortune and wouldn't. The least money-grubbing of men, he never talked in terms of what his paintings would bring: he talked only in terms of their importance to him. Dying before our eyes, he sacrificed everything for his art, and so did his family, but none of them saw it as a sacrifice. When Clyff sold paintings, and it was always sparingly and occasionally, he watched over the sale of that work with tenacious care. Except for the two large groups of paintings he'd given to Buffalo and San Francisco, much of his work (more than twenty-five hundred oils, watercolors, drawings, and prints) remained in his estate. He left a complicated will stipulating that his art be donated to an urban museum that would guarantee the facilities he ordered, such as separate physical quarters and storage, and a reliable conservator and curator. The art cannot be sold or lent, or hung with anyone's work, and a certain percentage of it must be on view at all times. And there were further requirements, all of which have made the finding of a permanent home more than difficult, especially as he left no endowment for the work's upkeep. Few museums have the space or funds to satisfy such exacting obligations, and in addition, thoughtful staffs are opposed to freezing their institutions into eternal rigidity. It is nothing less than tragic that this body of work remains unavailable to a public long denied adequate contact with it. Perhaps trusting the future is wiser than trying to control it.

11
Isamu Noguchi
In Search of Home

Isamu Noguchi handled the problem of his legacy more pragmatically than most of his peers. Like Clyfford Still, he searched for a museum willing to guarantee an ideal permanent home for his life's work, but when this proved impossible, he created his own institution. He and Louise Nevelson considered establishing a joint museum to include only their own art. It was probably Noguchi's idea. They bandied the plan back and forth, but I believe it was Louise who realized it wouldn't work. Those two strong personalities could never have sublimated their wills to such interaction.

Located in Long Island City, the Isamu Noguchi Garden Museum is only one of the omnipotent projects this artist embarked on. At his home in Japan, on the island of Shikoku, he engaged in remaking the landscape. Toward the end of his life, with almost godlike authority and the occasional help of a bulldozer, he leveled hills, erected others, and redesigned his surroundings to approximate utopia, or at least his conception of utopia. Similar to Buckminster Fuller, who was one of his closest friends, Noguchi felt that no seriously inventive proposition was out of bounds. He didn't so much compete with nature as try to reshape and absorb it, for nature was his guiding light. He wanted to personalize it, to possess it. Why limit oneself to a single carving when all of nature is available to appropriate at will? Every plant, path, rock, and vista he tried to make his own. At this point in his life, he was less interested in accepted procedures than in overall conceptions. Like Rothko, who grew bored with easel painting, Noguchi found the pursuit of individual sculptures too circumscribed.

He approached his new museum in the same spirit. Very large, costly, carefully conceived, it accommodates his work with the utmost grace — possibly too much grace. The fact that the collection is static and composed entirely of the work of one man puts a heavy strain on it: no new points of comparison, no new insights. The museum badly needs frequent reinstallation in order to visualize Noguchi's development in multiple directions, and juxtapositions with the work of other artists might be fruitful. But it is essential for this one-man institution to both illuminate and educate the public about the sculptor himself — about his dependence on Japanese and other Asian sources, as well as on American and European influences. Information on his technical adjustments, his impact on associates, and his philosophic approach to his work are largely absent. I am not referring to lectures, but to comparative and concentrated exhibitions designed to *visualize* the museum's purpose. Otherwise there is the danger of a lifeless sleeping beauty.

Noguchi and I were born the same year, 1904. We met in the 1930s and remained friends until his death in 1988. We were both inveterate travelers; our paths crossed frequently, and after I moved to New York we saw each other more often. In 1941 I ran into him in San Francisco. He had driven from New York in a new station wagon accompanied by Arshile Gorky and Gorky's soon-to-be wife, Agnes Magruder. Late one afternoon, along with Isamu's good friend, the artist Jeanne Reynal, we all converged at a lavish cocktail party at the home of Dorothy Liebes, best known for her blond good looks and modern textile designs. Her apartment, with spectacular views of bridges and bays, was filled with West Coast artists and visitors like ourselves from other parts of the country. In a corner were two small boys about five and seven, playing quietly. I remember how impressed I was by their behavior. Shortly afterward I met their parents, Barbara and Serge Chermayeff, for the first time. Later I was to rent a summer house next door to theirs in Wellfleet, Massachusetts, and watch at first hand young Ivan and Peter grow up.

After we had eaten ravenously at the cocktail party, our small group, with no need of dinner and led by Noguchi, spent most of the night at a Noh theater. During the week, Jeanne Reynal, who was then living in San Francisco and had dyed her hair bright purple, piloted us to all the best and most unlikely haunts. During those days, I was repeatedly puzzled by Gorky's silence and his lethargic depression. Perhaps there had been a flirtation on Noguchi's part with Agnes Magruder, but I sensed something deeper between the two men. Gorky was hostile and hurt, Noguchi blithely untroubled. I think they were in competition not as artists but as personalities. Gorky felt almost superfluous; Noguchi shone.

Many years later when I was visiting Isamu in Japan, he spoke at some length of Gorky. He told me he was still burdened by a sense of guilt. Toward the end of Gorky's life when he was ill, bereft, and very disturbed psychologically, he often "came banging" on Noguchi's door. Isamu would try to quiet and reassure him, but finally one night when a friend was staying with him, the pounding came very late after they had retired. The door was not opened — and it was that night Gorky hanged himself.

My friendship with Isamu antedated San Francisco. A few months after I opened my gallery, I took on consignment a group of works from the John Becker Gallery, which had recently closed in New York. In the collection I inherited was a terra-cotta sculpture that Noguchi had made during a visit to Japan. I sold the lower part of this composite piece, called *The Queen* (1931), to Claire Zeisler. Claire, who later became a distinguished artist in her own right, was a budding collector with a brave eye. For the first year or two that I was in business, she was almost my only client.

Two of Noguchi's studios made indelible impressions on me. One was in Long Island City, located in an old factory building he used as a sculpture studio. He had invited me for dinner, and I was surprised to enter the discarded industrial building and find in its voluminous interior various works in progress, plus a small Japanese house that the artist and some of his friends had built without the help of even one nail, or so Isamu told me. Visiting that hidden house where no noise from the city obtruded gave one a sense of seclusion, and Noguchi, a small man of great physical beauty, fitted it to a *T*. He seemed to relax, expand, and belong there, to relinquish the tensions that usually drove him. From my point of view, the house was no less a work of art than many of the stone and metal sculptures nearby. This artist always created his own environment.

I also remember his studio and house in Mure on the island of Shikoku. I visited him there in 1973. Mure was then a small village given over entirely to stone carving, which had attracted Noguchi in the first place. Here he was able to find excellent assistants, and here, except to three or four people who knew him, he was just another stone carver and not an internationally famous artist. There was no sign of those hordes of tourists, both native and foreign, who were about to swamp Japan. Even at that time, Isamu, who was an admirer of and admittedly influenced by the temples of Kyoto and Nara, confessed he had given up visiting them because of the organized onslaught of Japanese schoolchildren led in swarms by guides with megaphones and identifying banners. I can vouch from experience that under such circumstances the contemplative meaning of any Buddhist temple is irretrievably lost. Friends who visited Noguchi's studio just before his death tell me that Takamatsu, the nearest large town, is now growing so greedily that its outskirts are about to invade Mure. But when I was there, the surroundings of that village were one of the few landscapes I saw that still retained the poetry of early Japanese prints.

Across the road from his outdoor studio, which at that time was entirely *en plein air* except for a small shed, Noguchi had a very beautiful seventeenth-century house that one of his Japanese associates had moved section by section from another village. Originally the home of a samurai, it was reassembled with loving attention and unobtrusive modernization. The house has a wonderful privacy, cloistered from the outside world by small gardens and massive stone walls. Similar walls protect the studio across the road, but there the large irregular slabs of unpolished rock have been deftly fitted together into a circular druid construction that as a work of art itself becomes an excellent foil for Noguchi's sculpture.

Life in that house, with the exception of breakfast, which often could be Western, was Japanese. Isamu explained that he had taught

The work yard at Noguchi's studio in Mure, on the island of Shikoku, Japan, c. 1970. Photograph by Michio Noguchi.

his excellent native cook to make bacon and eggs American-style, but that was his only concession to his divided birthright. And divided it remained until his death. He was never able to sort out amicably his two warring selves — his Western half from a devoted American mother and his Japanese debt to his famous father, the poet Yone Noguchi. To make matters more difficult, his parents never married and his father, who had a large Japanese family, refused until almost too late to acknowledge openly his relationship to his half-American son. Isamu talked quietly about his problems of identity, and always with some anguish. I was touched that after his father's death he concentrated on publicly memorializing him with his own sculpture, but as the years passed, he began to compete with Yone Noguchi's reputation. The poet had been elevated during his life to the lofty hierarchy of National Treasure and, though father and son were often acutely divided politically, Isamu, always an outspoken liberal, yearned for the same recognition. The last time I saw him in New York, he confided that he had just learned that the honor would not be long in coming. To this day I don't know or care about the outcome. What always saddened me was how much emotion Isamu invested in his climb to national recognition, not in one country but in two. His Japanese home and his persistent pursuit of his father were, as he well recognized, keystones to recovering his roots.

One evening in Mure, while we were drinking sake in his living room, Isamu said, "When I'm in Japan, I think I should be in the United States, and when I'm there I want to be back in Japan." But from what I observed, it was Japan that exerted the stronger pull, and to this his art bears witness. I asked him at that time if he followed any accepted religion. He thought a while and then said, "No, but if I did, it would be Shinto. You only need to look at my lamps to understand that. They are completely Shinto." I was surprised only because his work is so often categorized as Zen. But Shinto and its spontaneous life-fulfilling relationship with nature were what he identified with. Even when he was manipulating nature to conform to his personal wishes, Noguchi's love affair with the natural world never abated, which may explain his passion for unadorned rocks. He found boulders and weathered stones irresistible. When he finished work late in the afternoon, we climbed the hills — elevated to "mountains" in Japan — behind Mure, while he assiduously examined every rock in the hope of finding the precise one for his next sculpture. His courtyard studio was crowded with candidates. For him stone symbolized the unyielding strength of nature, and though he hoped to mold both stone and nature to his will, he well knew what he was up against. As he grew older he left most of the raw stone untouched, content to alter form, surface, and shape to a minimum.

Without Mure, Noguchi's greatest stone carvings might never have existed. Here in his outdoor studio before bulldozers reconfigured the landscape, he worked on a succession of single and occasionally composite stone sculptures. Influenced by Japan itself and the temporary security of his samurai home, he concentrated on works of restrained majesty.

At times Noguchi experimented with American technology, but never with the same conviction he brought to his major stone works. Although it was his public art, his gardens, playgrounds, and commissioned plazas, that he seemed to prize inordinately, I have always preferred his single carvings. The gardens, with their philosophic symbolism, have never seemed quite at home in the UNESCO headquarters in Paris or in the United States, where there are several. Climate, noise, and overactive surroundings not conducive to meditation all act as roadblocks. Similarly, the monuments that evolved from modern technology are too overpowering, too lacking in the subtleties that set a Noguchi sculpture apart from any other. Singularly disappointing are the public sculptures made from industrial sewer pipes — they are ingenious but so heavy-handed as to obliterate any trace of Noguchi. He cherished privacy as a person, and private too was the best of his art. It has always been a riddle to me as why this inner-driven artist laid such store by public projects that demanded constant subjugation to the will of architects and designers. Once he did tell me that some of his worst frustrations resulted from bruising encounters in just such situations.

After I had been in New York just a few months and was still quite lonely, Noguchi picked me up one evening and took me to his studio in a building near or next to Carnegie Hall. He wanted to show me a sculpture he had just finished, a balsa wood carving called *The Cry*. The immediate impact of that taller than seven-foot work was startling. I was afraid that if I so much as moved, it would capitulate. Its "ephemeral lightness," two words Noguchi used to describe similar but later sculpture, only partly evoke the taut relationship of its two attached parts. Their interaction is what gives the piece its sense of perilous instability. Later, cast in bronze, it lost much of its illusion, but fortunately the original wood version was acquired by the Guggenheim Museum. It is Noguchi at his best — introspective, secret, and enigmatic. *The Cry* is curiously silent; only the viewer is tempted to gasp. This artist was beguiled by metaphor and meaning, whether his work was carved out of stone or conceived in more fragile materials.

Black Sun, strategically framing Seattle as one leaves that city's art museum, is another mesmerizing sculpture. The dark stone wheel, adroitly shaped to be looked through and around from every possible angle, becomes part of the landscape, its emotive variations recalling Brancusi, Isamu's early mentor. Oriented to its surrounding world, the sculpture dominates only because it synthesizes.

Noguchi was a sculptor first and foremost, but he designed furniture and dance sets and wrote with lyric skill. His autobiography, *Isamu Noguchi: A Sculptor's World,* published in 1968, should be read between the lines. What he omits is frequently as challenging as what he elects to confide. Far from being an autobiography of the artist's life or a personal investigation, the book is an autobiography only of Noguchi's work. Originally John Becker, his former New York dealer, was engaged to write Noguchi's biography with the artist's cooperation. One day Isamu appeared at my apartment with an early portion of the book, which he wanted me to read. He claimed it was "too coy, too simplistic." Because Becker was an old friend of mine (we both were Chicagoans), Isamu hoped that I'd help him escape from the agreement, but I emphatically declined. He anguished over the problem until he finally solved it by deciding to write it himself as an autobiography. In the foreword, Buckminster Fuller observed, "Isamu has always been inherently at home — everywhere." I wonder if he felt at home anywhere. He loved India, had many friends there, and repeatedly visited the country, but never settled there. When I met him in

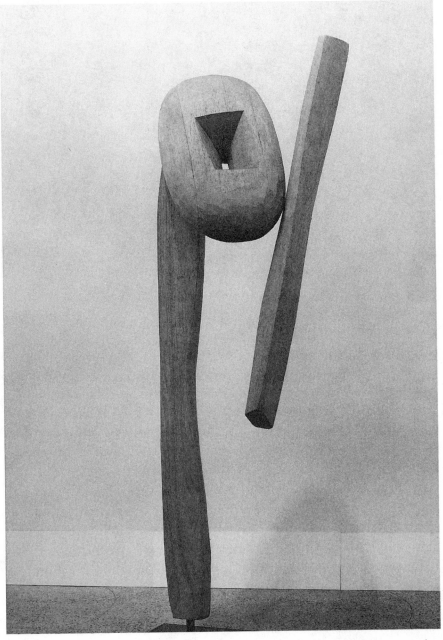

Isamu Noguchi, *The Cry*, 1959. Noguchi was at his best with stone and wood, the media he embraced as the most sympathetic to sculpture. The elegant verticality and weightlessness of *The Cry* suggest that Brancusi still influenced his thinking.

Black Sun in the process of being made, Mure, 1969.
Photograph by Michio Noguchi.

San Francisco with Gorky, he had decided to leave New York and permanently establish himself in California, but less than a year later he moved again. He was constantly in Europe, especially Italy and Paris, but he never seemed anchored to one place. The whole world was his domain but no one part of it, not even Mure, became his true "home."

Noguchi expressed himself in fluent, restrained prose superior to that of any of his critics, and in 1987, after he had opened the museum in Long Island City, he published a catalogue carefully written by him — and, for my money, the best such work I have encountered in a catalogue-clogged life. In pure, uncluttered English he tells how and why each work was conceived. No pretentious terminology mars this candid examination of his sculpture. Each word counts; there is not a superfluous one. To me, it makes other art catalogues seem heavy-handed and submerged in technicalities. This one I read from cover to cover at one sitting, engrossed by both content and method.

The stage sets and costumes for Martha Graham led to a long and close friendship. Isamu admired her extravagantly and though he was unknown when he started working for her, she quickly recognized his potential. He took his designs for her very seriously and considered them important works of art. Thus it was not surprising when he wanted the originals for his museum. He offered to have them duplicated so that Graham could release the original sets, but she refused. Legally, of course, she had no problem. Despite having paid only a pittance, she owned them, and, to be sure, she was as poor as he when she commissioned most of them. Isamu was hurt, certain that as a friend and fellow artist, she would understand, but she too viewed these works as part of her own creativity. After all, it was her choreography that had sparked them in the first place. Eventually some compromises were made and the old friendship was resumed well before Isamu died. But the fine point that the dispute raised was never resolved.

Another controversy involved my friendship with Isamu and recalls much about a certain era in American life. It occurred during the presidency of Lyndon Johnson at the height of the Vietnam debate. Somebody at the White House decided that a day devoted to artists, writers, and peripheral personalities in the art world would enhance the president's status and perhaps at least slightly reduce public antagonism toward him. It was all pretty transparent, and I for one refused to go. So did several others, including Robert Lowell and Stanley Kunitz. Noguchi, on the other hand, was going and became annoyed with me. He wanted us all to attend and then wreck the event with an angry demonstration, but I felt that to accept the invitation in the first place conferred an obligation to behave politely. I understand that Noguchi did attempt to sabotage the party, but because too few people followed him, the rebellion never became more than a tepid flurry. To this day, I'm not sure which of us was right, because for him the Vietnam War brought back memories of World War II and our government's attitude toward Japanese-Americans. About this time a deep-seated rage never ceased to torment Noguchi. He once said to me that his marriage to the Japanese movie actress Yoshiko (Shirley) Yamaguchi was terminated mainly because of bureaucratic problems with the United States government. Yet when I tried to untangle the facts, he became evasive.

The breakup of his marriage to the popular actress represented a

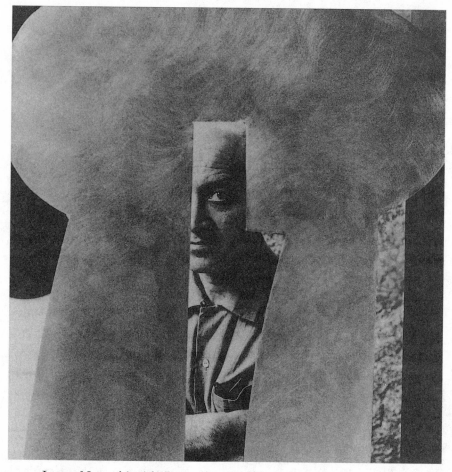

Isamu Noguchi with *Lunar,* late 1960s. Acutely conscious of his contradictions, Noguchi peers through a void, one part of his face divided from the other. Photograph by Vytas Valaitis.

defeat he was never willing to accept or perhaps fully able to understand. Wherever he went, he found interesting women. He told me once he'd had a brief affair in Mexico with Frida Kahlo. I knew Frida myself, and I asked him if he found her beautiful. His response was, "I only make love to beautiful women." Even when he was in his eighties he was still constantly traveling, a man lithe of step and totally involved in plans for the future, although to my mind he pushed himself into spending too much time on socializing in order to get his museum off the ground. He often complained to me about the endless dinner parties that he felt he had to attend.

The very fact that Noguchi was riven by his American and Japanese roots, torn between his ambivalence about and need of both heritages, made his struggle to enter history an even more demanding preoccupation. Only thus could he finally achieve a stable resting place. Otherwise he was a man torn between two countries, two ways of life, two kinds of art — public and intensely private, between abstract sculpture, theater design, and mass-produced objects, like lamps and tables. Ultimately I think of him as supremely civilized but searching for final answers that never ceased to baffle him. A photograph in *A Sculptor's World* shows Noguchi peering through an angular void in one of his stone carvings, his face divided as part of it looks for the other half.

12
Mark Tobey in Basel

I don't remember how I met Mark Tobey, but it was most likely through Marian Willard, whose gallery handled his work. We were certainly warm friends by the time I gave him a solo show at the Art Institute in 1955. An artist never fully appreciated in his own country, he eventually moved to Europe, settling in Basel in 1960 after a footloose life. He claimed, at least to me, that he'd left America because of exorbitant taxes; he saw himself as a helpless victim of the Internal Revenue Service. But I think he exiled himself to Switzerland to be nearer to a European audience which he found more perceptive than the one at home. He was the first American artist since Whistler to have been honored with an exhibition at the Louvre.

Tobey's paintings are distillations of energy, mass, and movement relying less on tangible models than on memory and associative interplay. They combine an almost metaphysical philosophy with an invented technique he called "white writing," which is based on linear webs connecting innumerable minute and often interlocking forms.

Mark Tobey in Seattle, August 1961. Photograph © Johsel Namkung.

Although his paintings are abstract and usually multileveled, they are also investigations of modern life. No one has caught better the luminosity of an American city at night, its myriad lights and amorphous speed. At one time Tobey lived in Japan in a Zen monastery, and for the viewer who is able to "read" his "writing," a complex world of East and West emerges. As for the white writing, it was more a metaphor than a system, but it always embraced a broken surface that produced its own ambience.

Though a loner, Tobey could be a sympathetic if idiosyncratic companion. We used to go to the movies together. Animals of all kinds interested him, especially untamed ones, and he loved films about wildlife. I remember a B movie we sat through twice, because he fell in love with the animals photographed in the African jungle. Riveted by their grace and oblivious to the banal plot, he opted to see it a third time, but I demurred.

His house in Basel was a four-story building on a respectable bourgeois street. I can barely describe the disorder within; I couldn't believe it. At first I thought a disaster had struck, but not at all: this was the way Tobey lived. A man of unmatched sensitivity, he was surrounded by incredible squalor. Under beds collecting dust were hundreds of little watercolors and drawings; more could be seen among and behind the cushions of chairs and sofas. One room was filled halfway to the ceiling with letters that had never been opened. There were files with papers hanging out at all angles, there were open suitcases still unpacked since Tobey's last trip. Behind a grand piano, all kinds of odds and ends, including pictures, were stashed helter-skelter. I was staggered by the mess, having regarded the artist as the epitome of balance and harmony. I offered to help him put a bit of order in the house, but he was implacable. "I don't want anyone organizing anything," he insisted. If it is true that an artist's environment mirrors his work, then perhaps the tempo of Tobey's shattered forms was reflected in the tangled maze at home. In each instance, however, an underlying order persisted, for he was always able to lay hands on the picture he was looking for, no matter where it was buried, and as for the paintings themselves, a basic structure prevents their dematerialized fragments from flying apart.

A strikingly beautiful man with crisply modeled features, Mark, who always seemed slightly remote, was a virtual recluse in Basel. He rarely left that tumultuous house, emerging perhaps on Sunday evenings to eat supper in the railway station restaurant with Mark Ritter, the companion who lived with him and looked after him selflessly. When Tobey's good friend, the painter Charmion von Wiegand, stayed with him, she was amused and flattered by his working habits. No sooner did she return from a walk or shopping expedition than he waylaid her, persuading her to discuss each brushstroke he'd applied since she'd left the house. "Shall we strengthen the left side? What about shifting this area? Should we make this stronger?" he would question conspiratorially. He was lonely for the fellowship of artists. Basel was scarcely a center of bohemia, but I'm convinced he chose to live there because it was isolated.

The last time I saw Mark was in 1970. I visited him in Switzerland on a beautiful October weekend, and he took me to the Basel Kunstmuseum. We walked there along a wide avenue where people were strolling in their Sunday best. Mark spied a small lame bird fluttering on the sidewalk, and with some difficulty (he was no longer young), sat down and began stroking it. Here, suddenly, was this portly bearded man, legs folded under him, nursing a little bird. At first the creature was frightened, but Tobey talked to it and soothed it. He sat on the sidewalk, so nicely and neatly dressed that the proper Swiss passersby enjoying their Sunday constitutionals thought him completely mad. No less moved by the beauty of the bird's translucent feathers than by its plight, he searched for a safe hiding place under a nearby tree and gently deposited his charge there. It was gone when we returned from the museum.

On our arrival there, Mark suggested that we visit the contemporary American section, hoping, he said, that I wouldn't "find him egomaniacal." I already knew that the Kunstmuseum had bought one of his most important recent paintings. On our way to the gallery, we passed a temporary exhibition of Josef Beuys, then a little-known avant-garde artist. Previously I'd seen his work only a few times, so when Tobey asked what I thought of it, I knew too little to have an opinion. "I don't understand it at all," he said. "Maybe I'm too old." Then he added, "Because, you see, I've never been interested in anti-art."

In the large room of contemporary American paintings there were superb paintings by Pollock, Rothko, and Kline, but the overwhelming presence in that gallery was the canvas by Tobey. Entitled *Sagittarius Red* and measuring 83½ by 152¾ inches, this large composition is carried out with the same meticulous transparencies and overlays that distinguish his smaller works. I don't see how he did it; the sheer size was antipathetic to his exacting inch-by-inch technique of applying layer upon layer of pigment. He was convinced that only in this way could he control every nuance of his painting. He worked on it for years, he told me, using a ladder-like adjustable platform. To me, it is his masterpiece.

Tobey was upset because the museum had not made a postcard reproduction of the painting to be sold at the door, which it often did with outstanding objects in the collection. Obviously this large, complicated, and fugitive composition would have lost much of its meaning if it were reduced to postcard size. I was touched that he thought in such elementary terms, and though he knew his own value, he worried that others did not. We sat down on a bench and soon a young man came in who was maybe nineteen or twenty. With his long hair and frayed jeans, he was a typical American art student of the 1970s. Galvanized by Tobey's painting, he kept repeating, "Terrific, God, terrific!" Then he sat down next to me and continued emoting. Mark listened to every word, yet never revealed who he was. I couldn't help feeling how much the boy would have enjoyed talking with him, but Mark preferred to remain incognito. His privacy came first, and his paintings are also curiously private. They are small messages to be "read" in seclusion.

We moved on to one of Mark's favorite galleries, the one containing the Kunstmuseum's extraordinary collection of Holbeins. Tobey seemed to prefer the drawings to the paintings; as he lifted each protective cloth from a framed sheet, he murmured, "Fantastic!" exclaiming about them with the same delight that the boy had brought to his own canvas. His favorite oil by Holbein was the down-to-earth group portrait of the artist's wife and children. It is curious that Tobey, who avoided the human figure in much of his work, was often seduced by it elsewhere.

Nearby was an entire room filled with a procession of Paul Klees. "You can't just look at Klees," he said. "They must be absorbed on multiple levels." For Tobey, Klee's work needed to be studied slowly, savored, and read. He, of course, wanted his own paintings read; he never conceived of them as related to walls. Influenced by Klee, at least in spirit, Tobey realized that for both of them walls could be barriers.

Although I'd been to the museum before, I'd forgotten how overwhelming a special section devoted to Picasso's early Cubist works was. A trifle apologetically Tobey admitted, "I've never been crazy about that fellow." But in the Braque room, he said, "This is the painter who appeals to me." Tobey disliked aggressive art, and he may have felt an affinity with Braque. Both men were discreet, low-keyed, and enamored of a certain Gallic aestheticism alien to the blunter voices of today.

Tobey's art preferences could give off conflicting signals, for though he was often repelled by fiery expressionism, a painter he esteemed most highly was Grünewald, a master of turbulent emotions.

He made frequent pilgrimages to Colmar to see the Isenheim Altarpiece. "When I look at Grünewald's *Crucifixion*," he once told me, "the sky grows darker, the Christ is never quite dead and the terrible anguish of the Magdalene with her soft white wringing hands — this for me is experiencing content in painting." In the Isenheim Altarpiece Tobey extrapolated something kindred to his own fervent celebration of light as a source of inner revelation.

One time when I was in New York during the early 1950s, Tobey took me to Lyonel Feininger's apartment on East 22nd Street. The two men were close friends who traded works and wrote forewords to each other's catalogues. In the small entrance hall, I spotted *City Radiance* (1944), a splendid example of white writing, and Tobey later told me that he was happy that this tempera belonged to a painter who often grappled with the same ephemeral theme: the magical light of a modern metropolis.

Feininger and Tobey shared similar attitudes toward art, saying that it was closer to poetry than prose. Both men were passionate about classical music. Once Mark had established a permanent home, he bought a grand piano and began taking music lessons and practicing seriously. Tobey looked on Feininger, who was the older of the two, as family, and the two men corresponded for years. Tobey may have found it easier to write than talk to him. Feininger had grown deaf, and at times his responsive face seemed baffled. He appeared to me always to be listening.

Though Tobey was never a "best-seller," he was an essential influence on twentieth-century American art. Even Jackson Pollock took note of his vision: in the mid-1940s, he expressed his regard for Tobey as a real painter. Tobey's approach was never limited to a single center of interest — with him there were no beginnings, no ends, no final destinations, but an all-over view of a fractured world where size was less important than degree. The painting in the Basel museum, for all its heroic dimensions, remains an intimate portrait of disintegration and re-creation. Pollock's work dealt with the same modern symbols, but with far more abandon. When a small canvas by Tobey is photographically enlarged, the similarity is striking. Yet on close examination, the kinship dwindles. Tobey's work is not related to Abstract Expression-

Mark Tobey and Lyonel Feininger, 1954. The artist Charles Seliger became
a close friend of Mark Tobey. He took the only photographs ever made
of Tobey and Feininger together, this one recorded in Stockbridge,
Massachusetts. Photograph by Charles Seliger.

ism, despite the occasional resemblance to it. His method, no matter
how inventive, was never the final message; it was merely an indispensable tool.

Because Tobey could endow the most casual occasion with special meaning, one tends to look back nostalgically on brief outings with
him. During a weekend at Marian Willard and Dan Johnson's place on
Long Island, several of us went walking on the beach. For Tobey it
was a random saunter of discovery. Every small object caught his eye,
every tiny twig, shell, bit of broken glass. He picked up a sliver of
abandoned wood, sat down on a log, and with his fountain pen ten-
derly transformed its notches and grooves into a rhythmic small Tobey
that he gave me and which I still prize. In his own way he left his personal stamp on everything he touched.

The only member of the New York School that Tobey really

Mark Tobey, *Edge of August*, 1953. This work was a source of Katharine's enduring fury toward the Art Institute's board of trustees. They decided against buying *Edge of August* on the flip of a coin.

admired was Mark Rothko, although perhaps more as a personality than as a painter. He didn't know Rothko well — they met chiefly at my house — but he respected his thinking. Both men repudiated "the Renaissance sense of space and order," as Tobey put it. And, to quote Tobey again, both men agreed that "painting should come through the avenues of meditation rather than the canals of action." Each claimed that his work, if not strictly religious, was related to realms of the spirit and conceived as contemplative experiences.

They operated on somewhat the same wavelength, though two people could scarcely have been more dissimilar. Rothko respected Tobey as an artist and enjoyed being with him, but their friendship always remained somewhat impromptu. During the 1960s when Tobey was in New York from time to time and came to see me, he would suggest that I ask "the other Mark" to join us. On such occasions the two men chiefly discussed art, and their talk included generous doses of gossip about the then-current art scene. They seemed strangely attuned to each other, particularly compatible in their disillusionments and aversions. They were both masters at demolishing an art world that held them in a similar love-hate bondage.

Rothko, younger by thirteen years, was endowed with robust appetites for food, drink, and women. Like his paintings, he was a large and enveloping personality but, unlike his paintings, he was strangely awkward and unkempt. Tobey was more than cautious when food and drink were concerned, he preferred men, and his quiet good manners protected an innate reserve. He was the observer, Rothko the activist. Tobey required solitude, whereas Rothko was a partygoer who needed people for reassurance. Both men were singularly articulate. They were able to communicate with each other, not always freely, but with considerable gusto. Their own work they rarely discussed; it was more the state of art and its corrupting antennae that engrossed them.

Counter to Rothko's preference for large canvases, Tobey's endearing habit of carrying many of his favorite paintings around with him in a suitcase was proof of how minutely he tended to work. He remains one of the few American artists who is able to encompass big ideas in surprisingly small dimensions. Like Klee, he tended to condense and distill his images, sometimes defining the energy of entire cities within a compass of a few inches. Once on a steamer en route to Europe, Charmion von Wiegand ran into him pacing the deck during a severe storm. He said to her, "Do you realize that if this ship goes down, most of my best work goes with it?" Compressing vast horizons, both visual and hypothetical, into modest areas, he depended on multiple and at times magical overlays of color and calligraphy to project an ever-shifting world. His diminutive works, based on the suggestion of unending boundaries, stretch uncurbed in all directions. Often of mixed media, they are less concerned with nature per se than with nature filtered through a subjective poetry.

When Tobey visited me, he always brought the suitcase, and as soon as he arrived we'd clear a large table and cover it with an array of dazzling small works. This traveling exhibition was a never-ending source of joy for both of us. He always watched my reactions intently and, with a showman's instinct, he kept the best, most fully achieved works for the last. I remember only one time when he shared the experience with Rothko, who studied each painting, occasionally murmuring a few words I couldn't catch. Finally he made no pronouncement whatsoever. The work may not have moved him, but he always spoke of Tobey with deference and told me several times that he considered him "an authentic artist," the highest accolade Rothko could give.

Tobey's paintings always indirectly reflected his personal interests. He embraced Baha'i doctrines at the age of twenty-eight and remained a disciple for the rest of his life. It permeated his thinking and his conversation, which was an unexpected mixture of Asian mysticism and Midwest American pragmatism. He told me that he was attracted by the Baha'i notion of the oneness of humankind, symbolized by the religion's nine-sided temples that are always unified at a central core. Tobey constantly referred to these ideas, relating them specifically to his paintings. This religion, free from all rigid dogma, encompassed more than aesthetics; it preached a utopian one-world philosophy that was close to his art. Several times when he visited Chicago, we drove to Wilmette to see a Baha'i temple located on the shore of Lake Michigan. He liked the idea of its multiple entrances, each a key to diversity but all eventually leading to the same destination.

For many of the years when I first knew Tobey, he was usually accompanied by Pehr Hallsten, an elderly Swedish-American whom he looked after with inexplicable tenderness. Pehr was rude, querulous, and impatient. From almost every point of view, he was a trial, if not for Mark, then certainly for his friends. I can remember endless occasions when the artist gave up his own long-anticipated plans in order to indulge some childish whim of Pehr's. When the two men visited me at the Art Institute, Mark usually wanted to see our new acquisitions, but no sooner did we get started than Pehr would demand to go shopping. He loved to spend money, and he whined until Tobey gave in. Mark explained that for some reason he was only attracted to old men and, if his relationship with Pehr was any indication, he must have stored up an overdose of love for this variety. The two men met on the docks of Seattle, where Pehr, who had worked on boats, was a penniless alcoholic out of a job. Mark took him in, and fed, clothed, and catered to him until his death. Then Mark was inconsolable. Even when I visited him in Basel, he still spoke of Pehr with nostalgia and gave me a primitive print that Pehr had made after what must have been considerable instruction by Tobey. He treated Pehr's work with far more solicitude than he accorded his own.

In Basel, Tobey was convinced that some of his smaller works were being stolen. He insisted that the culprit was the postman, one of the few townspeople who came to the house. It never occurred to Mark that the disorder made it impossible to find anything. How his fleeting watercolors ever survived is a miracle, doubly so because for many years he was constantly moving from place to place with no permanent studio. He painted in hotel rooms, in the houses of friends he was visiting, anywhere he found himself, which may explain why he often carried his work around with him and why he preferred small dimensions. Only when he settled in Basel, in a place with a proper studio, did he feel free to tackle a painting of heroic size, though fundamentally he never conceded that size had anything to do with the quality of a work of art.

Tobey was a man of unpredictable oppositions. He deplored the machine and everything it stood for, viewing it as an arbiter of death. He denounced the automobile and refused to fly, traveling to New York from Europe by steamer. On board, he reveled in all the shipboard amenities, from bouillon at eleven and long walks on deck to dressing for dinner and the daily bridge game. Yet he painted several (I know of two) compositions devoted to flying, how it looked and how it felt. One of these, *Above the Earth,* I acquired for the Art Institute in 1953. It condenses sensations of speed and space with almost supernatural forces. Another anomaly: Mark was neurotic about his health. He specialized in small problems that he never failed to describe in detail, but according to Marian Willard, when it was time to die, he stoically refused to eat, turned his face to the wall, and quietly waited.

13
A Day with Franz Kline

It was a heady spring morning when I arrived at Franz Kline's studio on West 14th Street. I believe the year was 1961. The place, buried in a sea of paintings, fairly exploded with raw power. But there was also a curious mystery about those canvases swathed in dark rivers of pigment that opened up only to close again. One moment the paintings seemed as clear and artless as translucent water, the next they were obscure, hidden, unreachable. Expecting to stay only an hour or two, I had gone there to check a few points of an earlier conversation for an article I was working on. Somehow my visit gradually took over the entire day, a day marked by casual activities and random conversations, all of which so typified Franz's offhand, yet wise acceptance of life that the day resembled a virtual microcosm of his world. A maverick if only because he was able to see himself and his work objectively, he was also a very special man — giving, kind, and full of love, but surprisingly elusive, too.

Kline was not in the habit of verbalizing about himself or his paintings: knotty aesthetic explanations he found suspect. He approached art head-on, accepting his work as a natural extension of himself. Always the great debunker, he viewed the creative process as a normal activity and not a privileged or esoteric one. Though I had known him for some time before this visit, I had never heard him discuss his work so freely. Very likely because the day was unplanned, he felt no pressure as he drifted carelessly from one idea to another.

Unlike most of his colleagues in the New York School, Franz was untroubled by a consuming ego. He gave little thought to promoting himself, choosing to roll with the waves. In fact, he is the only artist who has ever told me that he considered his work dispensable. On that spring day in his studio I was alarmed to notice a recent canvas already in perilous condition. The paint was lifting and the picture needed immediate restoration. "It's expendable," he said, "and so am I." Franz was fifty at the time. A year later he was to die. Despite periodic mild heart symptoms, he lived debonairly without regard to the fine points of self-preservation. Endearingly unpretentious, he rarely surrounded himself with the paraphernalia of public life or fame, though his reputation was already firmly established in both America and abroad. He enjoyed the act of painting, and for him that was enough.

Before I'd been at the studio an hour, Franz suggested that we have a drink, and he forthwith started on a diet of beer interspersed with shots of whiskey, a combination he recognized as dynamite. Because he believed in living for the moment — as in a sense he painted — caution and restraint were not for him. Now was what mattered. We sat across from each other on two straight-backed benches with a small table wedged between us, a bit like a booth in a bar or corner drugstore. As the day wore on, Franz talked intermittently about his work and elliptically about his life. He was well aware that his health could become a problem, but he made it clear that his chief interest was to live fully rather than carefully. "If a painting doesn't work, throw it out," he advised, and I think he felt much the same about his body.

There were several fine smaller canvases in the studio, but many more large ones, for Kline had discovered that the expansive dimensions made for a greater challenge. "I think you confront yourself much more with a big canvas. I don't exactly know why," he told me. For him any unnecessary confinement was anathema. He needed a large area where he could let himself go, where he could indeed "confront" himself. Much of the work in the studio was limited to his familiar black and white palette, but a few paintings showed traces of color — unexpected pinks, strong greens, blues, and dark reds. He had only recently started playing with color, yet it appeared to me that this addition was more an afterthought than an organic necessity. He approached color rather diffidently, set on proving to himself that it presented no insurmountable obstacles. "In using color I never feel I want to add to or decorate a black and white painting," he said. During the following year, which was to be the last he was able to work with total concentration, he slowly began to find a way to integrate color into the structure of his painting. He died too soon to go beyond that, but I have always wondered whether, given enough time, he might not have turned color relationships into a language of his own as he had done so eloquently with black and white.

Occasionally he got up to unstack a hidden canvas or two. I remember asking him why critics often related his work to Oriental calligraphy. "Calligraphy is writing," he answered, "and I'm not writing." He also said, "The Oriental idea of space is an infinite space. It is not painted space, and ours is." He made it clear that his paintings had nothing to do with black signs on white canvases; his white areas were as important as his black ones, and he frequently painted out the black with white or vice versa. At times he worked with such burning speed that he dashed on new paint before the underlayer had dried, which, of course, partly explains why certain canvases were apt to disintegrate prematurely. Before his work became successful, expensive artist's pigments were out of the question, so he used commercial products (often cheap enamel), which also may have brought on early surface erosion.

Franz looked on his works as "painting experiences" for himself and the viewer. He rarely identified them as separate framed objects. Once a canvas was finished, he was already champing at the bit for the next "experience." If symbolism had no part in his compositions, he admitted that sometimes imagery crept in uninvited. After all, only the most assiduous abstractionist (and he was not one) can always obliterate

Franz Kline in his studio at 242 West 14th Street, April 7, 1961.
Photograph © Fred W. McDarrah.

associations. "I don't decide in advance that I'm going to paint a definite experience, but in the act of painting, it becomes a genuine experience for me," he explained. Kline claimed that he never "painted a given object like a figure or a table" — he painted "an organization that became a painting." He avoided direct imagery because he felt freer without it, though earlier, after an academic art education in London, he had relied on both the object and the figure while also developing a respect for skilled draftsmanship. His youthful training may account for the potency of his abstract compositions, which often seem buttressed by the sinews and muscles of underlying supports.

Repeatedly that day Franz enlarged on his unorthodox preference for subtracting rather than adding as he worked on a canvas. While describing how he often started a painting and "then painted it out so that it became another painting or nothing at all," he applauded the idea of impermanence. He valued the freedom of following his intuition and hand wherever they led. For Kline, the idea of operating in reverse provided a quixotic twist that gave an added fillip to the final outcome of a canvas. And his technique of spontaneous trial and error responded sympathetically to oil paint, which permits frequent alterations. On the other hand, he sometimes made preliminary drawings for works that were deliberately planned in advance and carried out in detail. I have no doubt, though, that Franz preferred to paint directly as his immediate emotions dictated. Several large paintings stacked against a wall of the studio were unfinished, and these, he observed, were a group he was working on at the moment, going from one to another as the spirit moved him. He liked fluid pigment and a fluid life. Working on different canvases at the same time gave him and the paintings greater flexibility.

When he depended on sketches, he never merely enlarged them into finished compositions but conceived of each sketch as a separate area in a given painting, modifying the drawings and then incorporating them in a composite work. The most celebrated example to come out of innumerable preparatory sketches was a mural-like painting memorable for its remarkable breadth and seeming spontaneity that, considering the method used, was deceptive. *New Year Wall: Night,* now in the Bayerische Staatsgemaldesammlungen in Munich, was so called because it was executed on a studio wall made of homosote at the beginning of the new year of 1960. Its dark, burgeoning tonalities, like those of many other Klines, arouse nebulous atavistic memories of nocturnal encounters. Franz often relied on impulse, but he was aware that "what goes into a painting isn't just done while you're painting." Even his process of subtracting and adding by painting out strategic areas is convincing evidence that for him trial and error was also a judicial process that could require both time and analysis.

At some point when we grew hungry, Franz produced rolls and cheese. Only a few crises induce hysteria in me, but one of them is cockroaches. A couple of them ambled out of my bread in broad daylight, and to this day I'm still proud that not even a squeak on my part interrupted our conversation. We were talking about his titles, which Kline remarked were never descriptive, but were dreamed up as addenda chiefly for purposes of identification. I remember asking him about a canvas called *Bethlehem,* which he'd finished the previous year and was still in the studio. It was named after Bethlehem, Pennsylvania, which it did not resemble. Nor was it consciously connected with steel mills or industrialization. However, because he was born and had grown up in Pennsylvania, the designation was related to his youth. And he gave several paintings the same title. "Often you've thought of, let's say, four titles, that's about as much as you can think of, so when my paintings look somewhat alike, I give them the same titles," he told me. Gradually, he increased the repertory to include Scranton, Lehigh, Shenandoah, and several other towns in his home state. He pointed to an extremely bold canvas that was named *Dahlia* (now owned by the Whitney Museum of American Art) only because he liked the sound of the word. Nothing could have been less attuned to a flower than this bald testament to power. Sometimes the artist borrowed titles from places he had recently visited, though as usual the compositions involved were not necessarily identified with the sites. Take *Ravenna* and *Turin,* both of which were painted shortly after Kline made his first and only trip to Italy. "*Palladio* [now in the Hirshhorn Museum and Sculpture Garden] was done after I'd been to the Villa Malcontenta," he told me, "but it didn't have a thing to do with Palladian architecture."

During the autumn of 1955, when I was organizing the 1956 American section of the Venice Bienniale for the Art Institute of Chicago, a meeting with Franz emphasized how unconcerned he was with thematic matters. The fact that the projected exhibition had a definite subject and was labeled "American Artists Paint the City" put me in something of a bind, especially where the work of abstract artists was concerned. Moreover, I had made up my mind that Pollock, de Kooning, and Kline must be included whether or not their paintings had anything to do with cities. At that time I was inclined to believe that all three of them were at least partially indebted to New York. At Kline's studio, then located near Third Avenue, we selected two untitled canvases. I named one *New York* and he named the other *Third Avenue,* though needless to say, the artist frankly stated that both titles were convenient afterthoughts.

De Kooning's studio was only a few rooftops away, so we crawled through some sort of trapdoor and scurried over roofs to descend there directly. This was the favorite route used by the two friends when they visited each other. Still not dry, a breathtaking new canvas was leaning against the wall. Kline, who was devoted to de Kooning and a staunch admirer of his work, had warned me in advance that I'd "flip" over the picture and I did. Nothing could have pried me loose from that radiant melange of conflicting yet interlocking currents of energy, but again I was faced with inventing a title, the work obviously not specifically related to any given subject. After a sociable drink or two, I noticed the occasional and nearly invisible traces of newsprint pressed into the pigment. According to de Kooning, this technique gave texture to the painting and at the same time amused him, so the picture was promptly baptized *Gotham News.* Whereas de Kooning was easygoing about my arbitrary naming, Jackson Pollock vehemently disapproved of any theme. "Goddamn it," he said, "what a silly idea." I called his painting *Convergence* because the word had a little something to do with city life, and he was disgusted by the expediency. The misbegotten nomenclatures are presently dignified in a number of scholarly catalogues.

Along with Kline's *New York, Gotham News* and *Convergence* quickly entered the collection of the Albright-Knox Art Gallery in

Buffalo. That adventurous donor, Seymour Knox, purchased them as soon as I selected them and then loaned the paintings back to the Biennale. He and Gordon Smith, the museum's director, scrupulously checked to see if I wanted to buy any of the pictures for Chicago. Of course, I wanted them all — they were marvelous paintings and marvelous bargains — but my trustees wouldn't back me up, even though we had no Kline or Pollock then.

Tintoretto, Goya, and Rembrandt were among Kline's heroes from the past. Each, not surprisingly, was an outstanding innovator in the mysteries of chiaroscuro. But above all he was attracted by Velázquez, by his technique and authoritative deployment of lights and darks. Franz often mentioned Earl Kerkam, a contemporary of his whom he claimed as an important voice in his own development. The two had met in 1940 when they were both broke and exhibiting their work at the Washington Square Outdoor Art Show, and in 1950, when Kerkam was evicted from his studio, Franz promptly invited him to paint at his place.

Discussions with Kerkam frequently centered on drawing, as Franz found the other man's understanding of the process not only illuminating, but liberating. Through their mutual give and take, he was able to discard academic restrictions as he headed toward less and less orthodox solutions. It wasn't a teacher-student relationship, but simply a matter of talking things over together. Kline could not figure out why his friend, who was an excellent draftsman, never "made it." It grieved Franz and puzzled him. "Could it be," he asked me, "that his work hasn't caught on because he's always been so out-and-out honest about the artists who influenced him?" Kline himself freely acknowledged the painters from the past and present who had nourished him, yet it never occurred to him that he, too, might have affected his colleagues.

I asked him that day if he considered himself a distinctly American painter. He said yes, but went a step further and limited himself to New York, which, he added, "seems to be where I belong." Just why I don't know and neither did he, though I suspect that it was the speed and incalculable potency of the city, as well as the personal and far-reaching associations with provocative artists and writers. When he first settled in Manhattan, Franz was faced with dire poverty, yet he stuck it out and eventually made New York part of himself. Even though his paintings are never direct transcriptions of urban life, they reflect, for me at least, the tensile strength and shattering collisions that are part of any great modern metropolis. When once I suggested that his paintings seemed to mirror Chicago and its kinetic sprawl more closely than New York, he agreed but decided that propinquity was irresistible at times. It wasn't just the look of New York he loved — it was its entire ambiance that gave him security.

Franz lived to enjoy less than a decade of success which, when it finally came, he accepted lightly. Except for one extravagance, material possessions meant little to him. He was a pushover for beautifully designed and often costly automobiles, not only because of their performance, but equally for their aesthetic appeal. He delighted in the feel of them, in their obedient, well-tuned response. Two other modern painters shared the same enthusiasm — Robert Delaunay and Clyfford Still. With Delaunay, fast motorcars were an obsession, and as for Still, who always viewed frugality as a norm, expensive if conservative automobiles were, to my knowledge, his sole indulgence. It is possible that the three artists, each recognized as a leader of avant-garde twentieth-century painting, were understandably attracted by the most ubiquitous icon of their age and one that was likewise a symbol of speed and power. For Franz, speed was supreme. Only lately did I learn that he collected miniature trains as a hobby, fascinated at once by their mechanisms and evocation of speed. He even named pictures after famous trains, such as *Chief* and *Cardinal*.

When I was on the verge of leaving that day, Franz asked me to stay and do a small favor for him. It seems he was thinking about buying a house for himself, his companion Betsy Zogbaum, and her young sons. One nearby on 13th Street had recently come on the market, and because Betsy was sick, he hoped I'd substitute for her and go with him to take a look. Though Franz was married to a dancer he met in London, for many years she had been in a mental hospital. He visited her regularly, but it had been lonely for him, and when he and Betsy became seriously involved, he began to look forward to a reassuring family life.

Warning me that he knew nothing about houses, he refused to believe that I was equally inexperienced. In any case, we wandered over and were warmly received by a nice lady who fed us tea and then took us through the house, which I recall as being somewhat nonconformist, with occasional rooms sprouting from unexpected junctures. I also have vague memories of children's toys underfoot and a general sense of confusion, so after a pleasant visit we escaped no wiser than when we arrived. Franz urged me to return to the studio with him. He wanted to discuss the house room by room and even worried that we had overlooked the possibility of termites, but he soon realized that I was as much at sea as he. With great relief and pragmatist that he was, he said, "Forget it. I don't think it's the house we want anyway." Later, not too long before he died, he did purchase a house, but I don't believe he was well enough to move into it.

Our foray set him to reminiscing about times in his past when poverty was all-consuming and buying anything, let alone a house, was almost out of the question. He conjured up the 1940s after the New Deal federal arts projects were scuttled and when just keeping alive was a daily battle. Any work that came his way was accepted, and now, from the security of success, he looked back, wryly describing some of those jobs. He had particularly enjoyed painting a gaudy array of burlesque queens in a mural he made for a Greenwich Village bar. Nor did he regret the nights spent in another tavern where he drew rapid likenesses for fifty cents a portrait. He hailed that experience as "good practice and a not bad way of learning to draw." For a man who liked people and liquor, a bar was never to be underestimated. He always had a favorite one in New York near wherever he happened to be living.

Franz gave me the impression of a man at peace with himself, unscarred by the guilt that burdens most of us. And since he looked at art and life with unblinking eyes, he never romanticized either. He was not childish, but occasionally childlike in his appreciation of the immediate moment, a trait that concealed an understated weariness, a hint of quiet disenchantment. Somehow he always seemed to know the score, though he was not apt to expand on it. Above all, he was never an easy man to fathom, despite his gift for open camaraderie. As a rule, he spoke little about himself, and if he had anxieties, he rarely discussed them. It was as if he regarded himself as too run-of-the-mill to be considered an engrossing subject for conversation. Superficially he projected a happy-go-lucky personality that often served to protect his privacy.

Though Franz denied direct Asian influences, he confessed to a great affection for Japanese art. I wondered if the prevalent interest in Zen had touched him. He decided it probably had. Those cavernous paintings of his, their slashing pigment unleashed with such total integration of body and intuition, incorporated certain aspects of Zen if not deliberately, then unconsciously. He knew that as he grew older his work had "become looser, freer, so that the edges were not always as clearly defined." Now the paintings seemed to originate in hidden recesses of his accumulated experience.

Four decades after Kline's death, his work is no longer as widely heralded as during the last years of his life and immediately after he died, but I have no doubt that as time goes on he will again emerge as a focal influence on mid-twentieth-century painting. How can it be otherwise? No painter of the 1950s better expressed the inordinate power of America and yet at the same time projected the future with those late ominous, impenetrable compositions. He and his paintings were always more obscure than they seemed on first encounter.

When the day was finally over and I got up to leave, Franz offered to drive me home in his new car, parked on the street near the studio. It was a handsome, low-slung convertible with the top down. On that lovely late spring afternoon while driving through Central Park, he and the automobile appeared almost indivisible.

14
Jacques Lipchitz
at the White House

When I picked up the newspaper on Memorial Day weekend in 1973 and read on the front page that Jacques Lipchitz had died in Capri on May 26, I was filled with sadness. I grieved not just because the last great Cubist was gone, but also because this internationally admired artist had been an endearing friend, a salty combination of wisdom, poetry, optimism, and unexpected naïveté. Rather than write about his art and its wide influence, I prefer to recall a little-known incident involving Lipchitz and Lyndon Johnson, in a somewhat unlikely misalliance. It was an event I participated in peripherally, only because a young White House aide happened to know me slightly.

One spring day shortly after Johnson's inauguration in 1964, I received a phone call from that young aide to the president. He was asking me to recommend an American sculptor to design a medal that was being planned for high school students of outstanding achievement. The young people, to be known euphemistically — not to say

Jacques Lipchitz, 1970. Photograph by Frank Lloyd.

pretentiously — as Presidential Scholars, were to be honored at a well-publicized White House ceremony with none other than the president himself officiating. Furthermore, the medal was envisioned as an annual award, at least during the Johnson administration, and was accordingly to be issued in a fairly large edition.

There were, however, certain stipulations. Since this was a new venture and one in which the president was closely involved, the artist had to be a recognized sculptor of importance willing to carry out the assignment without pay. Johnson wanted the work completed in record time so that the awards to the honor students would coincide with the end of their school year. In addition, one side of the medal was to glorify a thirst for knowledge, the other to feature a portrait of Lyndon Baines Johnson.

I personally disapproved of the "no pay" clause and the demanding deadline, both of which I considered severe restrictions. Why the inevitable assumption that artists provide their services gratis while government officials are recompensed for theirs? Nonetheless I called back the White House. After expressing my dissatisfaction, which, alas, was brushed off, I suggested Jacques Lipchitz as the sculptor who best met the required qualifications. Whether he would be interested was, of course, up to him. What had stumped me was the idea of a portrait, for at that time there were relatively few distinguished American sculptors interested in this field. Yet Lipchitz, celebrated as a pioneer Cubist and later as an Expressionist, had from time to time created faithful, if not always realistic, likenesses, the most memorable of which were two busts of Gertrude Stein. Moreover, here at last, I thought, was a chance for an outstanding portrait of an American president instead of the usual flaccid, flattering whitewash. A deplorable bronze head of John F. Kennedy, kneaded into doughlike globs, had only recently gone on view in a New York museum. It would seem that, along with bank and university presidents, most top politicians, no matter how strong their personalities, prefer to be remembered as benign stuffed shirts, and to be depicted the same way while alive. Do they think that the public is reassured by these bland, blank images?

When I interviewed Lipchitz in the early 1960s, he told me, "A portrait is a special thing that is not only a work of art, but also has to do with psychology. Making a portrait is like getting married — you need to be nervously connected with your sitter. Sometimes it works, sometimes it doesn't click — again, just like a marriage. I feel strongly that the real aspect of the sitter cannot be eliminated from portraiture. When I was doing Gertrude Stein's portrait (you know, she didn't like sculpture at all), we had many conflicts. The first one I did of her in 1920–21 looked like a Buddha, but later, in 1938, when I made another, she had become so shrunken that she seemed like an old rabbi."

The White House asked me to call Lipchitz and find out if he would be interested in the assignment. I did, but I also outlined my objections to him. His final decision was to take on the project as stipulated. He made only one request: that he be given no less than two hours, though not necessarily at a single sitting, with the president in order to study and sketch his subject firsthand. There was no reason, he added, for Johnson to stop working. Lipchitz merely wanted to observe him in person, which seemed reasonable enough in light of the artist's attitude toward portraiture.

I conveyed the message, and it was decided that the artist would leave for Washington the next day. Lipchitz lived in Hastings-on-Hudson, a Westchester suburb about twenty miles north of New York City, and since he didn't like flying, he planned to travel by train. I think there were several reasons why he agreed to make the medal. First, he was touched that, though born in Lithuania seventy-two years earlier and having only settled in America in 1941, he still had been chosen to represent the White House. Czarist oppression and Nazism had cruelly dislocated his life, driving him from Russia and France. Though already respected as a sculptor, he was nevertheless exhilarated by recognition from the highest official of his adopted land because coming to America had given him a new life. Lipchitz told me that he arrived in this country "from Europe when I was completely worn out. There we were constantly waiting for death. I even carried poison in my pocket at all times. But when I first saw the harbor of New York, I was transported like a bird. I was particularly lucky because I came when I was fifty — at the beginning of my maturity — and I felt injected with youth."

Lipchitz regretted that his mother was no longer alive, for he said it would have given her deep satisfaction to know he had been so honored. He always credited her as a persuasive force in clearing the way for him to becoming an artist; his father had wanted him to be an engineer. Meanwhile, like any other American, he was curious about Lyndon Johnson, who as vice president had chafed uncomfortably in Kennedy's shadow after decades as an all-powerful insider on Capitol Hill. Who was this new president? What manner of man? To the ordinary public unfamiliar with the ins and outs of the Senate cloakroom, Johnson was a hidden, if not smothered, personality. Then too, Lipchitz must have felt, quite justifiably, that the project could add to his already illustrious reputation. (It is, after all, only since the Vietnam War and Watergate scandal that a connection with the White House has become more a burden than a blessing.) And last, he undertook the assignment because he was a genuinely generous person — this was only one of many instances when he graciously gave his services.

Lipchitz's method was to model a subject in clay as prelude to having it translated into marble or stone. He did not carve directly from wood or stone because, he said, ideas came to him "with [such] an unimaginable rapidity" that he had to "catch them and fix them as quickly as possible. And the technique best suited for this," Lipchitz continued, "is modeling, not the slower method of direct cutting." And so he went to Washington, wearing his ubiquitous beret and carrying with him on the train a sizable lump of damp clay wrapped in a calico cloth. With the clay he hoped to make rough sketches of the president, later to be the basis for his final portrait. Lipchitz assumed, as I did, that appointments for one or two sittings had been set up and that he would need to remain in Washington no longer than a day or two. On arrival he went immediately to the White House, but that day the president was too busy to see him. Each subsequent morning Lipchitz returned lugging the clay, which he conscientiously kept wet so that it could be used at a moment's notice, but Johnson was never available. As I recall, four or five days passed in what appeared to be an aimless runaround. Obviously the president was busy. What was doubtful, however, was whether he even knew Lipchitz *was* there and, indeed, who this artist was. It appears unbelievable that Johnson would not have found time had he realized that an internationally renowned sculptor was being asked to cool his heels while waiting to do a favor the White House itself had requested. The whole episode was turning into a kind of royal command performance with a disturbing lack of courtesy for the performer.

The artist was advised by administrative aides to wait in his hotel room until he was called: the president would try to fit him in. After a few days Lipchitz phoned me. He was upset for several reasons, but especially that he was wasting valuable time. Since he planned to leave shortly for Italy in order to supervise the casting of various works, specific dates, including his sailing, had already been arranged. In addition, he was lonely. Occasionally, it is true, he was taken out to a perfunctory lunch, and once a party was given for him at the home of Abe Fortas, the only social occasion at which he was honored. Most of the time, however, he sat in his hotel room. When he called me, I urged him to pack up and come home, which he agreed to do the next day, a Friday.

Shortly before Lipchitz was to leave for the station that day, a call came from the White House. The president would be free to see him early in the evening. Lipchitz canceled his return reservation and, carrying his omnipresent calico bundle, went to work. Johnson was occupied with a mound of official papers, but allowed the artist to set up a temporary table and embark on a clay sketch. It would be romantic to report that the two men enjoyed a warm conversation, but there was relatively little give and take. Both, immersed in their immediate tasks, were hounded by the pressures of time. Well before the agreed two hours were up, Johnson said that he had to leave and told the sculptor to return the next day if he wanted to. Lipchitz explained that he could not, because Saturday was his Sabbath.

Lipchitz returned home, his preliminary work incomplete. But he was not bitter; he was fascinated by the experience and, with his usual ebullience, forgot the days of waiting. For Lipchitz, Johnson projected an unforgettable visual presence — he found him a man of such gigantic physical dimensions as to be overwhelming. (Standing more than six feet tall, Johnson had a long nose, elephantine ears, and a midsection that spoke of a colossal appetite for food and drink.) "Everything," Lipchitz told me, "is enormous — his feet, his hands, his head, his ears — well, you know, *everything*."

The president reminded the sculptor of a powerful bull, a figure of consummate strength. And that is how he portrayed him. The portrait on the medal shows Johnson's face in profile, details eliminated and the sheer sweep of his head a manifestation of authority. The work is flawed, but it is still a serious likeness of a determined, decisive man, a potent interpretation that calls up memories of autocratic rulers. How Johnson felt about it was predictable. No better than the rest of us, he hated getting old and became ever vainer and more sensitive about his looks. If an artist told the truth about him, his stock gambit was that no likeness could do justice to his appearance. In 1967, with much fanfare, Peter Hurd was commissioned to paint the official presidential portrait. After the picture was unveiled, Johnson rejected it immediately, declaring, "That's the ugliest thing I've ever seen." Similarly, upon presentation of Lipchitz's medallion, Johnson said, "Looks like I've been dead three weeks, and maybe ought to be."

I also remember, according to certain members of the White House staff, that both Johnson and his aides were irritated because Lipchitz gave an interview to a newspaper columnist who heard he was in Washington and had gotten in touch with the sculptor. The writer and historian Eric Goldman, at the time handling cultural affairs for Johnson as the president's special advisor, suggested that it was hardly cricket to use a contact with the presidency for personal publicity. This was a somewhat ironic nicety, since a medal featuring Johnson's portrait was not exactly an act of reticence. One must ponder the double standard that in this case permitted a famous politician to exploit the opportunity for useful public exposure while denying it to a famous artist who needed exposure no less.

This small story about Lipchitz is a gloss on the bloated isolation of presidential power, but it is not for that reason that I recount it. Instead, it is on account of Lipchitz and his warm curiosity, his humanity, his emotional involvement in life, his ability to accept and savor each experience as it came along, his almost gullible trust in art and fame. The medal for Presidential Scholars will not go down in history as a major work by him, but given the difficulties he encountered, it symbolizes both his persistence and his humility. I especially remember the day he and I met at the New York foundry where the medal was

Jacques Lipchitz, *Presidential Scholars Medal,* 1964. Lipchitz's generous efforts were in inverse proportion to Johnson's appreciation of them.

being struck. Always the consummate artist and craftsman, he not only designed it, but patiently followed it through production. No chore was too menial for him. Each task, a component of his complete involvement with the casting and its finish, was an expression of his respect for art and the care he took in everything he did concerning his work and its expression in his favorite medium. Bronze, said Lipchitz, "is so alive, so direct, warm, and fluid. Each piece has my fingerprints all over it." One cannot help but wish that some of those young, well-tailored aides at the White House could have seen beyond the artist's beret and calico bundle.

15
Hans Hofmann in Provincetown

When I close my eyes I can still see the Hofmanns' house in Provincetown, buoyant with its boldly painted floors and whiter-than-chalk
walls hung with canvases by Léger, Miró, and especially Vivin. An entire sitting room was devoted to that French twentieth-century naive
artist whom Hofmann introduced to America and whose wise yet childlike scenes delighted him. In addition, numerous examples of Hofmann's own paintings provided a distilled if haphazard review of his
own work, revealing how consistently his art developed from earlier
compositions done directly from nature to later totally abstract ones.
Despite differences inevitable in any survey covering a long career, the
canvases unfolding from room to room constituted a coherently joyous progression, echoed by the house itself, which in a way was also a
work of art. Daring, unorthodox color was the keynote everywhere.
Paintings, building, and garden vibrated with it as splashes of ma-
genta, lemon yellow, green, and blue collided with each other.

On the surface at least, Hans always struck me as remarkably well adjusted, a rare phenomenon among artists of his period. He and his contemporary Edward Hopper were opposites, though they were separated by only two years in age and in the summers lived less than ten miles apart. Each man took from Cape Cod what he personally found there, or more likely what he brought with him. During the fifties and sixties, as the outstanding art patriarchs (along with Karl Knaths and Edwin Dickinson) at work on that narrow strip of land, they represented strikingly different traditions. Hopper was born in Nyack, New York, while Hofmann, who didn't settle in the United States until he was over fifty, came from Germany. In the summer Hans lived in Provincetown amid flowers, color, noise, traffic, and innumerable friends trooping in and out of his house. Hopper chose the most remote, treeless hill he could find in Truro. Here he worked in stark, isolated surroundings, the only visible color provided by the play of natural light on bare walls.

The two artists were of course acquainted, but I doubt if they ever went much beyond that. In only one way were they alike: each was a clear transcription of his own paintings, and intentionally so. Hopper insisted he concentrated on only one subject — himself — and though the main body of Hofmann's work is abstract, it nonetheless mirrors his joie de vivre, his genial presence, even his robust appearance. If Hopper's surfaces were dry, Hofmann's were juicy; where Hopper understated, Hofmann was euphoric. Hans told me, "My paintings are always images of my whole psychic makeup. You cannot deny yourself. You ask, am I painting myself? I'd be a swindler if I did otherwise."

Everything about Hans was welcoming. The minute you entered that house, you were enveloped in a wave of affection. First you walked through a radiant flower garden almost too lavish to absorb, and then into the front hall, where you were immediately assaulted by vivid primary colors covering wooden floors and a steep New England staircase. It was Hofmann's wife, Miz, who managed to transform an old Cape Cod house into an extension of both his paintings and his ebullient personality. Miz impressed me as an exemplary artist's wife, always ready to entertain her husband's friends, students, possible patrons, and even an occasional past mistress, though I must confess that some of the guests were not always stimulating. Miz put up with minor annoyances if she decided that they advanced her husband's career. Artists considerably younger than Hans, many of whom had studied with him, were frequent visitors; I rarely encountered older colleagues there. His overflowing vigor and enthusiastic espousal of the new were singularly adapted to youth. "I can't understand how anyone is able to paint without optimism," he once observed. For him the act of painting, the engagement with color, and the pursuit of light were intoxicating encounters that sustained him no less than his delight in nature.

As man and artist he was in love with life, embracing it with his whole being. Even when he was old, he looked like a fresh-cheeked,

Hans and Miz Hofmann in Provincetown, about 1951.
Photograph by Wilfrid Zogbaum.

beaming peasant, a product of soil and sun. His large, well-fed, and somewhat rotund body scarcely corresponded with the popular image of a struggling painter. Behind that rustic front, however, a sophisticated European versed in science, literature, and art history operated on several levels. Paralleling his nonobjective canvases was his ability to think abstractly. In various essays collected under the title *Search for the Real* (1948), he grappled with the metaphysical aspects of art, often in rather turgid prose. He was after certain imponderables that his ambiguous aphorisms tended to obscure. I found it more illuminating to talk informally with Hans than to read his writings.

The Hofmann house was designed for people; its capacious kitchen (decorated with a painting by Léger) and comfortable sitting rooms all opening into one another offered inviting spaces for large and small groups. One unwritten rule protected Hans from interruptions; no visitors were welcome before 5 P.M. Sometimes there were just two or three friends, sometimes overflow crowds with a liberal sprinkling of sycophants and hangers-on, for, as long as I can remember, the Hofmanns never turned anyone away. Especially conspicuous were numerous devotees of Hans, usually energetic old ladies who buzzed around him in adoring competition; there were also lonely young artists. The Hofmann largesse included them all. Before dinner, while we were having drinks, Hans would rush off to the fish market and buy vast quantities of live lobsters. Those feasts were heartwarming events that have never been duplicated for me. Every time I drive by that deserted house on Commercial Street — deserted, I always feel, because the Hofmanns are no longer there — I grieve for the riotous garden long since gone to seed.

Though Hans finally enjoyed considerable success, it came very late, which may explain why he taught for so many years. Clearly he needed the money, but there were other reasons. He was without question the foremost painting teacher in America during the forties and fifties, when he ran his own schools in New York and Provincetown. Students often followed him as he moved between his two homes. I think he loved the dual operation, though it was undeniably taxing. Once I asked him if he regretted all the time stolen from his own painting, for it was not until he was seventy-eight that he finally closed his schools. "I taught for so long," he said a bit sadly, "too long. You can teach art, but you can't make an artist." Whether he did, in fact, feel deprived because of those endless hours away from his easel is unclear. He was an inspired mentor who relied on no formula; for him each serious student represented an individual challenge, a neophyte with whom he often remained in close touch after the school relationship ended. Teaching for him was as much an art as painting and, though he gave generously to his students, he in turn received an invaluable feedback from them. He needed them.

I used to visit the school in Provincetown chiefly on days when Hans gave criticism before the entire group. Speaking in English with a strong German accent and interrupting himself repeatedly with the word *nicha* (a contraction of the German question *nicht wahr?* — not true?), he discussed each painting, no matter how unskilled, as an effort rating an honest opinion. He was incapable of unkind sarcasm; what he had to say was illuminating, encouraging, and tersely to the point, but generalized enough to benefit the whole school. Each student could take away what he or she needed. That word *nicha,* scattered through all Hofmann's conversation, was like a nervous tic that punctuated everything he said. Otherwise he always seemed serenely in command. No doubt because he had difficulty with English, *nicha* became a delaying tactic, giving him time to find the exact word he was looking for. His approach to life and art was sensuous; he loved the feel of things, the texture. That's why he preferred oil paint to watercolor — it had more body. Because he was indulgent, I sometimes asked him questions I hesitated to put to others. "What are you really after?" I wanted to know. His answer was poetic if also pat. "My aim . . . is to create pulsating, luminous, and open surfaces that emanate a mystic light." Perhaps the mystic light is not always there, but at his best he did produce remarkably free, unattached surfaces that seem to float in their own color ambiances. He felt that each medium had its intrinsic verity, that "the medium itself dictates the way." In other words, he wanted a painting to be purely a painting, not a re-creation of something else. In his best canvases, the spontaneity is so urgent that one almost senses the painter's hand at work slashing on rich, thick pigment.

Hofmann was one of the first artists in America to enunciate the basic premise of Abstract Expressionism, proclaiming that painting per se had its own inherent qualities governed by the potentials and limitations of the paint itself. He stressed that "all our ideas of the world go back originally to our emotional experiences," and it was his emotions as well as those of his students that he spent his life trying to liberate. A number of the members of the New York School, more often of the second generation, studied with Hofmann, and though several, who were considerably younger than he, became successful before he did, he remained serenely free of envy. Most of the pioneer Abstract Expressionists were beyond student age when he began teaching in this country, but often, if only through osmosis, they absorbed his ideas. He had much to do with shaping their attitudes, but it is also true that he and they may have come to certain conclusions simultaneously. A passionate involvement with gestural pigment and liberated expression was in the air, yet I have long wondered why Hofmann's influence on the movement was not more widely recorded. He, to be sure, never claimed the honor. In 1962 he produced a large painting called *Memoria in Aeternum* (now in the collection of the Museum of Modern Art) that was dedicated to his dead friends Arthur B. Carles, Arshile Gorky, Jackson Pollock, Bradley Walker Tomlin, and Franz Kline.

I remember how much Jackson Pollock's death upset him. Hofmann had become attached to the artist through Pollock's wife, Lee Krasner, who had studied with him. I saw Hans shortly after he received the news and he was devastated. He recognized the younger man as a major figure in American art well before it was popular to do so, and now he felt a sense of personal loss and also sadness at the terrible creative waste. Less surprised than grieved, he had been aware of Pollock's violence and previous tilts with destruction. The great difference between Hofmann and many of the Abstract Expressionists was not in their approach to painting but in his connection with life. Hans embraced each day with wonder while they often seemed bent on escaping life, chiefly through alcohol.

In a strange way, this confirmed European was one of the few older artists to applaud the American action painters. He was pivotal not only in teaching several of them, but also in encouraging the group as a whole. The fact that some of these men became household names while he was still better known as teacher than painter never interfered with his equanimity or his generous friendships. He was an artist without rancor.

The Hofmanns had no children of their own, and they probably poured affection on their younger friends because they were warmly parental. We came to them, especially to Miz, for advice. She was generous with her time, wise though sometimes acerbic with her words, and reliable as a confidante. Nothing shocked her. A 1901 portrait of her by Hans is difficult for me to relate to the Miz I knew — that older woman with her straggly short hair and lined, impassive face. The painting shows a strong, young Miz, withdrawn, sullen, and curiously sensuous. After she died, it was never quite the same. Hans was already eighty-three. All of us missed her, and so did the house. A year or two following her death Hofmann introduced me to a young German woman, describing her as his niece. Later they married, and after that I saw Hans only once and then all the glow had gone out of him. Suddenly he seemed old and frail. He died that same year at the age of eighty-six. During the second marriage he produced some of his most radiant paintings, notably nine canvases called the *Renate Series* for his young wife. This group, which she gave to the Metropolitan Museum of Art after his death, is graphic proof that at least creatively he had lost none of his earlier fire.

In many of Hofmann's pictures done in Provincetown, I find, or perhaps I imagine I find, the changing moods of the sea. That shining expanse of water immediately across from his house must have affected his sensibilities. It could be ominous and gray, luminous and blue, choppy, molten, or undulant, and so too were his paintings, depending on his mood. Though he did not as a rule work directly from nature, he was nonetheless swayed by it. "Nature is not limited to the objects we see," he explained. "Everything in nature offers the possibility of creative transformation." In one of his essays, he wrote, "The creative

process lies not in imitating, but in paralleling nature." He saw no reason why a painting could not become as alive, as vibrant, as nature's
own organisms. With this in mind, he relied on spontaneity, never in-
hibiting himself with preliminary sketches. In both his paintings and his
life, he fought to be free of all shackles, to open the windows and let
the air in, to open himself to unexpected and hidden stimuli. As he said
to me, "The first red spot on a white canvas may at once suggest to me
the meaning of 'morning redness' and from there on I dream further
with my color." Hofmann, not unlike Rothko, considered color a language in itself, a language that requires no further enhancement. For
him color was the final expressive force. He always insisted that a painting must "light up from the inside" and that this could be accomplished only through color. He wanted his surfaces to "breathe, to
move, to live."

Hans not only enjoyed the sea as a visual phenomenon; he experienced it actively, rolling around in it like a contented seal. When I
was living on Slough Pond in Wellfleet, Massachusetts, he used to
come early for appointments so that he could steal a quick dip in fresh
water, which for him was a treat. Each small experience he made his
own, and his constant rediscoveries of nature's daily delights were reflected in his work. It was not nature he was painting, but his reactions
to nature. Despite long years of teaching, Hans was a prolific artist
whose work as a result was uneven, sometimes coalescing in exhilarating color explosions, sometimes too fragmentary to hold together, almost as if overflowing emotions had jolted his hand out of control.

Hedda Sterne told me about running into Hofmann unexpectedly in Provincetown when she and her husband, Saul Steinberg, were
there one summer day. Hans was standing alone on the beach looking
out to sea. He turned to them with an ecstatic smile, disclosing that
for the first time in several years he could again "hear the waves." His
deafness had become a problem, but now, with the help of a sensitive
new hearing aid, he was suddenly able to listen to the ocean. For a
man who lived intensely through his senses, any cutoff from them must
have been an acute deprivation.

In 1961 I drove over to Provincetown to see what Hans had
been painting that summer. On the easel was a canvas he had just fin-

ished, the heavy impasto paint wet and gleaming. I fell in love with it and remember saying, "Hans, it's sheer joy." He took it off the easel and gave it to me. When I asked him to sign the canvas, he eased me out of the studio, explaining that the process required time and concentration. I joined Miz in the main house, which was attached to the studio, and we waited for him. In about an hour he appeared. Later he mentioned that it often took at least that long to decide on the right spot for his name since he always planned the signature as an integral part of the composition. Thus, his works started in total spontaneity and ended in careful premeditation.

On the back of the canvas he gave me, in an endearing spelling lapse, he inscribed the title *Yoy* and it is *Yoy* to this day. Incidentally, so generous was the opulent paint that it took nearly two years to dry. At a later date I asked him where he would like the painting to go when I died — which museum he preferred. He thought a while and then told me to leave it to whomever I wanted, but preferably to a museum connected with a teaching institution. To the end, his overriding concern was for education and the young.

Somehow I always associate Hofmann with Provincetown more than New York, though he lived equally in both places. I identify him with an out-of-doors life and comfortable informal summer clothes, with sandals and trendy garish shirts. When I knew him, there was never anything official about him, though earlier this may not have always been true. Louise Nevelson told me how drastically Hans changed after coming to the United States. As a young woman, she joined his school in Munich during its last season there and, if I understood her correctly, she was deeply disappointed. She had gone with high hopes at a difficult time in her life and she felt let down. The trip had been a severe sacrifice for her. Because Hofmann was beset with anxieties about his future, about leaving Germany and establishing himself in America, she found him a remote, unavailable figure who rarely came down from his pedestal to instruct her in the nitty-gritty of art. Much of the time she was handed over to an assistant. Shortly afterward she encountered him again, this time at the Art Students League in New York, where she was surprised to find him more understanding and, in her words, "more humble." She conceded that in the long run he had

Hans Hofmann, *Yoy–Divine Spark*, 1961. For many years, in deference to Hofmann's wishes, Kuh intended to leave *Yoy* to the Allen Memorial Art Museum at Oberlin College, but she changed her mind in the late 1980s and it went to the Art Institute of Chicago after her death. The Art Institute then sold the painting at auction.

probably influenced her thinking, specifically by his interpretation of Cubism as a system designed not merely to break up and rearrange form. He envisioned Cubism as a complex interaction characterized, as he put it, by the "push and pull" of organic tensions.

From time to time, Hans would talk about the period between 1904 and 1914 when he lived in Paris and where he began to unravel the mysteries of Cubism. He looked on those years as a time of growth that catapulted him into the heart of a new and provocative life. In

Paris he came to know Braque, Picasso, Delaunay, and Léger. If these men did not actively influence his work, they unquestionably broadened his outlook and forever pried him loose from any limited nationalistic stance. He told me how Delaunay had introduced him to Léger and how much even then in the first decade of this century these artists impressed him with their eagerness to break with the past, to investigate and innovate. It was the single-minded bravura of Delaunay that he most admired. About Germany Hans said very little except that his art school in Munich had achieved some renown before he emigrated to America in 1931. Not surprisingly the pre-Hitler atmosphere of his native land was repugnant to him. Moreover, his art only too soon would have been labeled "degenerate."

Like many other painters he transplanted himself, but at fifty-one it was far from easy. Fortunately, he knew several helpful young Americans who had studied with him in Germany; also, the year before he settled in the United States he had taught summer school at the University of California in Berkeley, so he had something of a head start. He didn't open his own school in New York for two years, but in the meantime he served on the faculties of institutions in California, New York, and Maine. As far as I know, he was never nostalgic for Germany, openly appreciating the vitality and "classless" democracy of his adopted land. Unlike many of his European colleagues, he did not return to Europe after the war. Instead he stayed in America, where he became a citizen.

Late one crisp fall day I dropped by Hofmann's Provincetown studio on Pearl Street, when his school was so large and crowded that he no longer could paint there. After he gave up teaching in 1958, the schoolrooms became his private work area, but the day I visited, he was still using a rented studio attached to a coal and lumber yard. To my amazement, I found Hans stretching canvases, most of them five to eight feet. There he was, kneeling, panting, hauling, and with craftsmanlike concentration turning out finished products of enviable precision. What astonished me was to see this artist then in his seventies expending energy on a physical chore that many younger men delegate to others. "I always stretch my own canvases, glue them, and prepare them in every way," he said. "It takes time, but I cannot paint on commercial canvases." As the years passed, he may have given up this activity, but I know he liked the idea of becoming acquainted with a canvas from the start and, almost like a progenitor, identified with it as a physical object before he applied even a single stroke.

Of all the painters I came to know well, Hofmann was the only one to discuss Rubens, Titian, and Tintoretto at length with me. These three old masters, particularly Rubens, were scarcely in tune with our century. Nor were the Italian primitives, whom he also took to his heart, claiming that "as an artist, you love everything of quality that came before you." To the baroque excesses of Rubens he gave a special salute, wistfully reliving the unprecedented concentrations of that painter's work in Munich and Vienna — a far cry indeed from Cape Cod. However, he placed Grünewald and Rembrandt above all others, and in the end it was Rembrandt he crowned.

Hofmann established no recognizable school of art. His students, encouraged to find their own way, remain an impressively varied group. I think of such disparate artists as Giorgio Cavallon, Alfred Jensen, George McNeil, Byron Browne, Fritz Bultman, Larry Rivers, Ludwig Sander, Richard Stankiewicz, Wolf Kahn, Lee Krasner, Tony Vevers, Helen Frankenthaler, Burgoyne Diller, Louise Nevelson, and too many others to list. The fact that their work adhered to no overall or rigid pattern but represents strong idiosyncratic personalities is, I think, a testament to their teacher. He never overpowered them, he left no limiting stamp. He helped them find themselves.

16
Josef Albers
The Color of Discipline

One Sunday morning in June 1941 when I was visiting Josef Albers at Black Mountain College, he joined me for breakfast and said, "Do you know what I just heard on the wireless? The Germans have marched into Russia." No one else at the college seemed faintly concerned, but Albers realized all too well what the news meant. Only eight years earlier, he and his wife, the weaver Anni Albers, had emigrated from Nazi Germany. Forgetting the food we had just collected in the school cafeteria, we rushed out to my car (which I had driven from Chicago) to search the neighborhood for morning newspapers. There was, of course, no television then. The rest of the day we tracked the pounding boots of a German army as it penetrated deeper into Russia.

The students, at least on the surface, appeared generally uninterested, though the possibility of an expanded world war that might well bring in the United States, once the idea percolated, must have jolted even their seemingly self-centered lives. Already the college, in its emphasis on multiple freedoms, predicted those future discords that were eventually to destroy it. At the top of the organization, no one voice took final responsibility; the goal was an unblemished democracy in which the joint input of living, learning, and teaching was indivisible. In those early years, the institution had not yet become a part of modern American cultural history nor were any of its alumni basking in stardom. All that was to come later. What I was experiencing was Black Mountain College in the raw, and I was too unfledged to understand how growth could develop in such an ambivalent environment. Based on both assertive individualism and an idealized communal life, the school was at once sapped and energized by these unresolved oppositions. Albers, I gathered, favored a more disciplined regime.

He and I had become friends when I showed his work at the Katharine Kuh Gallery. In 1937 I organized one of the earliest painting exhibitions for him in this country, and Albers told me that after seeing his work in my gallery, Claire Zeisler, the collector and fiber artist, purchased one of the first paintings he sold here. I didn't doubt it: Claire was my most enthusiastic client, and often the only one. She began with a Noguchi sculpture in early 1936, and went on to buy several Klees and a Picasso. She was the most independent, perceptive person in Chicago where art was concerned, and her belief in what I was doing gave me courage.

Albers was so wrapped up in every detail of Black Mountain that his own work may have suffered. Many years later, when he was teaching at Yale and living in New Haven, he discussed the problem, questioning whether his reputation as a teacher had interfered with his career. "I always think of myself *first* as an artist," he said. "Can it be that my paintings sell for less than they should because people think of me first as an educator?" The two outstanding art teachers in America at that time were Albers and Hans Hofmann, who also once lamented to me that he had jeopardized his own work by teaching "too long." It's curious that both men were expatriate Germans. Albers brought with him the philosophy and methods of the German Bauhaus, where as a faculty member he had fused his own convictions with those of the institution. Hofmann likewise came from a background of teaching, but, in his case, his school was his own brainchild, and a successful one that he was able to transfer to New York and Provincetown.

The day before that fateful Sunday, Albers suggested we drive to the nearby town of Black Mountain and see a bit of the North Carolina landscape. On arrival he steered me immediately to a large wooden bench at a corner of the main street and insisted that we sit down. I was puzzled. The surroundings scarcely rivaled the Spanish Steps or the Deux Magots for people-watching. Albers confided, "I come here every Saturday to watch the pretty girls go by."

I stayed at the college only three or four days, but for me it was an impression-filled visit. Because the Alberses lived in small quarters, they put me up in a dormitory and thus in close touch with the students billeted there. I must confess that the frequent emotional confrontations among them were hair-raising; one young woman became hysterical times several times while I was there. No wonder Albers fled to a bench in town. However, I doubt that this high-strung group was typical. In many cases students who could not make it in other schools were accepted at Black Mountain, and no doubt their tuition helped underwrite more gifted applicants who otherwise could not have studied there.

Beyond the instability in that special dormitory, which was very comfortable and probably reserved for the most affluent, I found reassuring signs elsewhere. The college, often financially strapped, expected its students to help construct the campus buildings and care for the grounds and vegetable gardens. What with studying and these added chores, there wasn't much time left over, but each student had a tiny "office" or private study room removed from group-living facilities. These havens were the sole escapes from a life of ceaseless interaction. Occasionally a student invited me for a quiet talk in his or her "office," and it was only then that I appreciated how invaluable were these small oases.

Albers envisioned the college as a new kind of self-contained institution where life and work were never separate. He encouraged his students to question, experiment, discard, and embrace their own philosophies, but his personal voice was so strong that, depending on the pupil, it could be either intimidating or inspirational. From Black Mountain have come such influential alumni as Robert Rauschenberg, John Cage, David Tudor, Kenneth Noland, Cy Twombly, and Merce

Cunningham. The interactions among them, which could be unnerving at times, were also a source of dynamic cross-fertilization. No other American school in so short a time span developed as many outstanding creative personalities. This small institution, isolated and intensely inner-motivated, burned itself out, but not before its message was delivered.

Recently the painter Dorothy Ruddick and I were discussing Black Mountain and Albers. Her work, in sharp opposition to his, deals with ephemeral tonal illusions far removed from his precise color experiments. In 1945 she left Radcliffe College for Black Mountain specifically to study with Albers. "He exceeded my expectations," Ruddick said. "He taught me to look in a new way with a kind of loving precision. He disappointed me because he inhibited self-expression. He was a complete disciplinarian, but I never resented it because he was riveting. The best of his students have not turned into little Alberses."

Norma-Jean Bothmer, an artist who studied with Albers at Yale, agreed that he produced no clones. "I think he would have been particularly hard on anyone trying to make Albers paintings," she told me. "He was interested in the thinking process, and during crits he might ask a student why he or she had changed a passage from, say, red to green. He could remember almost photographically all the various stages of our work. He expected his students to exercise control at every level and considered intuition a substitute and an unacceptable substitute for all-out concentration. He could be very difficult, ignoring you for days. I even recall him throwing a student's painting in the trash."

Bothmer, an accomplished draftsman whose work in no way resembles Albers's, claimed him as a pivotal stepping-stone in her development. "Just before I graduated," she added, "he called me into his office, looked at me with a very serious expression and said, 'Don't forget, Norma-Jean, it is more important to be a woman than an artist.' He couldn't get away with that today."

Albers remained at Black Mountain College until 1949 and was arguably the most cogent voice in the school's mandate. After he left, he founded and became chairman of the Department of Design at Yale University. Although Yale offered more prestige and his last years at Black Mountain were torn by strife, Black Mountain was always closer to his heart. I visited him in New Haven from time to time and will never quite recover from the immaculate purity of his studio in the basement of his home. The chairs were covered in something resembling cellophane to keep them from getting dirty. With not a drip of paint on the floor, not a discarded paper, not a personal memento or even a sketch tacked on the wall, his windowless workplace contrasted with the usual messy, object-strewn studios I was accustomed to. As a rule, such places provide autobiographical hints, and the almost antiseptic cleanliness of Albers's studio revealed much about his self-discipline. I couldn't see a sign that anyone had ever lifted a brush there, but such insistence on impeccable housekeeping was a personal signature in itself. The rest of the New Haven house was likewise strictly uncluttered, and its precision made me nervous. Yet his paintings, though reduced to essentials, were animated by an interior struggle for "action." Albers explained, "Action for me means intensity, relatedness, mutual interchanges."

It's interesting that, much as he deplored what he considered the overemotional excesses of Abstract Expressionism, Albers admitted to me a fondness for the paintings of Mark Rothko. "The only one of them I can abide," he said. Both men had the same preoccupation — color — yet how they used it and for what purpose differed sharply. Rothko wanted his work to expose his "most poignant" emotions about life; Albers, more specific, concentrated on the meaning and power of interacting color. And, he claimed, "Submitting to life is like any design — a recognition of restrictions." Albers kept a white margin on his paintings because he wanted them to have a beginning and an end. Rothko, who refused to frame his work, did not like to recognize the boundary between the edge of paintings and the environment surrounding them. Albers also knew Al Jensen personally, and it is worth noting that one point he and a colleague re-created a color triangle originally devised by Goethe, which indicates that he shared Al's interest in the philosopher's theories. But again, the similarity was more cosmetic than structural — the two artists had very different goals. Regina Bogat told me that once when Jensen and Albers ran into each other in the Museum of Modern Art's sculpture garden, "they had a sharp dispute about color. Al insisted that it was physical and prismatic, while Albers was vitriolically opposed. He insisted that color was psychological."

Albers, who lived during the great popularity of Abstract Expressionism, told me he came to hate the very word *expressionism*. He also said that for him "abstraction is real, probably more real than nature." He actually "preferred to see with closed eyes." That was his realism. He limited himself to the interrelationship of color and insisted it could assume infinite forms, a thesis with which he grappled much of his life.

If he scorned Expressionism, both American and German, he also had strong feelings about certain colleagues who taught with him at the Bauhaus, whether in Weimar, Dessau, or Berlin. For him Mies van der Rohe was a hero, Lázló Moholy-Nagy a villain. He tended to approach life in strongly delineated terms as, to be sure, do his paintings. Albers was in complete agreement with Mies, who maintained that Moholy had illegally appropriated both the name and ideas for his American school — the Institute of Design, originally called the Chicago Bauhaus. Mies had been the last director of the Bauhaus in Berlin when the school was closed by the Nazis, and the institution's bylaws stipulated that neither the name nor the curriculum could be adopted elsewhere without his consent, and he demanded that Moholy hold to this ruling. In a curiously stiff-necked stance, the two men never forgave Moholy. To be fair, they also found him an unrepentant self-promoter, and probably everything they claimed — that Moholy had presented Bauhaus ideas as his own without giving credit where credited belonged — was true. (Although I enjoyed Moholy's daring and effervescence — he seemed to have a million ideas a minute and one evening announced to me and his wife that he had slept with more than a thousand women — he was also aggressively centered on what he wanted, which was money to keep his school going. He was friendly and fond of me in a way, but I think he saw me mainly as a conduit. At a party I gave, he and some other guests were sitting around a table having drinks. Right in front of everyone, he leaned over to me and asked, "Which are the rich ones?") As for Gropius, who is often viewed as the father of the Bauhaus, his sympathies were with Moholy. I found it sad

Man Ray, Katharine, and László Moholy-Nagy, at the opening for "Modern Art in Advertising" at the Art Institute, April 27, 1945. The feuding among the Bauhaus exiles was constant, but Katharine remained friendly with the various antagonists. Man Ray's contribution to the exhibition is to his left.
Photograph by Gordon Coster.

that these men whom I looked on as giants in their professions were factionalized by such petty disputes. I learned that brave innovators are also human.

Anni Albers was always a conundrum for me. Just how this seemingly joyless marriage persisted for fifty years is a mystery. Her austere, color-reduced weavings were consistent with the almost monochromatic personality she offered the public. She was part of the Ullstein family, which ran a powerful Jewish publishing house in Germany, and though Josef was not Jewish, I'm sure he would have parted with the Nazis no matter what the grounds. His thinking was diametrically opposed to theirs. Whether Anni lived in a perpetual state of doubt about her husband's fidelity or was merely unsure of herself I never fathomed, but she was extremely jealous of me when I was at Black Mountain, even though I was accompanied by my mother. There was nothing sexual about my visit, but she couldn't figure out what I was doing there and suspected the worst. I didn't get to know her well, though in November 1941 I put on a small exhibition of her jewelry in my gallery. The space there was quite generous and divided into two sections by a freestanding wall, the front area much the larger. Behind the wall was an intimate space where in earlier years I had lectured on the history of art to support the gallery. It was in this back room that the jewelry was installed. Untraditional in both design and material, these ornaments were made of household items such as curtain rings, hairpins, paper clips, bottle caps, doorknobs, and kitchen gadgets from the hardware store. Inventive and witty, they had to do with a Bauhaus tradition that included daily objects as basic to art.

The painter who had star billing in the rest of the gallery was Charles Biederman, a young Constructivist from Minnesota who was convinced he had invented such a revolutionary new approach that art would never again be the same. I should not have been too surprised, for only months earlier Moholy-Nagy had told me that twenty years hence paintings on canvas would be curiosities. Constructions, projections, and light machines would make them obsolete. Also an ardent Constructivist, he never doubted that light and space were the sole arbiters of the future. Nothing else mattered. But Moholy realized that he was part of a movement, whereas Biederman saw himself as its prime activator, even progenitor. He had no doubt that his pure geometric conceptions were the final answer to the twentieth century and he even wrote a book on the subject that was more pedantic than persuasive. At that time he admired Cézanne, but he didn't fully acknowledge the pioneering leadership of European Constructivism, which was already solidly established, especially in Russia. A fiery young man, Biederman was outraged when he learned that his work was to share an exhibition with such "baubles as jewelry." Meanwhile, Anni Albers, though less voluble, was also disturbed at the thought of this unknown interloper.

In my years among artists, I found that keeping the peace could

Josef and Anni Albers at Black Mountain College, May 1949. The Alberses were married in 1925 and remained together until Josef's death in 1976. Nicholas Fox Weber, the art historian and director of the Albers Foundation, described the pair as resembling "a two-person religious sect" in their faith in art and devotion to work. Photograph by Theodore Dreier, Jr.

be tiring. The less known the artist was, the more difficult he or she was to deal with, due no doubt to insecurity. Public acceptance provided at least a semblance of confidence, but for even the most renowned art stars, sometimes there could never be enough obeisance. I will never forget the blowup surrounding an introduction I had been commissioned to write for a small publication celebrating Marc Chagall's gift of *The Four Seasons,* a large mosaic mural to be installed in a downtown plaza, to the city of Chicago in the early 1970s. The booklet was sent to him in advance. I believe that it was Madame Chagall who relayed word immediately that the artist refused to have his name appear with Picasso's. I had written that the two most widely known living

Anni Albers, *Necklace,* c. 1940. This necklace may well have been shown at
the Katharine Kuh Gallery in 1941. Anni Albers deplored the segregation
of the technological from the artistic. In her jewelry in particular,
she let herself be supremely stimulated by humble materials at hand
rather than standing in their way.

artists at the time were Pablo Picasso and Marc Chagall. Evidently Picasso was an insurmountable challenge, despite Chagall's international fame. Or was it only Madame Chagall who objected?

In contrast, Albers was both considerate and generous. In 1962, roughly thirty-five years after his exhibition in my Chicago gallery, he appeared at my New York apartment with a carefully wrapped package. "This," he said, "is in memory of your kindness during my first difficult years in America," and he unwrapped a drawing incised on plastic and mounted on wood that still stands on my living room bookcase. In his inimitable, impeccable handwriting, he had inscribed the piece to me on the back of the frame as exactingly as he painted.

Albers rarely lost touch with the students he believed in, and his impact on even those who opposed him was formidable. Robert Donnelley, a former officer at the First National Bank of Chicago, told me that when he was a student at Yale he learned more from Albers than from any other professor there, although he never studied with him. He had misquoted Albers in a college publication and was promptly invited for tea at the artist's house, where he recalled a car seat reupholstered in black leather that doubled as a sofa. "He taught me about life," Donnelly said. "I felt humble, because Albers discussed his philosophy of art with me. He proved to me devastatingly and meticulously how he could not possibly have said what I had written. I remember him saying, 'You listened, but you did not hear.' I think that this was a variation on his often quoted comment about understanding art — that 'cows look, but they don't see.'" One of the first paintings Donnelley bought for his own art collection was an *Homage to the Square,* which was in reality for him an "homage" to Albers himself. Almost thirty years after that single encounter, Donnelley still remembered the man as a beacon of unwavering certitude.

17
Edward Hopper
Foils for the Light

I associate Edward Hopper with Mexico City because it was there during the summer of 1943 that I came to know him more than casually. Yet I must admit that though I saw him periodically from that time until shortly before his death in 1967, I never felt I knew him well enough to call him by his first name. He was always Mr. Hopper to me, largely, I suppose, because of his austere silences. There was something private and withdrawn, almost unapproachable, about him.

This was his first trip to Mexico, and he hated the whole experience — the dust, the opulent Baroque architecture, the colorful Indian pageantry, the smells, the food, the ebullient Latins. It was all too sensuous for him; he was sixty-one at the time and not given to odysseys that upset his established way of life. He yearned for the cool light and laconic Yankee reserve of New England. Indeed, he often impressed me as the epitome of a Yankee — slow-moving, stiff-necked, frugal, monosyllabic, and supremely his own man.

I was walking along one of the downtown streets in Mexico City when I felt a tap on my shoulder and looked up to find the artist and his wife, Jo, greeting me. I had never met her before and only knew him slightly, so for a moment I couldn't place them. Hopper's tall, lanky frame towered above the Mexican street scene, his usually impassive face crinkled in the brilliant sunlight. Jo looked very strange, as if she were about to go milking. Almost hidden by an outsized pink sunbonnet tied under her chin, she immediately began their tale of woe. They were uncomfortable, the food was bad, Mexico wasn't what "he" had expected. I recall how often when I was with the Hoppers Jo referred to her husband not by name but as "he," or "him," evoking an omnipotent figure who needed no further identification. Invariably she did the talking, he only adding a word or two for emphasis when he disagreed, which, by the way, was frequently.

The Hoppers had been in Mexico for less than two weeks when we met. They were lonely and urged me to have dinner with them at their hotel. Euphemistically called the Ritz, the place was far from luxurious. Hopper confessed that he spent much of his time there and ate exclusively in the hotel dining room because it was the only restaurant in town where he could get a good steak. Highly spiced Mexican food was anathema to him, and so, too, was routine sightseeing. He mentioned that "all those gilded putti" unnerved him. At dinner he explained that their summer house on Cape Cod was unavailable until fall (apparently it was rented) and that he didn't want to return to their New York apartment during the summer heat, so he was "stuck" in Mexico. His dilemma was an inability to paint in that unsympathetic environment, for try as he might, he couldn't find a "motif" that satisfied him, by which he meant not so much a theme but a means for tackling his own distinctive perspective. This was a recurrent problem, one that tormented him even in congenial surroundings, when he sometimes wasted long months without coming up with a germinating point of departure.

Knowing that I had spent considerable time in Mexico and had traveled widely there, he asked me to recommend an area where he would feel more at home, a town, as he put it, with "no renowned monuments, no quaint or picturesque tourist attractions." I suggested the town of Saltillo, about 650 miles north of Mexico City, where I had visited when I was teaching in San Miguel de Allende. Saltillo had impressed me as somewhat down at the heels and honky-tonk, yet it turned out to be a lifesaver for Hopper. Resembling an anomalous outlying section of Chicago, it offered him a refuge from the distractions that appeal to most visitors in Mexico.

Edward and Josephine Hopper in their studio overlooking Washington Square, c. 1950. Photograph by George Platt Lynes.

When I saw Hopper in New York some months later, he showed me several watercolors he had painted from the roof of the modest commercial hotel where he and Jo stayed in Saltillo. That roof became his studio, his base of operation. Just what he and Jo found to do in Saltillo when he wasn't working is a mystery, but even a brief examination of the pictures he made there emphasizes how fertile the unobtrusive and commonplace were for him. He painted what others ignore, or ignore until they see what he painted.

The watercolors done from the hotel roof tell us less about Saltillo than about Hopper. What he chose to record were truncated chimneys and water tanks, the domes of humble churches, the tops of prosaic low buildings interrupted by a few discolored walls, all seen in bright sunlight with arid, treeless mountains as a backdrop. It could have been any small unlovely town, but Hopper made it his own, chiefly by the slant of his vision. His perspectives, building across the paper horizontally, were slightly tilted and cut by occasional diagonals, almost as if caught by an amateur's camera. But unlike a camera, the artist omitted more than he included, eliminating all fussy detail and any hint of ingratiating local color. Even when he concentrated on a single structure, such as the top of the house, which is the subject of a watercolor called *Saltillo Mansion* (now owned by the Metropolitan Museum of Art), he focused on what may appear to be a simple idea, but in fact was not. To create the illusion of solid form with little more than natural light and simultaneously imbue that form with its own personality was clearly a tour de force. Always interested in more than a purely technical exploration, he regarded light as a luminous force, explaining to me that "there is a sort of elation about sunlight on the upper part of a house." At that time he was talking about *Second Story Sunlight,* an oil now in the collection of Whitney Museum that he painted in 1960, many years after his Saltillo stay, and which he considered one of his most successful. All through his life the idea of liberated sunlight mesmerized him, early becoming his foremost consideration. Even the title indicates how important luminosity was for him, how secondary were details such as the two contrasting women, the background landscape, and the double facade of the house. They were there as foils for the light.

The watercolors that Hopper made in Saltillo were never intended as spontaneous sketches; each was carefully designed. In an interview some years later, Hopper told me that his watercolors, in contrast to his oil paintings, "were all done from nature — direct — out-of-doors and not made as sketches." Yet he added that he preferred working in oil because it was a slower and consequently more thoughtful process that permitted changes whenever necessary.

After their initial distaste, the Hoppers became so enamored of Mexico that they returned four times — in 1946, 1951, 1953, and 1955. In 1946 they again visited Saltillo, where the artist continued his rooftop series, this visit producing architectural juxtapositions that were considerably more complicated than those he had done three years earlier. No doubt knowing what to expect in advance gave him added assurance. In any case, the second series has always seemed more fully realized to me than the first.

Edward Hopper, *Saltillo Mansion*, 1943. After Katharine recommended the town of Saltillo to Hopper, his trip to Mexico became productive. This watercolor was one of four that resulted from the artist's stay there.

Paying a visit to the Hoppers could be trying at times, because it always necessitated climbing. The artist's obsession with upper-story light probably explains why both of his living places were located at the top of forbiddingly high flights of stairs. In New York, he lived and worked in an apartment at 3 Washington Square North, where four long flights of stairs punished his visitors and protected his privacy. I always pulled my way up the steps with horrible difficulty, but more intimidating than the steep stairs were those long silences of his. Often he seemed completely closed away, and when at last he was about to say something — and what he had to say was usually rewarding and unorthodox — Jo's interruptions would stifle him. At such times a fleeting grimace hovered over his face, quickly giving way to resigned wordlessness.

I specifically recall my visit to the New York apartment in the late 1950s, when I interviewed Hopper for *The Artist's Voice,* a book that was to include talks with sixteen other artists. My attempts to sound him out were exhausting, but far from futile. True, he never said an extra word, yet he also never made a statement that was routine or superfluous. Jo, who was always on hand, slowed our progress to a trickle with her constant interpolations. It was impossible to see Edward Hopper alone. In the twenty-four years that I knew him, I never did. The artist, who was ill at ease with small talk, probably relied on Jo's volubility, and at the same time was irritated by it, but there is no doubt that they both needed and depended on each other.

That day of the interview Jo sat on the floor directly at her husband's feet, a breezy guardian. Earlier she had been very kind to me when I was gasping up the four flights of stairs. Meeting me halfway with a pillow, she urged me to rest on one of the landings, all the while reassuring me that even she was beginning to find the steps a burden. Hopper lived to be eighty-five and, as far as I know, the Washington Square apartment remained his home to the end. The pillow must have helped him, too.

For Hopper to idealize himself, even minimally, was out of character, and one wry exchange that occurred during the interview was characteristic. When I asked the artist, "What part does color play in your paintings?" he replied, "I know I'm not a colorist. I mean, I'm not very much interested in color harmonies, though I enjoy them in nature. I'm more concerned with light than color." Jo was indignant, insisting that he was a strong colorist. "You should be careful what you say about color," she warned. "Why?" he answered. "Because I might offend color?"

Invariably Hopper brushed aside Jo's corrections and stuck to his original statements. He pondered each question carefully and then responded judiciously and with disarming candor. In no way did he romanticize himself, dramatize the earlier years when his work didn't sell, or indulge in wishful thinking. Nor was he even vaguely interested in public acclaim. He told me he painted only for himself, and I am convinced that was true. I have encountered no other artist, except for Clyfford Still, who so resolutely refused to compromise with daily demands. Yet the two men were very different; Hopper took his self-discipline for granted, Still saw his as an act of moral renunciation. "I would like my work to communicate," Hopper said, "but if it doesn't, that's all right, too. I never think of the public when I paint — never."

He once observed that a study devoted to the emotional character of an artist could reveal more about the man's paintings than the usual scholarly or critical account. After all, he added, "The man's the work. Something doesn't come out of nothing." He and his work were cohesively welded together, inseparable, less because the man identified with his paintings than because he was his paintings, so like them temperamentally as to exemplify a case of total fusion. He even looked like them, his unequivocally honest, lucid, and spare presence curiously close to a mirror image of his art.

Because Hopper resented easy generalizations, he took offense at the popularly held view of him as a disciple of the American scene. "I don't think I ever tried to paint the American scene," he told me. "I'm trying to paint myself. I don't see why I must have the American scene pinned on me. Eakins didn't have it pinned on him." That he referred to Eakins is not incidental, because if any figure in the history of American art left an imprint on Hopper, I have always felt it was Eakins. They were after the same kind of truth, the same American posture free of any concessions, for although Hopper denied his native roots, he couldn't escape them. One has only to look at his early work produced while he was in France to realize how alien was that other world.

When he could use a one-syllable word, he never used a two- or three-syllable one; he was doggedly unarty and unliterary. Had he been alive at the time of his 1980 retrospective at the Whitney Museum, I think he would have flinched during one of the video programs when several of his canvases were analyzed minutely in terms of deliberate symbolism. I couldn't help but recall how he insisted that symbolism in his paintings originated "in the eye of the beholder." He complained, "People find something in your work, put it into words, and then it goes on forever," a truism responsible for a variety of falsehoods not only about Hopper but many other artists.

Typical of such misconceptions, he felt, was the overworked stereotype designating loneliness as the core of his paintings. I think he preferred the word *solitude,* which avoided any suspicion of sentimentality. But if he did not intentionally evoke a feeling of aloneness, the fact remains that at least for the observer it is often there. His silent spaces, his frozen and uncommunicative human figures, his hard light all imply isolation.

As a rule, Hopper's attitudes toward artists of the past were predictable, yet he rarely discussed his own contemporaries with me. When the Abstract Expressionists were the heroes of the art world, he was quietly contemptuous, occasionally muttering about "the new academy," with its overemphasis on spontaneity and explosive emotions. He also punctured the idea of inspiration, claiming that only hard work and cerebral confrontation were the answers. As for artists of the past, he mentioned Eakins from time to time, but more often the nineteenth-century French etcher Charles Meryon, whose architectural compositions he esteemed, and Degas, for his mastery of veracity and his flawless technique. Above all Hopper revered Rembrandt, finding no other painter in history who approximated his stature. He even forgave the Dutch artist his heavy impasto paint, which he claimed was employed by him merely as "a by-product and never as an end in itself." When Hopper finally shed all French influence, he never again indulged in richly pigmented surfaces, fighting seduction as always with every tool at his disposal. His own evenly painted canvases gave no quarter to any hint of demonstrative involvement.

Nothing could be more impersonal than his occasional human figures, which, although sometimes differentiated, operate as props in the landscapes and cityscapes they inhabit. With him even female nudes were largely devoid of eroticism. Whether the figure was young or old, the artist depended on only one model — Jo, a painter herself, whom he married in 1924. I never learned if this arrangement was for Hopper's convenience or his wife's peace of mind.

Of all the images of Edward Hopper, it is those from Cape Cod that I remember most poignantly. First, his house in Truro — stark, white, isolated high on a bluff above the sea, a house he had designed himself precisely as he wanted it. Today, nearly forty years after his death, it stands there alone, a companion piece to the man and his work. Now when I drive from Wellfleet, where I live in the summer, to Provincetown, I often take the back road if only to glimpse that severe small building valiantly holding its own. I had always hoped it would be turned into a museum, for it tells us as much about Hopper as do his pictures, many of which were painted there.

To reach the Hopper house, one drove across a treeless sandy track on a makeshift road of little more than parallel ruts. Then a long precipitous flight of outdoor wooden steps led to an almost empty interior flooded with natural light. The view was quite wonderful, with the sea spread out in a vast panorama unbroken by any intervening land. Because the house was located as near the edge of the bluff as possible, one saw only water, as if from the deck of a lofty steamer. The intense sunlight still haunts me, pouring in from all directions and also bouncing back from the sea with exaggerated intensity. With unobstructed windows and no sign of a tree, the incandescent blaze could be blinding. One of Hopper's paintings, *Rooms by the Sea* of 1951, tells the whole story, for here, light, asserting its dominance and defining its own space, diminishes everything around it. The composition is virtually abstract, though Hopper would have undoubtedly denied it. He considered himself a realist, but once said, "I hope I'm not a realist who imitates nature." In *Rooms by the Sea*, Hopper was not concentrating on a realistic view of the interior of his house, though it did serve as his model. He was, however, preoccupied with a realistic report on the phenomenon of light as it played over and transformed unadorned walls and floors. He was dealing with the most ephemeral element a painter could address and doing it head-on.

In the front room that Hopper used as a studio and which may have also served sometimes as a sitting room, no concessions were made to comfort. A couple of armless straight-backed chairs and an easel in the middle of the space are all I remember. On one visit it was the easel that riveted my attention — perched on top of it was the artist's old felt hat and resting below was a pristine white canvas. Now at the end of the summer he was deeply depressed, for during all those weeks he could not decide what to paint. The whole summer had been a tragic loss, and the empty canvas stood there as an implacable re- minder. He was desolate and yet he refused to compromise. His spirit and even his body sagged with disappointment. Jo, always solicitous, treated him almost as if he were ill, which in a sense he was, since for him nourishment came from the act of painting.

The Hopper house, built among the dunes in Truro.

In 1963, four years before he died, Hopper painted what I have always considered a terse résumé of himself. Called *Sun in an Empty Room,* it is precisely that, yet much more. One sees only a corner of the room with a window and a suggestion of a leafy tree outside, but it is again the sheer luminosity that brings everything to life. Windows always played an important role in his pictures, probably because they supplied light while at the same time providing fragmentary glimpses of both an interior and exterior world. Intermittently one looks through his windows as well as out of them. *Sun in an Empty Room* is solidly, almost geometrically constructed, and proves once again how less can be more. Here, as in many of his late simplified compositions, viewers are given one or two brief clues and then left to their own devices. "The whole answer is there on the canvas," Hopper used to say, stubbornly refusing to analyze his work verbally. For him talk dissipated meaning, and though he agreed, as the years went on, that his paintings

Edward Hopper, *Sun in an Empty Room,* 1963. Katharine characterized *Sun in an Empty Room* as one of Hopper's most autobiographical canvases, and in his journal the artist tacitly confirmed her hypothesis.

became progressively purer and less literal, he nonetheless maintained that once he had found his own way, they never inherently changed. He, however, did — at least physically. The last time I saw him, about a year before he died, he was shockingly bent over, especially the upper part of his body. That once commanding figure was having trouble supporting itself, the head heavy and drooping below the shoulders. He who had always gazed down was now peering up at me.

Notes

Introduction: Sorting Out and Summing Up

5 **Sanity in Art was like an aesthetic "Moral Majority"** The Moral Majority, a political action group founded in 1979, was composed of conservative, fundamentalist Christians. During the 1980s, it sought to influence U.S. elections by backing conservative candidates who supported the teaching of creationism in public schools and opposed the Equal Rights Amendment, abortion, and gay rights.

5 **Jewett was a great-niece . . . animal breeding** See Sue Ann Prince, "Of the Which and the Why of Daub and Smear: Chicago Critics Take On Modernism," in *The Old Guard and the Avant-Garde: Modernism in Chicago, 1910–1940* (Chicago: University of Chicago Press, 1990), for further information on Jewett's life and professional career. "Jewett," Prince wrote, "did what was expected of a Chicago society woman: she wore the right clothes, married, raised four children, and upheld the moral virtues of her puritannical upbringing" (p. 104). Prince also

characterizes Jewett as "self-righteous," with a view of modern art as the by-product of "insanity, which reflected a diseased mind or worse yet, a diseased soul" (p. 112).

Jewett's animosity never waned. In November of 1951, she condemned Kuh and Rich for exhibiting abstract art, and called for the reactionary art writer and critic Thomas Craven, who was famous for his rejection of European modernism, to be given a position as "a director of nonmodern American art."

11   **The trial proofs were rejected**   Adams gave Kuh a trial print, which she later donated to the Art Institute.

15   **I asked $350**   The architect who bought the Kandinsky was James Eppenstein, and he kept the painting until his death. In November 1987, his children sold the painting at Christie's auction house in New York, where the work went for nearly twice its presale estimate, fetching $2.4 million. Kuh bequeathed her Kandinsky to the Art Institute of Chicago, and it went into the permanent collection in 1994; in 1956 she gave the 1914 Man Ray canvas (*Five Figures*) to the Whitney Museum of American Art. *Head of a Woman,* one of the Jawlensky paintings she bought, is now in the collection of the Frances Lehman Loeb Art Center, Vassar College.

29–30 Regarding the reluctance of Art Institute trustees to accept de Kooning's *Excavation,* the museum also let a superb early de Kooning slip away through tactlessness and ignorance. Kuh introduced the Chicago collector Albert Arenberg to de Kooning when the latter was in town in the 1950s, and the two talked and talked. Arenberg was an admirer of the artist from then on, and Kuh agreed to help obtain a good example of his work, provided that he left it to the Art Institute at his death. She found *Queen of Hearts* (1943–46), a painting of a seated woman, and advised Arenberg to buy it, which he did. It turned out that Arenberg's wife disliked how de Kooning portrayed his sitter and didn't want it in the house, so Kuh received it for display as a long-term loan at the museum. After Kuh's departure in 1959, John Maxon, Daniel Catton Rich's successor, removed the painting from the main galleries and relegated it to the basement. This enraged Arenberg, who immediately withdrew the picture from the Art Institute. Because he couldn't have it at home, he made a personal loan of it to Kuh, who was elated. It hung in her New York apartment for several years until

Joseph Hirshhorn happened to drop by. Hirshhorn said he had to have the painting, and by then Arenberg, with no hope of ever seeing his beloved picture on any wall in Chicago, was ready to sell *Queen of Hearts.* It is now one of the touchstones of the Hirshhorn Museum and Sculpture Garden's permanent collection.

36   The hidden figures in the *Grande Jatte:* Although the figures were not mentioned by anyone involved with the Art Institute's 1984 Seurat exhibition, in the catalogue accompanying the Art Institute's 2004 show, "Seurat and the Making of *La Grande Jatte,*" the existence of the two figures — one standing and the other lounging — is addressed.

1: Searching and Seeing

48   **assigned the object "doubtful status"**   Sidney Geist, *Brancusi: A Study of the Sculpture* (New York: Hacker Art Books, 1983), pp. 231, 257. In 2005 the sculpture is displayed in the Art Institute as being "attributed to Brancusi."

50   **Using ultraviolet inspection**   The description of the condition and history of *Saint Serapion* was confirmed and augmented by the entry on Zurbarán in *Italy and Spain, Fourteenth through Nineteenth Centuries,* ed. Jeanne K. Cadogan et al., volume 2 of *Wadsworth Atheneum Paintings* (Hartford, Conn.: The Atheneum, 1991), p. 328. I am grateful to Eric Zafran, curator of European painting and sculpture at the Atheneum, for providing me with this reference.

65   **in 1961, when I moderated a symposium**   The discussion took place on March 20, 1961, and besides Duchamp and Nevelson, the panelists were Larry Day and Theodoros Stamos.

2: Mies van der Rohe in Chicago

72   The rise of postmodern architecture to the perceived detriment of Mies's work: Since this essay was written, the International Style has not only been rehabilitated but exalted, and Philip Johnson became vocal in affirming his fealty and admiration for Mies. In 2001 the Museum of Modern Art and the Whitney Museum of American Art presented concurrent exhibitions on Mies and his European and

American commissions. Attendance was robust at both institutions, and the shows were critical and popular successes.

84   In 1997 Lord Palumbo opened the Farnsworth House part-time to visitors. In 2001 he decided to sell the house because he was in poor health. He offered it to the state of Illinois, which agreed to pay him $7 million and run it as a museum that would be open full-time to the public. In early 2003, however, the state authorities withdrew from the deal, stating that $7 million was too much to spend when the state was running a $5 billion deficit. Lord Palumbo began to look for private buyers, and when in October 2003 Sotheby's auction house in New York announced that it would be selling the Farnsworth House as the last lot in its twentieth-century design sale, architects, preservationists, and concerned citizens in Chicago and elsewhere were in an uproar about the administration's shortsightedness in abandoning an indisputable treasure of modern architecture. The National Trust for Historic Preservation and the Landmarks Preservation Council of Illinois then organized a joint campaign to buy the property. On December 12, bidding by telephone and competing against an unidentified buyer also on the phone, the preservationists won the Farnsworth House, paying $7.5 million. On December 17, 2003, the Farnsworth House was formally transferred to the National Trust, which purchased it with support from the Preservation Council and the Friends of the Farnsworth House, a group made up of individual donors who came forward at the last minute to save the house for the public.

4: Fernand Léger: Pioneering the Present

95   **organizing a Léger exhibition**   The exhibition was on view at the Art Institute of Chicago from April 2 to May 17, 1953; it traveled to the San Francisco Museum of Art for June 11–September 2, 1953, and the Museum of Modern Art for October 20, 1953–January 3, 1954.

104   **I asked the artist to list**   Léger's list of essential paintings has not been discovered to date, but Kuh's notes and correspondence indicate that *Composition,* then owned by the architect Wallace K. Harrison, and *The City* (Philadelphia Museum of Art) were on it. And after Kuh secured *The Card Players* of 1917 from the Kröller-Müller Museum, Léger felt that the 1916 *Soldier with Pipe* (Kunstsammlung Nordrhein-Westfalen, Düsseldorf) was a must, as an indispensable link between

the prewar work and the larger canvas. Kuh herself stated that no survey of Léger's work would be complete without *La Lecture,* discussed in the text and below.

105   *Three Figures,* **as the painting was temporarily titled**   The canvas was never really titled "Three Figures." In September of 1952 Lavera Pohl, the director of the Milwaukee Art Institute, told Kuh that the painting was called "Le Passage à Niveau" because this was the inscription pasted on the frame. Pohl also said that another title, "Pour Trois Portraits," was a later addition "apparently . . . given to the picture by someone working here." Kuh then wrote to Pohl saying that exhibiting the canvas as "Le Passage à Niveau" would only confuse the public and asked if she could title it "Three Figures," which would make more sense. Kuh did not want to use "Pour Trois Portraits" because she had given Léger photographs of the picture to study, and the artist had been adamant that the faces were not portraits, but fictional heads done from his imagination. In 1977 I. Michael Danoff in his catalogue *Fernand Léger: Study for Three Portraits* (Milwaukee Art Center, 1977, p. 10) stated that the inscription " — *sai pour 3 portraits"* was the original one and that "Le Passage à Niveau" was an incorrect appellation. The Milwaukee Art Museum now exhibits the painting as *Essai pour Trois Portraits.*

    Because Gimbel's bought Léger's painting in Paris in 1913 for an exhibition in the United States, the artist, after a forty-year lapse, later assumed — and said so to Kuh — that the painting had been in the Armory Show. Kuh stated this in her writings on Léger, which caused the mistaken information to be reported later in accounts of the Armory Show. Indeed, Kuh believed throughout her life that the painting she found had its American debut in the Armory Show. In March 1983 the scholar Aaron Sheon published an article on the obscure Gimbel's exhibition, "1913: Forgotten Cubist Exhibitions in America," in *Arts Magazine* 57, no. 7, pp. 93–107. He noted that Gimbel's capitalized on the publicity generated by the Armory Show and went on to prove that *Study for Three Portraits* was in the department store exhibition rather than in the Armory Show. Kuh was unaware of Sheon's article, and in these reminiscences I have corrected her confusion about where the painting was shown by substituting the accurate 1913 history.

110   **everything was intended for the Louvre**   *La Lecture* did go to France after the baroness's death in 1959; it is now in the collection of the

Musée National d'Arte Moderne, Paris. Yet Eva Gourgaud's fondness for Kuh, who continued to correspond and pay her visits after the Léger exhibition was over, did benefit the Art Institute. Between January 1954, after the tour of the Léger retrospective ended, until May 1956, when a major Léger show was being organized in Paris, the baroness allowed *La Lecture* to remain on loan in Chicago. *Nature Morte* (1927), the other painting she lent to Kuh's show, was also on exhibit in Chicago until the baroness's death, and in 1952 she made long-term loans of canvases by Braque to the Art Institute, possibly to help them fill the void left by the abrupt departure of the Chester Dale paintings. Kuh was devoted to *La Lecture,* and she did her best to secure it; in November 1956 success seemed in sight when the baroness went so far as to offer the painting to the Art Institute for $29,000. When Kuh started exploring the possibility of a sale, the baroness's attorney informed the museum that *La Lecture* was promised irrevocably to the Louvre. However, *Nature Morte* was not. It was sold at auction in New York in 1960, but by then, both Rich and Kuh, who were the most involved with the canvas, had left Chicago. Apparently no one else at the Art Institute was deeply enough interested in *Nature Morte* to retain it, and it was acquired by a private collector.

111   **"In 1934 we started from Antibes"**   Gerald Murphy, letter to Katharine Kuh, December 15, 1952, Box 9, Katharine Kuh Papers, Art Institute of Chicago Archives.

5: Stuart Davis and the Jazz Connection

116   **he wrote me a furious letter**   Strangely, Kuh consistently stated that Davis wrote her an angry letter because she couldn't sell anything. However, she did make one sale, and during the run of the show at that — an oil painting titled *Porte St. Martin,* which fetched $350. After sending Davis a check for $233.35, his share of the sale, she received a courteous and newsy letter from him dated February 18, 1939. He hopes for more sales, mentions that he's at work on two mural commissions, comments on the obtuseness of critics, and describes prospects for abstract painters. The letter is in Box 1 of the Katharine Kuh Papers in the Beinecke Rare Book and Manuscript Library, Yale University.

118   **"affirmed an urban continuity"**   This quotation and the extract that follows are from an unpublished statement by Davis dated December 1955, Box 12, Katharine Kuh Papers, Art Institute of Chicago Archives.

6: Constantin Brancusi: Elision and Re-vision

121 **"Nothing can grow"** Sidney Geist, *Brancusi: A Study of the Sculpture* (New York: Hacker Art Books, 1983), p. 2.

122 **"art in its most aesthetically pure form"** Isamu Noguchi, quoted in Paul Cummings, *Artists in Their Own Words* (New York: St. Martin's Press, 1979), p. 111.

123 **I had heard that we could purchase** *The Seal* was available for $10,000 rather than $20,000 because there was a small support in front and a tiny mended section. It is likely Kuh chose not to recommend the sculpture for acquisition because of the latter. Roché owned three sculptures, one of which he would permit the Art Institute to buy in 1952. They were *Two Penguins* (1914), a marble, for $10,000; *Torso of a Young Man* (1917), a bronze now in the collection of the Cleveland Museum of Art; and the crowning piece, *Adam and Eve,* for $20,000. There is no doubt that Kuh would have liked to have bought *Adam and Eve,* but perhaps the price defeated her. In 1961, after she was gone from the museum, the Art Institute bought *Two Penguins,* which Kuh had described as "Good, but not nearly as good" as the Arensbergs' *Three Penguins.*

129 ***Endless Column*, in its ever-increasing dimensions"** Sidney Geist, "Brancusi: The *Endless Column,*" in *The Art Institute of Chicago Museum Studies* 16, no. 1 (1990), p. 87.

8: Mark Rothko: A Portrait in Dark and Light

145 **"When young painters come to me"** Alfred Jensen, in unpublished notes of his conversation with Mark Rothko, February 14, 1956, collection of Avis Berman.

146 **"Since my pictures are large"** Mark Rothko, letter to Katharine Kuh, September 25, 1954, Box 4, Gallery of Art Interpretation Papers, Art Institute of Chicago Archives.

152 **"may, in fact, be a symbolic portrait of the couple"** Diane Waldman, *Mark Rothko, 1903–1970: A Retrospective* (New York: Solomon R. Guggenheim Museum/Harry N. Abrams, 1978), p. 45.

154 **"I wanted to paint my own size"** Alfred Jensen, in unpublished notes of his conversation with Rothko, April 23, 1956, collection of Avis Berman.

154 The Rothko murals in the Tate Gallery are no longer in the setting that Rothko and Kuh knew. In 2000 the Tate opened a second building — a former power station on the south side of the Thames — to house and exhibit its modern art collection by non-British artists. The Rothko murals were moved there and are on display.

160 **"two characteristics exist in my paintings"** Alfred Jensen, letter to Elise Donaldson, June 17, 1953, quoted in James E. B. Breslin, *Mark Rothko: A Biography* (Chicago: University of Chicago Press, 1993), p. 301.

9: Alfred Jensen: Competing with the Sun

170 **"The trouble with you, Jensen"** Alfred Jensen, unpublished reminiscence, c. 1955, collection of Avis Berman.

176 **"Your own tendency, Jensen"** Alfred Jensen, in unpublished notes of his conversation with Mark Rothko, July 23, 1956, collection of Avis Berman.

176 **"my psyche and evolutionary process of thinking"** Alfred Jensen, letter to Elise Donaldson, May 12, 1956, collection of Avis Berman.

178 **"a desperate man"** Alfred Jensen, in unpublished notes of his conversation with Rothko, February 8, 1955, collection of Avis Berman.

179 **"the only way one can expose"** Ibid.

184 **"The dark of the universe"** Quoted in *Alfred Jensen: Paintings and Diagrams from the Years 1957–1977* (Buffalo, N.Y.: Albright-Knox Art Gallery, 1978), p. 1.

184 **"Modern number abstractions"** Ibid.

184 **"One afternoon during the year 1921"** Ibid.

189 **"It does not matter whether society"** Alfred Jensen, in unpublished notes of his conversation with Rothko, April 22, 1956, collection of Avis Berman.

190 The full title of Jensen's painting that Hofmann admired, created in 1966, is *Das Bild der Sonne: The Square's Duality, Progression and Growth, and Squaring the 360 Day Calendar.*

10: Clyfford Still: Art's Angry Man

192 **"The men and their work"** Clyfford Still, "Notes and Letters," in *Clyfford Still,* ed. John P. O'Neill (New York: Metropolitan Museum of Art, 1979), p. 50.

11: Isamu Noguchi: In Search of Home

203 **"burdened by a sense of guilt"** Noguchi's sense of guilt, no doubt heightened by the pain he still felt from his own abandonment, may have overwhelmed his memory, or he may have telescoped and dramatized the story as the years went by. Actually, his behavior was much more exemplary toward his friend than he led Kuh to believe. Gorky did not kill himself the night that Noguchi refused to let him in. Instead, writes Matthew Spender in his biography *From a High Place: A Life of Arshile Gorky* (New York: Knopf, 1999), Gorky "spent the entire night on Noguchi's doorstep" (p. 368). Spender further relates that Noguchi, worried about Gorky's deteriorating mental state, drove him to his country house in Sherman, Connecticut, and arranged for the painter Saul Schary to look after him. Gorky committed suicide two days later.

12: Mark Tobey in Basel

221 Tobey's gift of the carved stick, as well as two of his works on paper that Kuh owned, went to the Art Institute after her death, as did the print by Pehr Hallsten.

14: Jacques Lipchitz at the White House

243 **"with [such] an unimaginable rapidity"** Quoted in Alan G. Wilkinson, *Jacques Lipchitz: A Life in Sculpture* (Toronto: Art Gallery of Ontario, 1989), p. 48.

246 **"is so alive, so direct"** Ibid., p. 51.

246 The Presidential Scholars program continues to this day, but it is now funded chiefly by private contributions. Up to 141 high school students are chosen each year for a week of festivities in Washington, D.C. Each winner is awarded a medallion, but no portrait of Lyndon Johnson adorns it. Nor, indeed, are there likenesses of any American president. The design that replaced Lipchitz's image is impersonal and nonpartisan: it has the Presidential Seal on the front and the White House on the back.

16: Josef Albers: The Color of Discipline

269 Albers's gift to Kuh was left to the Art Institute, and it is now in the museum's permanent collection.

17: Edward Hopper: Foils for the Light

281 **"The whole answer is there on the canvas"** If Hopper avoided analyzing *Sun in an Empty Room,* he left a revealing notation about it. In his record book, the commentary for this painting is, "White light uncompromising shadow. Stark." Quoted in Gail Levin, *Edward Hopper: A Catalogue Raisonné,* vol. 3 (New York: Whitney Museum of American Art in association with W. W. Norton, 1995), p. 376.

Photograph and Illustration Credits

Cover

Will Barnet. American, b. 1911. *Homage to Léger with K.K. (Katharine Kuh)*, 1982. Oil on canvas. 42 x 42 in. The Art Institute of Chicago. Gift of Mr. and Mrs. William Y. Hutchinson, 2002.634. Reproduction, The Art Institute of Chicago. © Will Barnet/Licensed by VAGA, New York, NY.

Preface

Katharine Kuh, c. 1919. Katharine Kuh papers, 1908–1994, Archives of American Art, Smithsonian Institution (hereafter KKP, AAA, SI). Rephotographed by Lee B. Ewing.

Katharine Kuh near Wrangell, Alaska, 1941. KKP, AAA, SI. Rephotographed by Lee B. Ewing.

Katharine and George Kuh, c. 1931. KKP, AAA, SI. Rephotographed by Lee B. Ewing.

Carlos Mérida. KKP, AAA, SI. Rephotographed by Lee B. Ewing.

Daniel Catton Rich, 1939. Allied News-Photo. Art Institute of Chicago Archives. Reproduction, The Art Institute of Chicago.

Katharine Kuh and workers at the Venice Biennale, 1956. KKP, AAA, SI. Rephotographed by Lee B. Ewing.

Introduction: Sorting Out and Summing Up

The Katharine Kuh Gallery, 1937. Photograph by Edmund Teske. © Edmund Teske Archives/Laurence Bump and Nils Vidstrand, 2001. KKP, AAA, SI. Rephotographed by Lee B. Ewing.

Ansel Adams, November 9, 1936. Photograph by Ansel Adams. KKP, AAA, SI. Rephotographed by Lee B. Ewing. Used with permission of the Trustees of The Ansel Adams Publishing Rights Trust. All Rights Reserved.

Ansel Adams. American, 1902–1984. *Portrait of Rosette Lowenstein,* 1902/84. Gelatin silver print, 58.8 x 23.6 cm. The Art Institute of Chicago. Gift of Mrs. Katharine Kuh, 1959.868. Rephotographed by Greg Williams. Reproduction, The Art Institute of Chicago. Photograph by Ansel Adams. Used with permission of the Trustees of The Ansel Adams Publishing Rights Trust. All Rights Reserved.

Vasily Kandinsky. French, b. Russia, 1866–1944. *Houses at Murnau,* 1909. Oil on cardboard, 49 x 64 cm. The Art Institute of Chicago. Bequest of Katharine Kuh, 1994.33. Reproduction, The Art Institute of Chicago. © 2005 Artists Rights Society (ARS), New York/ADAGP, Paris.

Front facade, The Art Institute of Chicago, c. 1950. Art Institute of Chicago Archives. Reproduction, The Art Institute of Chicago.

Walter and Louise Arensberg with Marcel Duchamp, August 17, 1936. Photograph by Beatrice Wood. Gelatin silver print. Philadelphia Museum of Art.

13–1972.9(163). Gift of Jacqueline, Paul, and Peter Matisse in memory of their mother, Alexina Duchamp.

Sun room in Walter and Louise Arensberg house, Hollywood, California, c. 1944. Photograph by Fred R. Dapprich. Gelatin silver print. Philadelphia Museum of Art, Walter and Louise Arensberg Archives.

Georges Seurat. French, 1859–1891. *A Sunday on La Grande Jatte,* 1884–86. Oil on canvas, 207.6 x 308 cm. The Art Institute of Chicago. Helen Birch Bartlett Memorial Collection, 1926.224. Reproduction, The Art Institute of Chicago.

Katharine Kuh, Daniel Catton Rich, and Marc Chagall at the Art Institute of Chicago, 1958. KKP, AAA, SI. Rephotographed by Lee B. Ewing.

1: Searching and Seeing

Constantin Brancusi. French, b. Romania, 1876–1957. *Wisdom,* c. 1908. Limestone, ht: 56.5 cm. The Art Institute of Chicago. Ada Turnbull Hertle Fund, 1955.646. Reproduction, The Art Institute of Chicago. © 2005 Artists Rights Society (ARS), New York/ADAGP, Paris.

Francisco de Zurbarán. *Saint Serapion,* 1628. Oil on canvas, 47.563 x 41 in. 1951.40. Wadsworth Atheneum, Hartford. The Ella Gallup Sumner and Mary Catlin Sumner Collection Fund.

Vincent van Gogh. Dutch, 1853–1890. *The Bedroom,* 1889. Oil on canvas, 73.6 x 92.3 cm. The Art Institute of Chicago. Helen Birch Bartlett Memorial Collection, 1926.201. Reproduction, The Art Institute of Chicago.

Katharine Kuh and Marcel Duchamp, October 1949. KKP, AAA, SI. Rephotographed by Lee B. Ewing.

2: Mies van der Rohe in Chicago

Ludwig Mies van der Rohe, 1963. Photograph by Dick Nichols. Hugo Weber papers, 1932–1971, AAA, SI. Rephotographed by Lee B. Ewing.

Crown Hall, Illinois Institute of Technology, Chicago, Illinois. Photograph by Hedrich-Blessing. HB-18506-P4. Chicago Historical Society.

Ludwig Mies van der Rohe in Crown Hall. Photograph by Hedrich-Blessing. HB-18506-M4. Chicago Historical Society.

Exterior view of Farnsworth House, Plano, Illinois. 1951. Photograph by Hedrich-Blessing. HB-14490-T. Chicago Historical Society.

3: The Two Vincent Van Goghs

Vincent Willem van Gogh in Laren, c. 1948–49. Photograph by Peter Pollack. Art Institute of Chicago Archives.

Unidentified artist. *Still Life: Melon, Fish, Jar,* n.d. Oil on panel, 55.2 x 46.3 cm. The Art Institute of Chicago. Helen Birch Bartlett Memorial Collection, 1926.201. Reproduction, The Art Institute of Chicago.

4: Fernand Léger: Pioneering the Present

Fernand Léger in the window of his studio, c. 1952–54. Photograph by Alexander Liberman. Alexander Liberman Photographic Collection and Archive. Research Library, The Getty Research Institute, Los Angeles (2000.R.19).

Fernand Léger in Chicago, 1945. KKP, AAA, SI.

Fernand Léger. *Essai pour trois portraits* (Study for three portraits), 1910–11. Oil on canvas, 76 3/4 x 45 7/8 in. MX. 5. Milwaukee Art Museum, Anonymous Gift. © 2005 Artists Rights Society (ARS), New York/ADAGP, Paris.

Katharine Kuh at La Grange, Yerres, 1952. Photograph by Eva Gourgaud. KKP, SI, AAA.

Fernand Léger. *La Lecture,* 1924. Oil on canvas, 44⅞ x 57½ in. Musée National d'Art Moderne-Centre de Création Industrielle, Centre Georges Pompidou, Paris. Bequest of Eva Gourgaud, 1965. Photograph by Bertrand Prévost. Reproduction, CNAC/MNAM/Dist. Réunion des Musées Nationaux/Art Resource, NY. © 2005 Artists Rights Society (ARS), New York/ADAGP, Paris.

5: Stuart Davis and the Jazz Connection

Stuart Davis, early 1950s. Courtesy of Earl Davis.

Stuart Davis. American, 1892–1964. *Ready-to-Wear*, 1955. Oil on canvas, 142.9 x 106.7 cm. The Art Institute of Chicago. Gift of Mr. and Mrs. Sigmund Kunstadter and Goodman Fund, 1956.137. Reproduction, The Art Institute of Chicago. © Estate of Stuart Davis/Licensed by VAGA, New York, NY.

6: Constantin Brancusi: Elision and Re-vision

Constantin Brancusi. French, b. Romania, 1876–1957. *Leda,* c. 1920. Marble on concrete base. 66 x 48 cm at widest point. The Art Institute of Chicago. Bequest of Katherine S. Dreier, 1953.195. Reproduction, The Art Institute of Chicago. © 2005 Artists Rights Society (ARS), New York/ADAGP, Paris.

Constantin Brancusi. *Self-portrait in the studio,* c. 1955. Modern print. Musée National d'Art Moderne-Centre de Création Industrielle, Centre Georges Pompidou, Paris. Reproduction, CNAC/MNAM/Dist. Réunion des Musées Nationaux/Art Resource, NY. © 2005 Artists Rights Society (ARS), New York/ADAGP, Paris.

7: Three Encounters with Bernard Berenson

Bernard Berenson and Nicky Mariano, late 1950s. Courtesy Berenson Archive, Villa I Tatti, Florence. Rephotographed by Donato Pineider.

Katharine Kuh and Daniel Catton Rich in Rome, c. 1954. KKP, AAA, SI. Rephotographed by Lee B. Ewing.

Bernard Berenson and Harry S. Truman, 1956. Foto Levi, courtesy Berenson Archive, Villa I Tatti, Florence. Rephotographed by Donato Pineider.

8: Mark Rothko: A Portrait in Light and Dark

Mark Rothko, 1952. Photograph by Kay Bell Reynal. Photographs of Artists collection, AAA, SI. Rephotographed by Lee B. Ewing.

Mark Rothko. *Slow Swirl at the Edge of the Sea,* 1944. Oil on canvas, 191.1 x 215.9 cm (75¼ x 85 in.). The Museum of Modern Art, New York. Bequest of Mrs. Mark Rothko through The Mark Rothko Foundation, Inc. (429.81). Digital Image © The Museum of Modern Art/Licensed by SCALA/Art Resource, NY. © 1998 Kate Rothko Prizel and Christopher Rothko/Artists Rights Society (ARS), New York.

Mark Rothko, 1960. Photograph by Regina Bogat, Photographs of Artists Collection I, AAA, SI. Rephotographed by Lee B. Ewing. © 2005 Regina Bogat/Artists Rights Society (ARS), New York.

9: Alfred Jensen: Competing with the Sun

Alfred Jensen in his studio, c. 1973. Photograph by Regina Bogat, courtesy of Regina Bogat. © 2005 Regina Bogat/Artists Rights Society (ARS), New York.

Alfred Jensen. *Girl and Boy and Numbers,* 1978. Panels I and II; panels III and IV. Oil on canvas, 86 x 192 in. (four panels, each 86 x 48 in.). Private collection. Photographs courtesy of PaceWildenstein. © 2005 Estate of Alfred Jensen/Artists Rights Society (ARS), New York.

10: Clyfford Still: Art's Angry Man

Clyfford Still. *1957-D No. 1,* 1957. Oil on canvas, 113 x 159 in. (287.02 x 403.86 cm). Collection Albright-Knox Art Gallery, Buffalo, New York, Gift of Seymour H. Knox, Jr., 1959.

Clyfford Still in San Francisco, 1976. KKP, AAA, SI.

11: Isamu Noguchi: In Search of Home

Work yard, Noguchi's studio, Mure, c. 1970. Photograph by Michio Noguchi, courtesy of The Isamu Noguchi Foundation, Inc. © 2005 The Isamu Noguchi Foundation and Garden Museum, New York/Artists Rights Society (ARS), New York.

Isamu Noguchi. *The Cry,* 1959. Balsa wood and steel. Overall 84¼ x 29½ x 19¼ in. (219.1 x 75 x 49 cm). Solomon R. Guggenheim Museum, New York,

66.1812. Photograph by Robert E. Mates © The Solomon R. Guggenheim Foundation. © 2005 The Isamu Noguchi Foundation and Garden Museum, New York/Artists Rights Society (ARS), New York.

Black Sun in the process of being made, Mure, 1969. Photograph by Michio Noguchi, courtesy of The Isamu Noguchi Foundation, Inc. © 2005 The Isamu Noguchi Foundation and Garden Museum, New York/Artists Rights Society (ARS), New York.

Isamu Noguchi with *Lunar,* late 1960s. Photograph by Vytas Valaitis, courtesy of The Isamu Noguchi Foundation, Inc. © 2005 The Isamu Noguchi Foundation and Garden Museum, New York/Artists Rights Society (ARS), New York.

12: Mark Tobey in Basel

Mark Tobey, August 1961. Photograph © Johsel Namkung. Kenneth Callahan papers, 1932–63, AAA, SI. Rephotographed by Lee B. Ewing.

Mark Tobey and Lyonel Feininger, 1954. Photograph by Charles Seliger, courtesy of Charles Seliger.

Mark Tobey. *Edge of August,* 1953. Casein on composition board, 48 x 28 in. (121.9 x 71.1 cm). The Museum of Modern Art, New York. Purchase, 5.54. Digital Image © The Museum of Modern Art/Licensed by SCALA/Art Resource, NY. © Mark Tobey Estate/Seattle Art Museum.

13: A Day with Franz Kline

Franz Kline, April 7, 1961. Photograph © Fred W. McDarrah. American Art Expositions, Inc. records, AAA, SI. Rephotographed by Lee B. Ewing.

14: Jacques Lipchitz at the White House

Jacques Lipchitz, 1970. Photograph by Frank Lloyd. Courtesy, Marlborough Gallery, New York.

Jacques Lipchitz. *Presidential Scholars Medal,* 1964. Bronze, 3 in. diam., ⅛ in. (rim) to ½ in. (relief) high. Foundry: Metallic Art. Courtesy of the

Lyndon Baines Johnson Library and Museum, Austin, Texas. © Estate of Jacques Lipchitz, courtesy, Marlborough Gallery, New York.

15: Hans Hofmann in Provincetown

Hans and Miz Hofmann, c. 1951. Photograph by Wilfrid Zogbaum. Lillian Kiesler papers, 1920s–1990s, AAA, SI. Reproduced courtesy of Rufus Zogbaum.

Hans Hofmann. *Yoy–Divine Spark,* 1961. Oil on canvas, 38 x 30 in. Collection Helen L. Kimmel, New York. Photograph courtesy of Sotheby's, New York. © 2005 Estate of Hans Hofmann/Artists Rights Society (ARS), New York.

16: Josef Albers: The Color of Discipline

Man Ray, Katharine Kuh, and László Moholy-Nagy, April 27, 1945. Photograph by Gordon Coster. KKP, AAA, SI. Rephotographed by Lee B. Ewing.

Josef and Anni Albers, May 1949. Photograph by Theodore Dreier, Jr., courtesy of The Josef and Anni Albers Foundation.

Anni Albers. *Necklace,* c. 1940. Metal-plated drain strainer, chain, and paper clips. Drain strainer: 3.1 in. (7.9 cm) diameter; chain: 16 in. (40.7 cm) length. Collection The Josef and Anni Albers Foundation, AAJ16. Photograph courtesy of The Josef and Anni Albers Foundation. © 2005 The Josef and Anni Albers Foundation/Artists Rights Society (ARS), New York.

17: Edward Hopper: Foils for the Light

Edward Hopper and Josephine Hopper, c. 1950. Photograph by George Platt Lynes. George Platt Lynes photographs, 1926–1950, AAA, SI. Reproduced courtesy of George P. Lynes II. Rephotographed by Lee B. Ewing.

Edward Hopper. *Saltillo Mansion,* 1943. Watercolor on paper, 21¼ x 27⅛ in. (54 x 68.9 cm). The Metropolitan Museum of Art. George A. Hearn Fund, 1945 (45.157.2).

The Hopper house in Truro. Collection of Avis Berman.

Edward Hopper. *Sun in an Empty Room,* 1963. Oil on canvas, 29¼ x 40 in. Private collection. Photograph by Neil Greentree.

Acknowledgments

Producing a book like this, which combines someone else's voice inflected with the tones of your own, engenders its own special set of obligations, and it gives me great pleasure to thank the many people who made it easier for me to bring Katharine Kuh's memoirs into being.

Katharine began her career in Chicago, and it is to the staff members of the Art Institute of Chicago, the institution she loved and railed against, that I owe more than I express. For assistance past and present, for favors that can never be repaid, for answering questions, and for help in locating documents and images, I am delighted to thank Judy Barter, Amy Berman, Jack Brown, Stephanie D'Alessandro, Gloria Groom, Eva Panek, Susan Rossen, Bart Ryckbosch, Daniel Schulman, and John Smith.

I am also grateful to a number of individuals at other museums, libraries, and scholarly organizations who have aided me with this volume over the years. At the Archives of American Art, Smithsonian Institution, I was assisted by Richard Wattenmaker, Judy Throm, Trina

Yeckley, and Joy Weiner. Special thanks go to Catherine Gaines, who organized and photocopied segments of Katharine's papers in the Archives for me, Wendy Hurlock, who pored over multitudinous boxes in search of photographs I wanted to reproduce, and Lee B. Ewing, who rephotographed those images. Nicholas Fox Weber and Brenda Danilowicz of the Josef and Anni Albers Foundation have always been models of kindness and rectitude, and their suggestions and solicitude were no exception when it came to research on Katharine Kuh. I also wish to acknowledge Jon Mason, PaceWildenstein; Amy Hau and Carl Riddle, Isamu Noguchi Foundation; Anita Duquette, Whitney Museum of American Art; Susan K. Anderson and Holly Frisbee, Philadelphia Museum of Art; Scott Nussbaum, Sotheby's; Eric Zafran, Wadsworth Atheneum; Ann Mark and Karen Kadlecsik, Marlborough Gallery; Rebecca Foster, Society for the Preservation of American Modernists; Colleen Beckett, Chicago Historical Society; Julian Cox, J. Paul Getty Museum; Tracy Schuster and Anne Blecksmith, Getty Research Institute; Michael MacDonald, Lyndon Baines Johnson Library and Museum; Vivian Bullaudy, Hollis Taggart Galleries; Esther Shafran and William Turnage, Ansel Adams Publishing Rights Trust; Fiorella Superbi, Villa I Tatti; Andrea Mihalovic-Lee, VAGA; Janet Hicks, Artists Rights Society; and Humberto De Luigi and John Benicewicz, Art Resource, for their patience and concientiousness.

Katharine had many friends and colleagues in New York who contributed to these reminiscences in innumerable ways. Chief among them is Will Barnet, who was unstintingly generous in giving his permission to reproduce his portrait of Katharine on the cover of this book. Dixie Sheridan, who took the jacket photograph, was equally good-hearted. Others from whose warmth, advice, and encouragement I have benefited are Regina Bogat; Norma-Jean Bothmer; Patrice Cotensin; Earl Davis; Tina Dickey; Robert Donnelley; Helen L. Kimmel; Robert and Arlene Kogod; Miani Johnson; Mary and Richard Lanier; Susan Larsen; George P. Lynes II; Kathleen Mangan; Eleanor Munro; Francis V. O'Connor; Dorothy Ruddick; Naomi Sawelson-Gorse; Charles and Lenore Seliger; Matthew Spender; and Rufus Zogbaum.

After Katharine's death, I required time to find and sort out the manuscripts I had inherited. I am grateful to Thomas E. Keim, executor of Katharine's estate, and William H. Roth, her attorney, for their support in securing the archival materials I needed to continue what Katharine started. For aid in the final stages of work, I wish to thank my agent, Ann Rittenberg, for all her labors. At Arcade, Jeannette Seaver edited the manuscript with precision and understanding, Winfield Swanson indexed it thoughtfully, and Casey Ebro was unfailingly reliable throughout the entire publication process.

My deepest thanks are reserved for the Renate, Hans, and Maria Hofmann Trust and the New York Foundation of the Arts. Both of these remarkable foundations were critical to my work in the middle phase, when I had reached an impasse in editing and researching a good portion of the book's chapters. The extremely liberal grant awarded to me by the Hofmann Trust and administered by NYFA made it possible for me to finish this book and get it into suitable shape for a publisher's evaluation. In particular, Robert Warshaw, acting for the Hofmann Trust, demonstrated extraordinary belief and understanding. The funding I received was indispensable to this enterprise and, without it, more time than I care to imagine would have elapsed before Katharine Kuh's tales of her life and career would have seen print.

Publication History

Portions of chapter 2, "Mies van der Rohe in Chicago," chapter 12, "Mark Tobey in Basel," and chapter 17, "Edward Hopper: Foils for the Light," appeared in "An Interview with Katharine Kuh," conducted by Avis Berman and edited by William McNaught, *Archives of American Art Journal 27*, no. 3 (1987), pp. 2–36.

Portions of chapter 4, "Fernand Léger: Pioneering the Present," were published as "Remembering Léger, Champion of Nuts and Bolts," *New York Times,* February 8, 1998.

Chapter 6, "Constantin Brancusi: Elision and Re-vision," originally appeared in a slightly different form as "Constantin Brancusi: Master of Elision and Revision" in *Saturday Review* 3, no. 25 (September 18, 1976), pp. 36–38.

Portions of chapter 10, "Clyfford Still: Art's Angry Man," were published as "Cantankerous Clyfford Still's Palette of Green and Black," *Washington Post,* June 17, 2001.

Chapter 14, "Jacques Lipchitz at the White House," originally appeared in a slightly different form under the same title in *Saturday Review World* 2, no. 16 (July 31, 1973), pp. 46–47.

Chapter 15, "Hans Hofmann in Provincetown," was published as "Hans Hofmann: A Memoir" in *Hawthorne to Hofmann: Provincetown Vignettes, 1899–1945* (New York: Hollis Taggart Galleries, 2003), pp. 58–65.

Index

NOTE: *Italic numerals indicate that the information is given in a caption.*

Above the Earth, 226
Abstract Expressionism, 65, 67, 252, 263, 264
Adam and Eve, 125, 289
Adams, Ansel, 11, *13, 14,* 284
Albers, Anni, 259, 265–66, *267,* 268
Albers, Josef, 79, 259–69, *267,* 292
  other artists, 263–65
  studio, 263
  teaching, 260, 262–63
Albright-Knox Art Gallery, 193, *194,* 233–34
Algren, Nelson, xix–xx
Archipenko, Alexander, *3*

Arenberg, Albert, 127, 284
Arensberg, Louise, *18,* 21, 45–46
Arensberg, Walter, 17–23, *18, 19,* 24, 45–46, 193
Armour Institute, School of Architecture, 72–73
art appreciation, 36–37
  curator's role, 41–44
  evolution, 56–61
  history, 55
The Artist's Voice, 39, 276
Art Institute of Chicago, xxi, xxiii–xxv, 15–20, *17,* 23–24, 29–30, *64, 124, 222, 256, 265,* 284–85, *286,* 288, 291, 292
  Mies van der Rohe and, 75–76
  artists, xxiv–xxv, 37, 38–39, 266–67
Asher, Elise, 150

authenticity, 50
Avery, Milton, 157, 175–76
Avery, Sally, 170, 175–76

Baltimore Museum of Art, 170
Barcelona Exposition, German
    Pavilion, 73–74, 76
Barr, Alfred H. Jr., xvi–xvii, 33,
    44–46, 47, 73–74
Bauhaus, 264, *265*
    Chicago, 79, 264
    German, 73, 260, 264
Baur, John I. H., 35–36
Becker, John, 208
The Bedroom, 52, *53*, 91
Behrens, Peter, 73
Beistle, Mary Alice. *See* Rothko,
    Mell
Berenson, Bernard, 131–41, *134*,
    138
Berenson, Mary, 132, 134
Berlage, H. P., 73
Bethlehem, 232
Beuys, Josef, 218
Biederman, Charles, 266
Bird in Space, 125
Birth, *34*
Black Mountain College, 259–63
    alumni, 261–62
Black Sun, 208, *210*
Block, Leigh and Mary, 28
Bogat, Regina, *161*, *174*, 175, 176,
    179, 180, 186, 188, 189,
    263–64
Bosch, Hieronymus, 54
Bothmer, Norma-Jean, 262
Box in a Valise, 193
*Branch of an Almond Tree in
    Blossom*, 89, *90*
Brancusi, Constantin, 20, 47–48,
    49, 121–29, *124*, *127*, 285,
    289
    childhood, 124–25, 127
Braque, Georges, 55

buckyballs, 62
Calder, Alexander, 11–12, 89, 95
Callery, Mary, 82
Canaday, John, xi
Caravaggio, Michelangelo Merisi da,
    55–56
The Card Players, 286
Cavallon, Linda and Giorgio, 149
Cayton, Horace, xxi
Chagall, Marc, *34*, 267, 269
    Picasso and, 267, 269
Chermayeff, Barbara and Serge, 203
Chicago Renaissance, xxi
Chicago Tribune, 5–6, 30
The Chief, 126
City Radiance, 220
The City, 286
Clifford, Henry, 139
collectors, 24, 28–30. *See also*
    Arensberg, Walter and Louise;
    Dale, Chester
Composition, 286
conceptualism, 59–60
The Construction Workers, 103
Convergence, 233
criticism, xii
Crown Hall, 76, *77*, *78*
The Cry, 208, *209*
Cubism, 55, 58, 239, 241, 256,
    287
    German Expressionism vs.,
    54
Culberg, Maurice, 29

Dada, 58, 60
Dahlia, 232
Dale, Chester, 22–23, 24
Danoff, Michael, 287
Das Bild der Sonne, 190, 291
Davis, Earl, 114
Davis, Roselle, 114
Davis, Stuart, 113–20, *115*, *119*,
    288
    studio, 115–16

writing, 117–19
Day, Larry, 285
deaccessioning, 43–44
Degas, Edgar, 25, 91, 278
de Kooning, Willem, 29–30, 233, 284–85
Delaunay, Robert, 235, 256–57
de Menil, Dominique and John, 144–45, 163
democracy, and art, 24–26
de Montebello, Philippe, 198
Depression, xxiii, 3–5, 12, 236
d'Harnoncourt, René, 33
Dickinson, Edwin, 248
display, 31, 32
Divers on Yellow Background, 103–4
Donnelley, Robert, 269
Dreier, Katherine, 20
Dreier, Theodore Jr., 267
Dubuffet, Jean, 29, 100–101, 177, 178, 194
Duchamp, Marcel, 17, 18, 20, 21–22, 58, 59, 60, 63–66, 64, 193–94
    painting, 64–65
Dunham, Katherine, xxi
Dymaxion House, 61, 62

Eakins, Thomas, 43–44, 277
Eddy, Arthur Jerome, 12–13, 15
Edge of August, 30, 222
Endless Column, 126, 128–29, 289
Eppenstein, James, 284
Essai pour trois portraits. See Three Figures
Expressionism, 59–60, 264. See also Abstract Expressionism

Farnsworth, Edith, 81, 82–84, 83, 286
Farnsworth House, 82, 83
Fauvism, 15, 16
Feininger, Lyonel, 220, 221
First National Bank of Chicago, 38

Five Figures, 284
Fogg Art Museum, 113, 118
Fortas, Abe, 244
The Four Seasons, 267
Frances Lehman Loeb Art Center, Vassar College, 284
Francis, Sam, 181
Friebert, Joseph, 104–5
Friendly, Judge Henry, 140
Fromboluti, Sideo, 172–73, 176
Fuller, Buckminster, 61–64, 95, 201–2, 208
funding, federal, 24–25, 27

Gardner, Isabella Stewart, 133
Gebhard, Eva. See Gourgaud, Baroness Eva
Geist, Sidney, 48, 126, 129, 285
German Expressionism, Cubism vs., 54
Gimbel's, 287
Girl and Boy and Numbers, 182–83
Goethe, Johann Wolfgang von, 168–69, 187, 263
Goldman, Eric, 245
Goodrich, Lloyd, 36
Gorky, Arshile, 202, 203, 291
Gotham News, 233
Gourgaud, Baroness Eva, 107–110, 287–88
Gourgaud, Baron Napoleon, 108, 110
Graham, Martha, 210–11
Grande Jatte. See Sunday on La Grande Jatte
Granoff, Katia, 44, 45
The Green Box, 193
Greyed Rainbow, 30
Gris, Juan, 31, 33
Gropius, Walter, xi, 79, 80, 264
Grünewald, Matthias, 54, 219–20
Guggenheim Museum, Solomon R., 46, 47–48
Guttoso, Renato, 137

Halévy, Daniel, 25
Hallsten, Pehr, 225, 291
Hand, Judge Learned and Frances, 140–41
Harrison, Wallace K., 286
Hayakawa, S. I., 12
Head of a Woman, 284
Henry Ford Museum, 62
Hess, Thomas B., 198
Hilberseimer, Ludwig, 74–75
Hirshhorn, Joseph, 285
Hirshhorn Museum and Sculpture Garden, 232
Hodes, Barnet, 128
Hofmann, Hans, 170, 177, 189–90, 247–58, *249, 256*
  deafness, 254
  other artists, 248, 252, 255–58
  Provincetown, 247, 248–49, 250
  teaching, 250–51, 255, 257, 258, 260
Hofmann, Miz (Maria), 248–*49,* 253, 255
Hofmann, Renate, 253
Hofstadter, Richard, 161–62
Holbein, Hans, 219
Homage to the Square, 269
Hopper, Edward, xi, 96, 248, 271–82, *273, 275, 280, 281,* 292
  Cape Cod, *279–80*
  Mexico, 271–73, 274, *275*
  other artists, 277–78
  Washington Square, *273,* 276
Hopper, Josephine, 272, *273,* 274, 276, 277, 279, 280
Houses at Murnau, 15, *16*
Hurd, Peter, 245

Illinois Institute of Technology, 75, 76, *77*

Indian artifacts, 38
International Style, 80, 285
Iris, 45
Isabella Stewart Gardner Museum, 132–33
Isamu Noguchi Garden Museum, 201, 202

Jackson, Martha, 189
Jawlensky, Alexei von, 13, 284
jazz, Stuart Davis and, 113–20
Jensen, Alfred, 154, 167–90, *174, 182–83,* 263–64, 290–91
  childhood, 169–70, 177
  numerology, 179, 180, 183–84, 186–87
  other artists, 173, 175–76
  Rothko and, 167–69, 172–79, 189, 190, 289, 290
Jensen, Anna, 179, 181
Jensen, Peter, 181, 188
Jewett, Eleanor, 5–6, 283–84
Johns, Jasper, 157, 173
Johnson, Dan, 221
Johnson, Lyndon B., 239–*46*
Johnson, Philip, 72, 155–56, 285

Kahlo, Frida, 212
Kandinsky, Vasily, 12, 13, 15, *16,* 57, 284
Katharine Kuh Gallery, *3,* 260, *268*
  employment bureau, 4–5
  opening, xviii–xix, 2–4, *3*
Katzen, Lila, 171–72, 173
Kepes, Gyorgy, 73
Kerkam, Earl, 170, 234
The Kiss, 126
Klee, Paul, 66–67, 74, 219
Kline, Franz, 170, 227–37, *230*
  Asian influence, 229, 237
  other artists, 234
  titles of paintings, 231–32, 235

Knaths, Karl, 248
Knox, Seymour, 234
Koetser, David, 50
Krasner, Lee, 252
Kröller-Muller Museum, 88, 89
Kuh, George, xvii–xviii, *xix*
Kuh, Katharine Woolf, ix–xxvi, *xiv,*
    xvi, xix, xxiv, 1–2, *38, 64, 110,*
    137, 265, 284–85.
    Art Institute of Chicago, 30,
      75–76
    art interest, xii–xiii, xvi–xvii
    childhood, xii–xiii, 2
    dealing with artists, xxiv–xxv,
      266–67
    education, xv–xviii
    feminism, xxiii–xxiv
    love affairs, xvii, xviii–xxii,
    xx
    marriage, xvii–xviii, xx, 2–3
    Mexico, xx–xxi, 7–11
    polio, xii–xiii, xv, xxv, *64,*
      133
    (*See also* Katharine Kuh
    Gallery)
Kunitz, Stanley, 150, 161, 162–63
Kunstmuseum, Basel, 218–19

La Lecture, 110, *111,* 287, 288
The Large Glass, 65, 193
Leda, 124
Léger, Fernand, 63, 95–112, *98, 99,*
    111, 113, 114, 256–57,
    285–88
    studio, 97–99, *98*
Léger, Jeanne Lohy, 96, 111–12
Léger, Nadia Khodossievitch, 96–97
Levy, Louis, 132
Liebes, Dorothy, 202–3
Lipchitz, Jacques, 239–46, *240,*
    246, 291–92
    childhood, 242–43
    portraiture, 241–42
Lloyd, Frank, 159, 164–65, *240*

Lowenstein, Rosette, 11, *14*
Luce, Clare Booth, 109
Luce, Henry III, 173
Lunar, 212
Lurçat, Jean, 107

Magruder, Agnes, 202, 203
Mann, Thomas, 12
Man Ray, 13, 22, *265,* 284
Man Ray, Juliet, 22
Mariano, Nicky, 134–35, *134,* 136
Marlborough Gallery, 159, 164–65
Marx, Lora, 74, 81–82
Marx, Sam, 74
Matisse, Henri, 157, 163
Maxon, John, 37, 284
May, Saidie Adler, 170–71, 177–78,
    188
Memoria in Aeternum, 252
Mérida, Carlos, xx–xxi, *xx,* 6–7, 8,
    9, 135
Meryon, Charles, 278
Messer, Thomas M., xxii
Metropolitan Museum of Art,
    198–99, 253, 274
Miller, Dorothy, xvii, 146
Miller, Henry, 12
Milwaukee Art Institute/Museum,
    105, 287
Miró, Joan, 5, 29
Mlle Pogany, 123, 126
modern art, acceptance of, 4, 57
Moholy-Nagy, Lázló, 79, 264, *265,*
    266
Mondrian, Piet, 89, 113–14
Monet, Claude, 44–45
Moral Majority, 283
Morgan, Maud, xxv
Murphy, Gerald, 110–12, 288
Musée National d'Art Moderne,
    Paris, 123, 288
museum directors, 35–36
Museum of Fine Arts, Boston,
    26–27

Museum of Modern Art, 43–46, 66,
    252, 285–86
    fire, 31–33
    Rothko, 159–60
museums, role, 34–36

National Gallery of Art,
    Washington, 23–24
Nature Morte, 288
Nef, John U., 33–34
Nevelson, Louise, 65, 157, 201,
    255–56
New Year Wall: Night, 231–32
New York, 233
Newhall, Nancy, 62
Newman, Barnett, 157
Newman, Muriel Kallis, 28–29
1957-D No. 1, 193
Noguchi, Isamu, xi, 62, 122, 127,
    193, 194, 201–13, *209, 210,*
    212, 289, 291
    biography, 208–9
    Gorky and, 202–3, 210, 291
    studio, 203–5, *205*
Noguchi, Yone, 206

Palladio, 232
Palumbo, Lord Peter, 84, 286
Perkins, Frances, 139
Peterhans, Walter, 74–75
Phillips, Duncan, 23, 28
Phillips Collection, 152–53
photography, 58–59
Picard, Lillian, 188–89
Picasso, Pablo, 48, 50, 54–55, 58
    Chagall and, 267, 269
Pogany, Margit, 126
Pohl, Lavera, 287
politics, art and, 26–27, 57
Pollock, Jackson, 30, 220, 233, 252
Pomerantz, Louis, 31
Porte St. Martin, 288
Portrait of Nancy Cunard, 126
Presidential Scholars, 241, 245–46,
    246, 292
press, 5–6, 26–27, 30
Princess X, 125

Queen of Hearts, 284–85

Ravenna, 232
Ready-to-Wear, 118, *119*
Reinhardt, Ad and Rita, 156
Reis, Bernard, 159
Rembrandt (Rembrandt Harmensz
    van Rijn), 157–58, 163, 258,
    278
Renate Series, 253
Reynal, Jeanne, 202, 203
Rich, Bertha Ten Eyck James, xxii
Rich, Daniel Catton, xvii, xxi–xxiv,
    xxiii, 15, 18, 22–23, 27–28,
    31, 33, 55
    Amsterdam, 85, 89–92
    Italy, 133–37, *137*
Rijksmuseum, Amsterdam, 89–90
Ritter, Mark, 217
Robie House, 76
Roché, Henri-Pierre, 123, 289
Rodin, Auguste, 46, 121
Rooms by the Sea, 279–80
Roosevelt, Franklin Delano, xv
Rosenberg, Harold, 43
Rothko, Christopher (Topher), 144
Rothko, Kate, 150–51, 158–59
Rothko, Mark, 118, 143–66, *147,*
    153, 161, 187, 263, 289–90
    childhood, 158
    his paintings, 146–48,
        153–54, 160, 164, 176,
        186
    Jensen and, 167–68, 169,
        173–75, 176, 178–79, 189,
        190
    lawsuit, 159
    other artists, 145, 156–57,
        162, 223
    Provincetown, 161–63

Still and, 194–97
suicide, 165–66
Rothko, Mell, 143–44, 149,
150–51, 152
Rothko Chapel, 144–45, 154, 158,
163–64
Rousseau, Theodore, 85, 89, 91
Ruddick, Dorothy, 262

Sagittarius Red, 218
Saint Serapion, 50, 51, 285
Saltillo Mansion, 274, 275
San Francisco Museum of Art (now
San Francisco Museum of
Modern Art), 151–52, 193
Sandberg, Willem, 88–89
Sanity in Art, xxi, 5, 6–7, 74, 283
Sargent, John Singer, 133
Saturday Review, 26, 30
Schary, Saul, 291
Schniewind, Carl, 42
The Seal, 289
Search for the Real, 250
Sebree, Charles, xxi, 5
Second Story Sunlight, 274
Seliger, Charles, 221
Seurat, Georges, 31, 32, 37, 285
Sheon, Aaron, 287
Slow Swirl at the Edge of the Sea,
151–52, 153
Snowdon, Lord, 198
Society for Contemporary Art, 28
Soldier with Pipe, 286
Solomon R. Guggenheim Museum,
46, 47–48
Soviet Union, 27, 57, 97, 103
Spender, Matthew, 291
Speyer, Nora, 173, 176
Stamos, Theodoros, 143, 159, 285
Stedelijk Museum, 88–89
Stein, Gertrude, 241, 242
Steinberg, Saul, xxv, 199, 254
Stendahl, Earl, 22, 45
Sterne, Hedda, xxv, 114, 162, 254

Still Life: Melon, Fish, Jar, 93
Still, Clyfford, xi, 185–86,
191–200, 194, 195, 235, 277,
291
other artists, 192
Rothko and, 194–97
Still, Patricia, 197
Study for Three Portraits. See Three
Figures
Sun in an Empty Room, 281, 292
The Sun Rises Twice, Per I–IV, 174
A Sunday on La Grande Jatte,
31–33, 32, 36, 37, 285
Surrealism, 54–55, 58
Sweeney, James Johnson, 46–48
Sweeney, Laura, 46–47
Sweet, Frederick, xxv

Tate Gallery, London, 154, 155–56,
290
I Tatti, 131, 132, 133, 134, 136,
138–40
technology, art and, 61, 66
theft of Renoir painting, 31
Third Avenue, 233
Three Figures, 104, 105, 106, 107,
287
Tiepolo, Giambattista, 135–36
Tinguely, Jean, 66
Tobey, Mark, 30, 46, 215–26, 216,
221, 222, 291
house, 216–17, 225
other artists, 219–20,
221–23
Tomkins, Margaret, xxv
Torso of a Girl, 125
Torso of a Young Man, 289
Tretyakov Museum, Moscow, 27
Truman, Bess, 139
Truman, Harry S., 138–39, 138
Tugendhat House, 76
Turin, 232
Turner, J. M. W., 155, 185
twentieth-century art, 58–59

Two Penguins, 289
Tworkov, Jack, 165

Valentin, Curt, 47–48
vandalism, 30–31, 32
van der Rohe, Ludwig Mies, xi–xii,
     xxi, 46–47, 69–84, 71, 78,
     264, 285–86
  apartment, 70–71
  architecture, 72–73
  Art Institute and, 75–76
van der Rohe, Waltraut, 80–81
van Doesburg, Theo and Nelli,
     69–70
van Gogh, Theo, 86–87, 91
van Gogh, Vincent, 37, 52–53,
     90–94, 90
  letters, 92
van Gogh, Vincent Willem, xv,
     85–94, 90
  home in Laren, 89, 90
van Gogh-Bonger, Johanna, 87
Venice Biennale (1956), xxiii–xiv,
     137–39, 233, 234

Wadsworth Atheneum, 50
Waldman, Diane, 152, 289

Weber, Nicholas Fox, 267
Weston, Edward, 12
Whitney Museum of American Art,
     149, 232, 274, 278, 284,
     285–86
Wiegand, Charmion von, 217, 224
Willard, Marian, 215, 221, 226
Wisdom, 48, *49*
Women's Garment Workers Union,
     50, 52–53
Woolf, Morris, xii–xiii, xv, 132
Woolf, Olga Weiner, xii–xiii, xv–xvi,
     132–33
World War I, 58, 104, 127
World War II, 4–5, 15, 58, 74, 88,
     94, 108
Wright, Frank Lloyd, 76, 79–80
Wright, Richard, xxi

Yale University, 156, 262–63
Yamaguchi, Yoshiko (Shirley),
     211–12
Yoy—Divine Spark, 255, 256

Zeisler, Claire, 203, 260
Zogbaum, Betsy, 235
Zurbarán, Francisco de, 50, *51*, 285